WITHDRAWN

Dialectics of Labour

Dialectics of Labour

Marx and his Relation to Hegel

C. J. Arthur

Basil Blackwell

Copyright © C. J. Arthur 1986

First published 1986

Basil Blackwell Ltd
108 Cowley Road, Oxford OX4 1JF, UK

Basil Blackwell Inc.
432 Park Avenue South, Suite 1503,
New York, NY 10016, USA

All rights reserved. Except for the quotation of short passages for the purposes of criticism and review, no part of this publication may be reproduced, stored in a retrieval system, or transmitted, in any form or by any means, electronic, mechanical, photocopying, recording or otherwise, without the prior permission of the publisher.

Except in the United States of America, this book is sold subject to the condition that it shall not, by way of trade or otherwise, be lent, resold, hired out, or otherwise circulated without the publisher's prior consent in any form of binding or cover other than that in which it is published and without a similar condition including this condition being imposed on the subsequent purchaser.

British Library Cataloguing in Publication Data
Arthur, C. J.
Dialectics of labour: Marx and his
relation to Hegel
1. Marx, Karl   2. Hegel, Georg Wilhelm
Friedrich   2. Marxian school of sociology
I. Title
301'.092'4   HX39.5
ISBN 0-631-15218-0

Library of Congress Cataloging in Publication Data
Arthur, C. J. (Christopher John), 1940–
   Dialectics of labour.

   Bibliography: p.
   Includes index.
   1. Marx, Karl, 1818–1883.   2. Hegel, Georg Wilhelm
Friedrich, 1770–1831—Influence.   3. Labor and laboring
classes.   I. Title.
B3305.M74A87   1986   335.4'12   86-11757
ISBN 0-631-15218-0

Typeset in 10 on 12 pt Garamond by Alan Sutton Publishing Limited
Printed in Great Britain by The Camelot Press, Southampton

Contents

Acknowledgements	vi
Introduction	1

PART ONE   Marx's Theory of Alienation

1	Alienated Labour	5
2	Private Property	20
3	Communism	35

PART TWO   The Critique of Hegel

4	Marx and Hegel	45
5	Hegel's Phenomenology	49
6	Marx's Criticism	59
7	The Influence of the Phenomenology	77
8	Hegel on Wage-labour	93

PART THREE   1844: The Turning Point

9	Marx and Feuerbach	105
10	Towards an Assessment	127
11	The Continuing Importance of 1844	141

APPENDIX Problems of Translation	147
Notes	152
Bibliography	174
Index	180

Acknowledgements

Earlier versions of some of the arguments of this book appeared in *Radical Philosophy* (Nos. 26, 30, 35) and *New Left Review* (No. 142). I am grateful to the editors of *Radical Philosophy*, and especially to Roy Edgley, Joe McCarney and Jonathan Rée, for advice and encouragement. I thank also my friend, and fellow-thinker, Gülnur Savran.

Introduction

In V.I. Lenin's little article 'The three sources and three component parts of Marxism' the said sources are identified as 'German philosophy, English political economy and French socialism'.[1] There is widespread agreement that this is indeed the case.[2] But what is the thread that links these disparate intellectual sources together? The answer is that Karl Marx effected this synthesis once he grasped the importance of *human labour* in the history of society. The idealist dialectic of the German philosopher G.W.F. Hegel, presented in his *Phenomenology of Spirit* as the self-movement and self-estrangement of spirit, Marx re-read in terms of human practice – centrally in terms of the *alienation of labour*; English political economy (Adam Smith, David Ricardo), he discovered, based itself on the *labour theory of value*; French socialism protested against the exploitation of the labourer and counterposed to the *division of labour* the principle of 'association'.

It was in Paris in the year 1844 that the young Marx first drew these threads together and put material labour at the centre of his research programme. In his manuscripts of that year we can see this new synthesis taking shape.[3] They begin as a simple set of notes on his reading of economic texts; then he breaks off to write the section (now justly celebrated) on *estranged labour;* he goes on to reflect on the meaning of communist doctrines in this light; along the way he conducts a running debate with the shade of Hegel, especially around the central question of our time – that of alienation. It should be noted that most works on Marx's theory of alienation are defective because they do not recognize that *all* the sections of the manuscripts are equally essential and inform each other.

For Marx, from 1844, the problem of alienation in modern society is understood to gravitate around the estrangement of labour. All other spheres of estrangement are to be related to this.[4]

What we find, then, in the *1844 Manuscripts* is the emergence of a new theory of extraordinary scope and fertility.[5] As such it is one of the most exciting texts in the history of modern philosophy. At the same time, it is one of the most difficult, partly because of its fragmentary character; even more, because of the complexity and originality of Marx's new ideas. Indeed the vast scope of the project sketched out in these manuscripts defeated Marx himself. Only a part of the programme he outlined for himself was undertaken, namely the researching and writing of *Capital* – and even that project remained incomplete at his death. The critique of Hegel, by contrast, was never taken up; although Marx continually promised himself that he would write some sheets on what is rational in Hegel's dialetic.

This book sets out an interpretation of Marx's *1844 Manuscripts*. It will attempt to clarify what is obscure and to complete thoughts Marx left incomplete. A special effort is made to assess Marx's relationship to Hegel, which is one of extraordinary complexity; the influence of Hegel on Marx is enormous, yet Marx's embrace of materialism sets him poles apart from Hegel. Not surprisingly, the matter is a controversial one. The evidence offered by the *1844 Manuscripts* of Marx's own understanding of his relation to Hegel has been insufficiently studied (except by Georg Lukács in his masterly work *The Young Hegel),* and never properly explicated. The question is not without its importance; for the central role played by labour in Marx's thought, and its character as 'the activity of alienation, the alienation of activity', is much illuminated by tracing Marx's route out of Hegel. Above all, this book aims to bring out fully the *dialectical* aspects of Marx's thought at this important turning point. The book ends by indicating the continuing importance of the themes of 1844 in Marx's later work.

Although an enormous literature exists on Marx's theory of alienation, and although certain remarks of his about Hegel's philosophy are frequently quoted, there has been no thorough study of the *1844 Manuscripts* themselves, and certainly no detailed exegesis of Marx's critique of Hegel's dialectic therein. That is why it is worthwhile to devote a whole book to the study of this important turning point in the birth of Marxism.

PART ONE

Marx's Theory of Alienation

1

Alienated Labour

Introduction

In 1844 a turning point occurs in Marx's philosophical development. For the first time he attributes fundamental ontological[1] significance to *productive activity*.[2] Through material production humanity comes to be what it is. Through the process of production the worker realizes his potential and becomes objective to himself in his product. He develops his productive powers and knows himself in and through his activity and its result. It is important to observe that this is possible only because there exists raw material with which to work. Marx says that 'the worker can create nothing without *nature*, without the sensuous external world'.[3] It is the material in which his activity realizes itself, and, in the absence of any distortion of the relationship, this material production is the *'mediation'* in which the unity of man with nature is established.

The category of 'mediation' Marx takes from Hegel, and it is as central to his work as it is to Hegel's. It is to be contrasted with 'immediacy'. In the present case, someone who argues that man is nothing but a part of nature, a natural being subject to natural laws, is taking the position that man is in *immediate unity* with nature. By contrast, someone who takes a dualistic position, representing man as separate from the natural realm, developing himself spiritually, and struggling against the power of nature latent in himself as well as the influence of external determinants, is taking man to be *immediately opposed* to nature.

Marx's position is much more complex. On the one hand, he speaks of nature as 'man's inorganic body' and says that 'he must maintain a continuing dialogue with it if he is not to die . . . for man is a part of nature'.[4] On the other hand, he says that 'it is in his fashioning of the objective world that man really proves himself'; through such productive activity 'nature appears as *his* work and his reality . . . and he can therefore contemplate himself in a world he himself created';[5] this process is characterized as *'objectification' (Vergegenständlichung)* – another important category Marx employs.

In truth, man is neither passively dependent upon nature, nor is he able to create his world from nothing. It is rather the case that through industry, productive activity, a dynamic relationship between man and nature is established in which both poles are transformed. In a discussion of this problem in the *German Ideology* (1846) Marx and Engels explain that 'the celebrated "unity of man with nature" has always existed in industry . . . and so has the "struggle" of man with nature . . .'.[6] In summing up Marx's position we may therefore refer to the relationship of man and nature as *mediated* in that it is not immediately given, and forever untransformed, but is one in which productive activity, interposed as a third 'moment', provides a principle of development, transformation and self-transformation. On the objective side there is the development of productive powers, which enable society to appropriate natural materials to human use with decreasing effort. On the subjective side, Marx elaborates the idea of the constitution of a 'wealth of human needs',[7] and the development of 'the richness of . . . *human* sensibility (a musical ear, an eye for beauty of form – in short, senses capable of human gratification, senses affirming themselves as essential powers of man)'.[8]

The mediation of productive activity (objectification) Marx views as ontologically fundamental to the whole social and historical development of mankind (see figure 1).

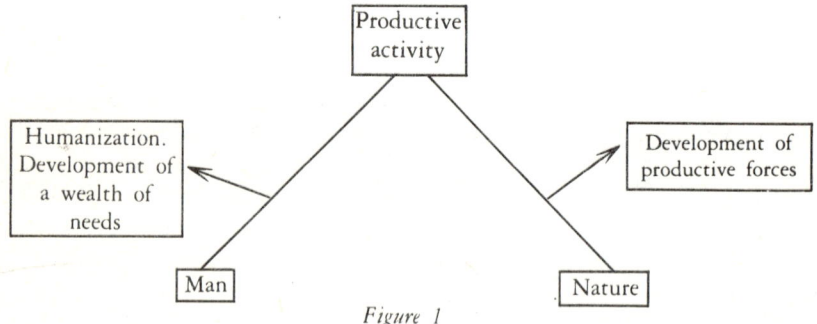

Figure 1

Where idealist social ontologies try to purge social categories of the natural, and biological reductionists evacuate the social mediations, the strength of Marx's category of 'productive activity' lies precisely in its double determination as the linking element between the human and the natural, the ideal and the material, teleology and causality. Productive activity is at the same time both a *material interchange* (the combination and transformation of raw materials into goods for human consumption) and a human *social process* – whereby the cunning of human practice realizes its aims within the context of definite, historically determined and transformed, socio-economic relationships.

The perspective just outlined is admittedly very general, but it underpins Marx's theory of alienation as it is sketched in the well-known chapter of the *1844 Manuscripts* – 'Estranged Labour' – to which we now turn. (For notes on the German terms for alienation/estrangement see the Appendix, pp. 147–9.)

Estranged Labour

Marx's *1844 Manuscripts* are justly famous for conceptualizing the situation of the wage-labourer as one of *alienation*. Because the worker has no property in the means of production his labour-power is excluded from the instrument and object of production owned by another; his labour realizes itself therefore only through the wage-contract whereby it is alienated to the master and works in his behalf. The labourer treats his labour as a commodity; as a consequence he has no interest in the work itself but only in the wage; labour does not belong to itself but to private property. Marx comments trenchantly on the situation endured by the worker: he executes plans he does not form; he objectifies himself in his product only to have it taken from him; he produces palaces but lives in hovels; his labour creates beauty but deforms himself; the more intelligence is embodied in the design of the factory system the more machine-like and stupefying the routine of work, so much so that the labourer faces machinery as a competitor for his place; at work he does not feel at home; he feels himself only when he is not working; his work is not voluntary therefore, but is forced labour; in it the worker belongs not to himself but to another.[9]

Marx's diagnosis of 'estranged labour' is a complex shifting one in which he continually comes back to elaborate themes initiated earlier. Because we have before us a first draft, the *presentation* is not clearly organized. However, the underlying *structure* of Marx's thought articulates the different moments of the system of estranged relationships by mapping the alienating mediations on to the ontologically fundamental relationships already outlined.

Marx's frame of reference is the relationship man – activity – nature. In his production man works upon the naturally given object of his activity and develops himself and his powers on a corresponding basis. Marx thematizes alienation in the same dimensions. Alienating activity estranges man from the object of production and his essential human qualities. Although the *active* moment is the central one, in his exposition Marx finds it convenient to deepen the analysis in the sequence object – activity – man. Let me elaborate these moments (see figure 2).

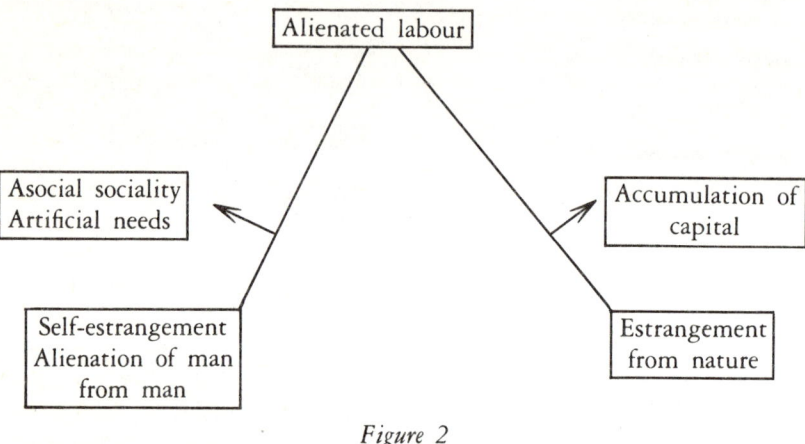

Figure 2

1 The worker is confronted by the *product* of his labour 'as an alien object exercising power over him' says Marx; not only does he lose the product to the capitalist, but its sale by the latter reinforces the power of wealth over the labourer; and, likewise, nature, the basis of production, is monopolized by the propertied class and appears as 'an alien world inimically opposed to him'.[10] 'The product of labour', says Marx, 'is the *objectification {Vergegenständlichung}* of labour', but, given that labour is separated from its objective conditions of realization (namely the material and the instruments of production) by their status as private property, the objectification of labour is at the same time its *alienation*, and the outcome is the estrangement of the worker from the material basis of his existence and life activity.[11]

2 'The relation of labour to the *act* of production within the *labour* process', Marx says, 'is the relation of the worker to his own activity as alien . . .' Marx derives this aspect from the first by means of the argument that, if estrangement is manifest in the result of production, this means that production itself must be alienating, 'the activity of alienation, the alienation of activity'. The wage-labourer has no satisfaction in his work and only endures it for the sake of the wage,

subordinating his activity to an alien power. 'His life-activity', says Marx, 'does not belong to him.' Since, for Marx, activity is the central determinant of human being (for as men express their life so they are), the alienation of labour is at the same time self-estrangement. Marx concludes: 'Here we have *self-estrangement*, as previously we had the estrangement of the *thing*.'[12]

3 'Estranged labour', Marx says, 'turns *man's species being* . . . into a being alien to him, into a *means* for his *individual existence*.'[13] What does Marx mean by '*species being*'?[14] He explains that 'man is a species being . . . because he looks upon himself as a *universal* and therefore free being.'[15] The most important species activity is 'productive life'.[16] It is worth quoting an extended passage in which this is thematized:

> The practical creation of an *objective world*, the *fashioning* of inorganic nature, is the proof that man is a conscious species being . . . It is true that animals also produce. They build nests and dwellings, like the bee, the beaver, the ant, etc. But an animal produces only what is immediately needed for itself or its young; it produces one-sidedly, while man produces universally; it produces only under the pressure of immediate physical need, while man produces even when he is free from physical need and truly produces only in freedom therefrom; it produces only itself, while man reproduces the whole of nature; its product belongs immediately to its physical body, while man freely confronts his product. An animal forms things only according to the standard and need of the species to which it belongs, while man knows how to produce in accordance with the standard of every species and knows how to apply to each object its inherent standard, hence man forms things in accordance with the laws of beauty.
>
> In fashioning the objective world, therefore, man proves himself really to be a *species being*. This production is his active species life. Through it nature appears as his work and his reality. The object of labour is therefore the *objectification* of the species-life of man: for he duplicates himself not only intellectually, in his consciousness, but actively and actually, and therefore he sees himself in the world he has created.[17]

The characteristic of human productive activity that marks it off from a merely animal mode of subsistence is its universal and creative power. A man can 'put his hand to anything'. But the labourer subordinated to the division of labour obtains no satisfaction in his work because the universal power of the species is realized in capitalism as the annexation of the individual to a particular set routine. The work is a mere means towards a living wage. 'In degrading spontaneous, free activity to a means, estranged labour makes man's species life a means to his physical existence',[18] complains Marx. In this light, Marx argues that an increase in wages 'would therefore be nothing but better *payment for the slave*, and would not win either for the worker or for labour their human status and dignity.'[19]

At the same time, the social character of production takes on an *asocial* quality in so far as the worker and the capitalist both depend on each other, yet are thrown into confrontation over the destiny of the product. Thus man is estranged from man.[20]

So this, in schematic outline, is Marx's account of estranged labour. We are not concerned here with thematizing other spheres of estrangement; but there is one corollary worth noting. Marx writes a special section on the estrangement involved in capitalist *consumption*. The significance Marx attaches to the development of 'the wealth of human needs' was noted briefly above. In principle, Marx regards each new product as 'a new enrichment of human nature'. Under private property, however, this relation of production to consumption reverses its significance; for the former now dominates the latter in an alienating way, he argues. The capitalist 'speculates on creating a *new* need in another so as to drive him to fresh sacrifice, to place him in a new dependence'. In this context 'every new product represents a new potentiality of mutual swindling.'[21] In a remarkably prescient passage, Marx diagnoses the essence of advertising:

> Subjectively . . . the extension of products and needs becomes a contriving and ever-calculating subservience to inhuman, sophisticated, unnatural and imaginary appetites . . . No eunuch flatters his despot more basely or uses more despicable means to stimulate his dulled capacity for pleasure than does the industrial eunuch – the producer – in order to sneak a few pieces of silver . . . out of the pockets of his dearly beloved neighbours in Christ. He puts himself at the service of the other's most depraved fancies, plays the pimp between him and his need, excites in him morbid appetites, lies in wait for each of his weaknesses – all so that he can then demand the cash for this service.[22]

As for the purchaser of these goodies, he is incapable of truly enjoying anything *for itself* because all the senses have been estranged by private property in favour of 'the sense of having'.[23]

Marx is struck above all by the quasi-magical power of money seemingly to acquire for its possessor every human power he lacks. It is 'the alienated ability of mankind'; 'it makes contradictions embrace'.[24]

Of course, one could say that such a criticism of capitalist priorities and perversions is not difficult to mount: Charles Fourier, with his theory of the passions, had already connected the richness of need and enjoyment with 'association' of labour, and inveighed against production for the sake of production; the work of M. Hess on the category of 'having' is explicitly cited in Marx's text; furthermore, Marx is able to draw on the resources of literature[25] in so far as it depicts the system of estrangement — in the final pages of his notebook he quotes passages from Goethe and Shakespeare in his critique of money.[26]

What is new in Marx, as we shall see, is the way in which such insights are situated in a comprehensive theory of capitalism which grounds the necessity of communism in a real historical transition.

Let us now try to get an overview of our progress so far. At the beginning I showed that the category of 'productive activity' has general ontological significance for Marx. Already in 1844, therefore, we have the first glimpses of the science of historical materialism, because this mediation provides the possibility of a historical dimension to human existence in so far as men's relationships to nature and to each other are transformed through it.

The actual development of this activity, however, has become subsumed under a further set of mediations; in the present economic conditions we find that productive activity itself is mediated through the division of labour, private property, exchange, wages, in sum a system of estrangement in which productive activity loses itself and falls under the sway of an alien power. István Mészáros has termed this 'a set of *second-order* mediations . . . i.e. a *historically specific* mediation of the *ontologically fundamental* self-mediation of man with nature.'[27] The most important distinction between the two orders is that initially it is presupposed that productive activity is in immediate unity with its object, whereas with the imposition of the estranging second-order mediations labour is immediately confronted by its object as something separate from it. This immediate opposition is not ontologically given in the nature of things but is the result of historically determinate mediations. (It is necessary to note that the categories immediate/mediate do not divide elements into two different classes; rather, the same relation may be mediated from one point of view and immediate from another.)

For Marx, what requires historical explanation is not the unity but the separation of these moments, through a process whereby 'man alienates the mediating activity itself', and hence becomes the slave of an '*alien mediator*'.[28]

It is important to understand that the emergence of the second-order mediation does not substitute itself for the first – it further mediates the mediation itself. This means that it would not be correct to erect a dichotomy between them such that everything true of one side is untrue of the other (a strategy typical of analytical thought); this, in turn, would facilitate a faulty diagnosis of the problem of alienation in terms of an opposition of the ideal and the real.

Let us note in particular that, if through productive activity man objectifies himself and lives in a world he has himself made, this is no less true when he alienates himself and fails to recognize himself in the system of estrangement brought about through alienated objectification. It is this conceptual *inflection* rather than mutual *exclusion* of the categories 'objectification' and 'alienation' that permits theoretical space for grasping the objective necessity of a historical supersession, which would otherwise be a utopian 'demand'. Equally, the possibility of historical supersession depends on a refusal to identify the second-order mediation with the first (easy to do because in recorded history the rule of private property bulks large), thus building into the theory the inevitability of alienation, whatever philosophy may endeavour to reconcile us to it. In order to overcome estrangement, the alienating mediations must be overcome. But this does not mean that Marx rejects all mediation, for the 'first-order mediation' – productive activity as such – is an absolute ontological dimension of social life; Marx opposes only its specific alienated form, imposed through second-order mediations which are historically surpassable. If this distinction is not drawn, and social philosophy collapses the two levels into one, such that private property and exchange are taken to be as absolute as productive activity itself, then it is not possible for such a philosophy to grasp the conditions of a *positive supersession* of estrangement; it must descend to apologetics and pseudo-solutions.

The Concept of 'Labour'

Confusion is evident on this last point in some of the secondary literature on Marx's *1844 Manuscripts*. One reason for this is that Marx's terminology is not always understood. To make further progress in elucidating his thought, it is necessary to deal with a point on this avoided so far.

This is that the second-order alienating activity is often identified by Marx as '*labour*' – not 'wage-labour' or 'alienated labour' but 'labour' pure and simple. If this category 'labour' (*Arbeit*) is identified in reading the text with the productive activity as such that is ontologically fundamental, hopeless misunderstanding can arise. It need not arise if a commentator is sufficiently sensitive to the context to discount such a 'literal' reading. However, this point on terminology needs to be grasped, not only for pedantic exactness, but also because an important conceptual point hangs on it, as will be shown below.

To begin with, let us attend to the textual problem. This problem is a special case of the difficulty of reading Marx's early work through spectacles acquired by a knowledge of the later work, thus imposing anachronistically the meanings of *Capital* on the young Marx. The category 'labour' (*Arbeit*) had settled its meaning by the time Marx wrote *Capital*, as one of his fundamental ahistorical categories. Thus, the chapter in *Capital* on the labour-process starts with the assertion that this can be examined without reference to the social form within which it is carried on. He goes on:

Labour is, first of all, a process between man and nature, a process by which man, of his own accord, mediates, regulates, and controls the metabolism between himself and nature . . . Through this movement he acts on external nature, changing it, and simultaneously changes his own nature.[29]

Another quotation from *Capital* shows that at this time Marx equates 'labour' with productive activity in the sense of our first-order mediation:

Labour as such, in its simple character as purposive activity, is related to the means of production not in their determinate social form, but rather in their concrete substance . . ., the earth as non-produced means of labour, the others as produced.[30]

The usage of the term 'labour' is different in the early writings. In such texts as the *1844 Manuscripts* and the *German Ideology* (1846–7) Marx restricts the term to *productive activity carried on under the rule of private property*. It is *not* the term he uses when he wishes to thematize that activity which is the universal ontological ground of social life. Still less does it apply to future unalienated free activity.

It is a testimony to the incapacity of people to read what is written in the 1844 text that when Lukács takes from it the appropriate distinction he does not use Marx's own terminology. Instead, he elevates the term '*Arbeit*' to an ahistorical universal, as in the following diagnosis:

In his discussion of economics Marx, drawing on his knowledge of empirical evidence, distinguishes sharply between objectification in labour in general and the estrangement of subject and object in the *capitalist form* of labour.[31]

If Lukács can overlook the point, it is not surprising that lesser thinkers do so. Thus Herbert Marcuse (in his 1932 review of the *1844 Manuscripts*) speaks of 'Marx's positive definition of labour', and (in his *Reason and Revolution* of 1941) he states that in the *1844 Manuscripts* Marx holds that 'labour in its true form is a medium for man's true self-fulfilment'.[32] T.I. Oizerman says in his paraphrase of the *1844 Manuscripts*: 'To analyse private property, one has above all to analyse the form of labour which creates it ... Marx ... explains that private property and everything that springs from it is not created by labour in general, but by *alienated labour*, a historically definite form of human activity.'[33] These are examples of 'positive' readings, which would conform with Marx's usage only if the phrase 'labour in general' were to be 'productive activity' instead.

Let us now turn to some examples of 'negative' readings. Raya Dunayevskaya, without citing exact references, says:

> So hostile was Marx to labour under capitalism, that at first he called, not for the 'emancipation' of labour, but for its 'abolition'. That is why, at first, he termed man's function not 'labour', but 'self-activity' ... No matter how the language changed, the point remained that labour, in a new society, would in no manner whatever be the type of activity it is under capitalism where man's labour is limited to the exercise of his physical labour-power.[34]

Erich Fromm follows Dunayevskaya closely.[35] Robert Tucker sums up the matter correctly as follows:

> By 'labour' or 'alienated labour' – terms that he employs interchangeably – Marx means productive activity performed by man in the state of alienation from himself. He declares that all human activity up to now has been labour ... Consequently, man has never been fully himself in his creative activity. This activity has never been 'self-activity', by which Marx means free creativity in which a person feels thoroughly at home with himself, enjoys a sense of voluntary self-determination to action, and experiences his energies as his own.[36]

Mészáros detects some ambiguity:

> In the *Manuscripts of 1844* labour is considered both in general – as 'productive activity': the fundamental ontological determination of 'humanness' – and in particular, as having the form of capitalistic 'division of labour'. It is in this latter form – capitalistically structured activity – that 'labour' is the ground of all alienation.[37]

G. Petrović detects a similar inconsistency:

> In the *Economic and Philosophical Manuscripts*, Marx as a rule opposes 'labour' to 'praxis' and explicitly describes 'labour' as 'the act of alienation of practical human activity', but he is sometimes inconsistent, using 'labour' synonymously with 'praxis'.[38]

I would not claim that Marx is absolutely consistent, but I would say that his normal usage of 'labour' refers it to the more specific meaning and that examples that look like the more universal sense are often simply aspects of the former because, as we have already explained, labour is, at the same time, productive activity.

Let us now establish the textual evidence for Marx's early 'negative' definition of 'labour' and his anticipation of its 'abolition'. In the first three sections of the first manuscript it has not yet occurred to Marx to organize the material under the rubric of estrangement. His main critical category is 'abstraction'. Capital, landed property and labour are separated from each other and this 'abstraction' is 'fatal for the worker'.[39] Marx shows that the evidence of the political economists themselves proves this; but they do not recognize 'that labour itself . . . is harmful and pernicious' – even though it follows from their own arguments.[40] This is partly because the political economist does not consider the human being of the worker but merely his function as a labourer – one who lives 'by a one-sided abstract labour' – hence 'in political economy *labour* occurs only in the shape of the activity of *earning a living*'.[41] This might leave open the possibility of some other 'shape' of labour, but in the following discussion of estrangement Marx says more conclusively that 'political economy *conceals the estrangement inherent in the nature of labour*'.[42]

In the following pages there is a summarizing passage in which 'labour' is equated with 'the act of estranging practical human activity'[43] and in which '*the act of production*' is said to become 'an alien activity' turned against the worker, within 'the *labour* process'.[44]

In the second manuscript a very important passage includes the following definition: 'Within the private property relationship there is contained latently . . . the production of human activity as *labour* – that is, as an activity quite alien to itself, to man, and to nature.'[45] In this passage 'labour' is defined as productive activity transformed by the private property system into an activity alien to itself. Were it not that this is simply ignored by political economy, simply not understood, then 'alienated labour' would be a pleonasm. In this sense of 'labour', human activity as such is distinguished from it as free activity which harmoniously relates man and nature, the producer and his object.

In the third manuscript Marx says that the history of industry presents – albeit 'in the form of estrangement' – an 'open book of man's essential powers'. 'This was not conceived in its connection with man's essential being but only in the external relation of utility', he goes on, because 'all human activity hitherto has been labour', that is 'activity estranged from itself'.[46] Here there is a clear distinction between the positive side of the history of production, in so far as it mobilized 'man's essential powers', and the negative side, constituted by the forms of estrangement within which it has developed. 'Labour' is clearly assigned to the latter as 'activity estranged from itself'.

Later, in a fragment on the division of labour in civil society, the same negative definition of 'labour' appears again; since 'labour is only an expression of human activity within alienation' then the division of labour is 'the estranged and alienated form of human activity as an activity of the species'.[47]

A couple of years later Marx worked with Engels on another manuscript, known to us as the *German Ideology*, in which even more striking formulations occur. He proposes not only the end of the division of labour (for which 'private property' is an 'identical expression'[48]) but also the *abolition* of labour. For example: 'In all previous revolutions the mode of activity always remained unchanged and it was only a question of . . . a new distribution of labour . . . whilst the communist revolution is directed against the hitherto existing *mode* of activity, does away with *labour* . . .'[49] There followed the beginnings of a further amplification: 'the modern form of activity under the rule of . . .' – but this was crossed out; nevertheless it is clear that 'labour' is understood as an activity which is not free and falls together with private property.

The 'abolition of labour' ('*Aufhebung der Arbeit*') is spoken of on several occasions later in this text,[50] of which the most interesting states:

> Labour, the only connection which still links them with the productive forces and with their own existence, has lost all semblance of self-activity and . . . while in earlier periods . . . the production of material life was considered a subordinate mode of

self-activity, they now diverge to such an extent that material life appears as the end, and what produces this material life, labour (which is now the only possible but, as we see, negative form of self-activity) as the means.[51]

All these passages show that 'labour' is defined as alienating activity, to be distinguished from self-activity, free activity, human activity. In all these passages, also, the context makes it clear that the labour defined negatively is not productive activity itself (the manifestation of 'essential power') but only that carried on within the division of labour and private property. Equally, abolition of labour does not do away with work itself (not even manual work) but sets it in the framework of 'free' and 'universal' activity. If we want to know the immediate source of this way of talking about 'labour', we need look no further than Marx's own acknowledgement of the influence of M. Hess on his thought. In the Preface to the *1844 Manuscripts* Marx says that 'the only *original* German works of substance in this science' include 'the essays by *Hess* published in *Einundzwanzig Bogen*'.[52]

This refers the reader to some essays by Hess, in a book published abroad in 1843 to defeat the German censorship. The first of these is a review of a book by Lorenz von Stein on French socialism and communism, which made a big impact on radical circles in Germany. At the time he wrote the review, Hess was already in Paris and so had first-hand knowledge of the Fourierists and other socialist currents. In his review Hess declares that in communism 'the opposition of enjoyment and labour disappears'. This is because 'every man has an inclination to some kind of activity, even to very different sorts of activity, and out of the multiplicity of free human inclinations and activities arises the free, living and everyouthful organism of free, human society, free, human occupations that cease to be 'work' and become identical with 'pleasure'.'[53]

There is no doubt, therefore, that in his *1844 Manuscripts* Marx is writing under the immediate influence of such views.

Two of the commentators we cited earlier as failing to notice that in the *1844 Manuscripts* 'labour' is the term construed as a 'negative' form of self-activity, as alienation, are yet struck by the fact that Marx calls for the 'abolition of labour' in the *German Ideology*; and they provide similar solutions to the problem – which will serve to introduce our own reflections on the matter.

Marcuse (in his *Reason and Revolution*) makes the following comment:

> These amazing formulations in Marx's earliest writings all contain the Hegelian term '*Aufhebung*', so abolition also carries the meaning that a

content is restored to its true form. Marx, however, envisioned the future mode of labour to be so different from the prevailing one that he hesitated to use the same term 'labour' to designate alike the material process of capitalist and of communist society. He uses the term 'labour' to mean what capitalism actually understands by it in the last analysis, that activity which creates surplus value in commodity production, or, which 'produces capital'.[54]

Oizerman permits himself to express the view that in speaking of the abolition of labour Marx adopts 'a form of expression which is not very apt terminologically';[55] and he excuses it with much the same reasons as Marcuse, namely that Marx is simply borrowing the category of the political economists and that, in any case, *'Aufhebung'* does not quite mean 'abolition'.[56]

The problem is clear — in some sense the alienated form of activity seems to demand a distinct concept which is correlative with the other moments of the bourgeois totality, notably capital, that is a concept which is historically specific; in another sense there is a continuity of reference when we discuss productive activity under the rule of private property, and under socialism.

Curiously enough, a similar terminological problem was addressed by Engels in his editorial work on Marx's *Capital*. In a footnote in *Capital*,[57] Marx already noted that English writers of the seventeenth century liked to use an Anglo-Saxon word for the actual thing, and a Latin word for 'its reflection'. In a later note inserted in the fourth German edition such a case arises, when Engels over-enthusiastically claims that where German just has *'die Arbeit'* English has the advantage of two separate words for two different aspects of it: that which 'creates use-values . . . is called "work", as opposed to "labour"'; that which 'creates value . . . is called "labour", as opposed to "work",' says Engels.[58] English usage does not accord with Engels' distinction — as expressions such as 'look for work' show — but the important point is that it would be useful to have two such separate expressions.

There is a conceptual difference that needs to be marked between the material process of working and the inflection given to this activity when it is socially specified within exchange as value-producing labour. It is no longer just work but has a determinate social form which marks it out within the generic activity.

Earlier I mentioned that there is a conceptual problem underlying the sense in which 'labour' is used. This is because, throughout the *1844 Manuscripts*, Marx continually relates labour to private property in a very intimate way, as 'the subjective essence of private property'. Since private property is understood by Marx as a historically specific system, to be superseded, it must surely follow that its *essence* cannot be a first-order mediation but must be equally determined within the framework of second-order mediations. *Either* Marx should have said that the essence of private property is 'alienated labour', reserving the term 'labour' for the ontologically prior level; *or*, if 'labour' as such is to be 'the subjective essence', then we need some other term for the relevant first-order mediation. If we take the second alternative, then a reading of Marx's *1844 Manuscripts* and the *German Ideology* readily gives us a candidate, namely 'activity' or, more precisely, 'productive activity'; 'labour' may then be defined as 'alienated productive activity', or, if that is to beg the question, as 'activity within the relationships of private property'. The next chapter investigates these private property relations.

Summary

Marx's *ontology* comprises the complex totality man – activity – nature. In the history of human society the mediating moment is *productive activity*. But imposed on this *first-order mediation* is a set of *second-order mediations*, principally *private property*, estranging man from himself, his powers, his activity and his object. *Objectification* is then at the same time *alienation*. Within the system of second-order mediations, productive activity, now an alienating activity, is redefined as (alienated) *labour*.

Marx's project is to conceptualize the positive supersession of this system of estrangement.

2
Private Property

Introduction

The first chapter brought out the character of estranged labour by showing how the fundamental mediatedness of social development, articulated through the complex man – activity – nature, becomes transformed in all its dimensions: man is specified socially as labourer or exploiter; productive activity becomes alienated labour; and the object is constituted within the sphere of private property as an independent power, as capital.

This chapter will take a closer look at this set of second-order mediations. In particular, it will discuss the way in which Marx conceives of the relation between alienated labour and private property; the dialectic of the movement of private property; and the contradictions that require resolution.

The Movement of Private Property

At first sight it appears that the worker's alienation in his labour is due to the subordination of labour to *private property*. His estrangement follows from the separation between labour and private property, and the power of private property over the immediate producer. The only certainty in the worker's life is that his destiny depends upon private property – on whether it has any use for the labour he offers. The *immediate* precondition of alienated labour thus appears to be private property in the means of production which excludes the worker.

Unwary readers of the section on 'estranged labour' in the *1844 Manuscripts* – assuming that what is being claimed is that the worker is alienated because he works under the sway of the property owner – are then astonished when Marx suddenly turns round and says that private property is not so much the cause as the consequence of alienation. Here is the passage in question:

> Private property is . . . the product, result, and necessary consequence, of *alienated labour*, of the external relation of the worker to nature and to himself . . . It is true that we took the concept of *alienated labour* . . . from political economy as a result of the *movement of private property*. But it is clear from an analysis of this concept that if private property appears as the ground, the basis of alienated labour, it is much more its consequence, just as the gods were *originally* not the cause but the effect of the confusion in men's minds. Later, however, this relationship becomes reciprocal.[1]

It is of the first importance to understand what Marx is saying here, and the significance of his view of private property as the product of alienated labour.[2] A clue to the direction of his thought is given a few lines later, when he comments: 'In speaking of *private property* one imagines that one is dealing with something external to man. In speaking of labour one is immediately dealing with man himself.'[3] This reminds us that private property is a social institution. It is simply a way of organizing human relationships in the production and distribution of material goods. Ultimately it has to be grasped as a *human* creation. Otherwise one would be illegitimately *naturalizing* (treating as a *given* basis of human existence) what is produced and reproduced in and through human history.

None the less, as we shall see in a moment, in the case of pre-capitalist society one is not going too far from the truth in seeing property, e.g. landed property, as a prior *condition* of labour's realization: but developed private property, held as capital, is different. Capital, as a store of value, is *internally* related to value-creating labour.

In the first part of the *1844 Manuscripts* Marx stays close to his sources in political economy and shows from facts admitted by political economy itself that the more the worker produces the less he can call his own and 'the more he falls under the domination of his product, of capital'.[4]

In its theory political economy says that labour is the basis of production and exchange; Adam Smith is quite clear that the real 'wealth of nations' lies in the *labour force* and in improvements in productivity brought about by the division of labour. The economy appears to be founded on the movement of private property, on buying, selling, investing, profiting; but behind these relationships lies labour and *its* relations and development. Marx says that there is therefore a paradox in that 'political economy starts out from labour as the real soul of production, and yet gives nothing to labour and everything to private property'! 'Proudhon has dealt with this contradiction', Marx continues, 'by deciding for labour and against private property'; but that is insufficiently dialectical; what we are faced with is 'the contradiction of estranged labour with itself'.[5] Today, private property is, paradigmatically, *capital*, which is nothing but a store of value. What is the origin of value? What is its substance? Why – *labour*! Every time the worker labours, therefore, he creates a value which, when realized on the market by the employer, adds to his capital. The worker produces and reproduces that which dominates him – capital.

The relation of cause and consequence is grasped here from the point of view of the self-reproduction process of the totality rather than an external conjunction of antecedent and consequent. Abstract alienated labour, and capital, stand in an internal relation which structures the whole of capitalist society in such a way that its reproduction depends on the constant reflection of these moments into each other (for 'moment', see Appendix). To prioritize labour is not to overlook the power of capital; but capital's effectivity as the proximate moment in the worker's estrangement does not prevent Marx from grasping it as the mediating moment in labour's self-alienation, established by labour itself as its own otherness. In grasping this dialectical relation of reflection in otherness we are dealing not with the constant conjunction of otherwise unrelated elements but with a polar relation in which, although one can follow the movement of private property as its current principal aspect, the ultimately overriding moment must be labour, which alienates itself in the capital to which it is subordinated.

Marx says:

> The labourer produces capital and capital produces him, which means that he produces himself; man as a labourer, as a commodity, is the product of this entire cycle.[6]

In relating labour in its alienation to fully developed private property, that is, capitalist property, in this way, Marx is well aware that relationships were different in previous social formations. When he gives priority to labour over property he is not posing it as historically antecedent but rather as ontologically more fundamental in the social totality established by their dialectic. However, this dialectical relationship between labour and private property is itself a historically developed result. Hence, it had not merely to be discovered, but to be created. If one looks, as Marx does in the first manuscript, at pre-capitalist formations, there is no *internal* economic dialectic between labour and property as there is between labour as the substance of value and capital as 'stored up labour' — as Marx defines it (following Adam Smith).[7]

In the main form of pre-capitalist property, namely landed property worked by serfs, or yielding tithes, there is certainly an opposition between labour and property in that, in virtue of the political ties of lordship and bondage, the exploitation of the propertyless mass of labourers is effected. But this process of exploitation does not sustain the property relation itself in purely economic fashion. Romanticism views this state of affairs as the absence of alienation — for the market is very marginal to life and the land is inalienable. But, despite the absence of the activity of huckstering in the daily round, estrangement is still present as a permanent condition. 'Feudal landed property is already by its very nature', Marx says, 'huckstered land, which is estranged from man and hence confronts him in the shape of a few great lords.' Thus, the basic condition of labour, the earth, appears as 'an alien power over man'. Hence 'the rule of private property begins with property in land; that is its basis'.[8] However, it does not yet appear as an *economic* power, because it is *politically* enforced and reproduced. From an economic point of view feudal property is an externally enforced condition determining one's place in production and the possibility of gaining wealth; for example, the serf is condemned to be an appurtenance of the land, the land itself is inalienably linked to the system of primogeniture.

But when private property is fully developed it is free from all such restrictions and is universally alienable. Along with the development of markets in all kinds of commodities goes the reduction of land and labour themselves to alienable commodities. Possession now depends no longer on political mediation, but on the effect of the *purely economic movement*. It becomes inevitable, Marx says,

> that the rule of the property owner should appear as the naked rule of private property, of capital, divested of all political tincture; that the relationship between property owner and worker should be reduced to the economic relationship of exploiter and exploited; that the personal relationship between the property owner and his property should come to an end, and that property itself should become merely *objective* material wealth . . .[9]

It is noteworthy, moreover, that Marx commonly speaks of the power of property or of capital rather than the domination of the property owner or the capitalist. Much more is involved here than a rhetorical figure. This usage represents Marx's insight into the real conditions of social relationships in bourgeois society. This is: that the nature of the relationship between persons follows from their relationships to things. If one asks of two persons going into a factory why it is that one can boss the other around, the answer cannot be given in terms of the personal qualities of the individuals concerned but only in terms of their differing relation to capital. The one who owns (or acts on behalf of) capital is thereby the master of the other. Marx says:

> Capital is the *power to command* labour and its products. The capitalist possesses this power not on account of his personal or human properties but in so far as he is the *owner* of capital. His power is the *purchasing* power of his capital, which nothing can withstand.[10]

Throughout his work Marx never tires of contrasting the relationships of personal dependency in pre-capitalist society with the liberation from personal dependence established by the bourgeois revolution; but then there comes the common dependence on impersonal relations; through the mediation of money and capital new social dependencies arise.

In feudalism there is the appearance of a meaningful unity between the individual and the means of production in that land is *individuated* with its lord and its serfs – just this particular estate is *his* and they belong to *it*. Hence the proverb: 'No land without its lord'.[11] Developed private property, by contrast, has an *abstractly universal* form: value. One can put one's wealth 'into' anything – factories, land, works of art – without ceasing to be 'worth' so much. Money dissolves all feudal fixity and we find the modern saying 'Money has no master' expressing the absolute contingency of the relationship between property and personality. In the *Communist Manifesto* Marx and Engels (following Carlyle[12]) will declare that there remains 'no other nexus between man and man than naked self-interest, than callous "cash-payment".'[13] We no longer bow the knee to princes, but now, says Marx, 'an impersonal power rules over everything'.[14]

What Marx traces in his treatment of pre-capitalist forms is a movement from a situation where property is a politically enforced condition of labour (for example, one just finds that one is *obliged* to work as a serf for the propertied) to that in which property rests on the exploitation of the 'free' labourer in the capital relation. There is a shift from a *state* of estrangement between labour and its conditions of actualization (appearing over against it as another's property) to the constitution of a *process* of alienation sustaining the system of estrangement of labour from its object and itself.

The first relation (politically effected estrangement) is a historically prior condition of the second complex; but in the movement of the economic totality that is now constituted by the relations of labour and capital, labour establishes private property as its estranged self. Marx says: 'It is only at the culminating point of the development of private property that this its secret re-emerges, namely, that on the one hand it is the *product* of alienated labour, and on the other it is the *means* through which labour alienates itself, the *realization of this alienation.*'[15]

The relation of immediate exclusion between labour and its object remains in the new dynamic, not now as a precondition, but as a mediated result, as the recurring moment at which the worker is forced to sell his labour-power because he has no other property. The whole system, including the reproduction of this very moment, is sustained by labour's continual self-alienation.[16]

Private property, originally *other* than labour, becomes in practice labour's *own* other, private property *as* alienated labour. Private property is unmasked as itself a *structure of alienation*, rather than the (apparently external) cause of estrangement.

Let us now summarize the position we have reached – in so doing, perhaps, elaborating it rather more sharply than it is explicitly articulated in the text.

It is necessary first to recognize the fact that we have now seen two senses in which private property is less fundamental than productive activity. In the first place the general level of discussion of these issues has led us to emphasize the importance of conceptualizing the system of private property as a historically specific form of organizing the material life of society. In principle it is possible to envisage material production going on without it, and it is possible to discuss the work-process in abstraction from it (as Marx does in the first section of the chapter on 'the labour-process' in *Capital*). The question of the origins of the alienating second-order mediations is something Marx does not attempt to tackle in the *1844 Manuscripts*. (In the *German Ideology* he links back private property to the development of the social division of labour.) But this question is not relevant to his purposes in any case, because what counts from the point of view of the dynamic of the supersession of the private property system is its present articulation and contradictions. This in turn leads us to the second striking aspect of Marx's theory of alienation. As we have seen, even if we take it that private property, and hence the estrangement of labour from its object, is historically given, study of the movement of private property itself leads Marx to conclude that in its reciprocal relationship with labour it is ultimately best understood as the consequence rather than the cause of alienated labour. The state of estrangement between labour and private property is developed, historically and conceptually, to a process of *active alienation of labour from itself.*

At the level of first-order mediation Marx puts at the centre productive activity. At the level of second-order mediation he puts at the centre, correspondingly, alienated labour.

The Contradictions of Private Property

In the *1844 Manuscripts* 'labour' is understood fairly broadly as activity enforced on the immediate producers by external constraints, such as the social division of labour and the rule of private property. It is understood also, more narrowly, when related to capital ('stored up labour') as *'the subjective essence of private property'*. Important consequences follow from such a conceptualization.

The point is developed best in the second manuscript (which is passed over in silence by most commentators, but which is crucial to Marx's whole argument), and in a couple of closely related comments on it from the beginning of the third manuscript.[17] Consider first the following highly dialectical exposition of the private property relationship:

> The relationship [*Das Verhältnis*] of private property contains latently within itself the relationship of private property as *labour*, the relationship of private property as *capital*, and the connection [*Beziehung*] of these two terms to each other. On the one hand we have the production of human activity as *labour*, that is as an activity wholly alien to itself, to man, and to nature ... the abstract existence of man as a mere work-man [*Arbeitsmenschen*] ... on the other hand, the production of the object of human activity as *capital* – wherein all the natural and social specificity of the object is *extinguished* ... in which the *same* capital stays the *same* in the most diverse natural and social instantiations [*Dasein*], totally indifferent to its actual content. This contradiction, driven to the limit, is necessarily the limit, the culmination, and the downfall of the whole system.[18]

In considering this passage we need first to attend to the term *'Verhältnis'* (relationship). Bertell Ollman (in his book *Alienation*) has already drawn our attention to the central role of this term in Marx's work. He claims that within such a relationship each 'factor' internalizes the relationship itself such that if the latter alters 'the factor itself alters; it becomes something else'. On this view, Ollman continues, interaction is, more properly speaking, 'inneraction' because the factors form an organic whole.[19]

Ollman also explains that in discussion of such a system of 'internal relations' it is possible for any term to extend its reference beyond its 'core' to related moments and even the whole. With our passage in mind he says: 'Perhaps the major service performed by Marx's conception of private property is as a meeting-place for various strands in his thinking'; it is a relation 'which contains many others'.[20]

It is also interesting to note the Hegelian origins of this term '*Verhältnis*'. M.J. Petry explains that Hegel employs the cognate term *Verhalten* 'to refer to a relationship, *one* factor of which tends to be predominate or to take the initiative'.[21] Gillian Rose goes further. She says that for Hegel something in the condition of relation (*Verhältnis*) *subordinates* its object to itself.[22]

Of course, we cannot be sure that Marx used this common term[23] in the same way as Hegel. None the less, when Marx speaks of '*Das Verhältnis des Privateigentums*' (the private property relation), he may well have in mind the sort of relationship in which each side develops itself only through the subordination of its 'other', which always remains in some sense a 'barrier' it must set itself to incorporate.

Let us see how Marx explains in the passage above the transformation of productive activity brought about through 'the relationship of private property'.

At the level of first-order mediation we are concerned with 'human activity' and its 'object', but these are now related within the second-order mediations, summarized as the private property system, such that the first is constituted 'as labour', an activity 'wholly alien to itself', while the second is now held 'as capital' over against the labourer. Their participation in the relationship of private property *changes the nature* both of activity and its object. Furthermore, they now stand in a relation of mutual opposition; but this opposition is itself a relationship, in which each defines itself through exclusion from its other.

Marx goes on to explain that this contradiction emerges in all its purity only with the full development of the private property system. Earlier, historically specific distinctions existed both in forms of property-holding and in the sites of labour. Labour had 'not yet reached the stage of *indifference* to its content';[24] but now it is merely a 'source of livelihood' and as such the worker has no genuine identification with the work as it is *determinate*, a specific job. Liberated from all traditional ties to a foreordained occupation, the 'free worker' of the industrial revolution is a labour-power machine to be slotted into any job as required, subject to the needs only of capital accumulation. Likewise, while landed property still existed apart from industrial capital, it was still 'afflicted with local and political prejudices'.[25] Marx gives a graphic description of the ideological battles fought by the representatives of movable property and immovable property ('this distinction is not rooted in the nature of things', he says, 'it is a *historical* distinction'[26]); and the subsequent development 'results in the necessary victory of the *capitalist* over the *landowner* – that is to say, of developed over underdeveloped, immature private property – just as in general, movement must triumph over immobility, open self-conscious baseness over hidden unconscious baseness, cupidity over self-indulgence, the avowedly restless, adroit self-interest of *enlightenment* over the parochial wordly-wise respectable, idle and fantastic self-interest of *superstition*, and *money* over the other forms of private property.'[27]

At all events, the upshot of the development of the system of private property is a pure contradiction between two poles: Labour ('indifferent to its content') and capital (likewise 'indifferent to its real content'). The two terms (opposed and united) of the property relationship, labour and its object, the propertyless and the propertied, were previously chained together in particularized fixed units. Now, each side has become free to move and has attained abstractly universal form; both enter into a systematic totality, and become *posited by the private property relationship itself*.

Marx notices that the real history of private property is paralleled by the development of the theory of political economy. He says that the real process 'repeats itself in the scientific analysis of the *subjective* essence of private property, *labour*. Labour appears at first only as agricultural labour, but then asserts itself as labour in general'.[28] Marx draws two conclusions. It is only with the victory of industrial capital 'that private property can complete its domination over man and become, in its most general form, a world historical power';[29] and 'only when *labour* is grasped as the essence of private property can this economic process be analysed in its actual specificity'.[30]

This contradictory unity of labour and its other is important for Marx's dialectical development of the downfall of the whole private property system as it is drawn out in this and other passages. For example, the communist movement has the historic task of overthrowing private property assigned to it by Marx: but what is the ground of this necessity? If it were simply a matter of a discrepancy between wealth and poverty, an opposition between those who own property and those who have nothing, this might lead to a 'call for' the rectification of this antithesis based on some criterion of social justice applied externally to the existing situation. Marx, however, is able to root the necessity of the communist movement in the contradiction *internal* to the development of modern private property. In so doing he has to reinterpret the antithesis of property and propertylessness as that of capital and labour, because only in the latter form does the possibility arise of understanding the relation in a suitably dynamic fashion. It is true that throughout the *1844 Manuscripts* Marx more often speaks of private property than of capital, but it is perfectly clear that his reading of political economy had allowed him to grasp the central importance of the capital – labour contradiction. The following passage puts the matter beyond all doubt:

> The antithesis [*Gegensatz*] between *propertylessness* and *property*, so long as it is not comprehended as the antithesis of *labour* and *capital*, still remains an indifferent antithesis, not grasped in its *active connection*, in its *internal* relation, not yet grasped as a *contradiction* [*Widerspruch*]. It can find expression in this *first* form even without the advanced development of private property (as in ancient Rome, Turkey, etc.). It does not yet *appear* as having been established by private property itself. But labour, the subjective essence of private property as exclusion of property, and capital, objective labour as exclusion of labour, constitute *private property* as its developed state of contradiction – hence a dynamic relationship driving towards resolution [*Auflösung*].[31]

Private property in 'its developed state of contradiction' is characterized by the simultaneous identity and exclusion of two poles, labour and capital. Hence there can be no harmonious synthesis – only a drive towards dissolution. This important feature of the dialectic of second-order mediation (private property and exchange) distinguishes it markedly from that of the first-order mediation.

In working on the object of production a reciprocal transformation occurs, at the level of first-order mediation. On the one hand the object becomes adapted to some specific human use, as means either of consumption or production. On the other hand, human productive power is extended and developed. Over time there results an ever-growing mediatedness of the relationship between social man and the rest of nature. Within this, the recalcitrance of the objective world to human use is actively overcome on the basis of theoretical knowledge and practical experience of its determinate potentials. The manner in which the object is appropriated depends upon the specificity of its relation to the relevant mode of affirmation of human power and enjoyment.[32]

But all this is perverted in the context of estranging second-order mediation. Private property constitutes a determinate mode of externality of man to himself and to the conditions of his activity. If nature is man's 'inorganic body' because it is posited in his activity as its essential object, then to separate human productive power from its conditions of realization through constituting the latter as private property (whether or not the means of production are in fact monopolized in consequence) is already to constitute the object as external both to itself and to productive power. The latter is now thrown back (because of the *contingency* of this external relationship to the means of production) into an abstract 'subjectivity' estranged from its objective realm of expression. If the potentially monopolizable means of production are then in fact monopolized by a particular class of non-producers, the subjective moment too has to become external to itself since labour-power can now actualize itself in objective activity only in so far as it is alienated through the wage contract, becoming a commodity like any other. The aspiring producer thrown back into 'subjectivity' faces the purely objective conditions of his activity as absolutely recalcitrant to his appropriation because they are held as the private property of another. Hence this estrangement of the factors of production from each other makes necessary the active alienation of his powers to the other if he is to work at all. The 'unity' established through the wages system of the estranged moments is achieved through a 'second alienation' so to speak. This 'negation of the negation' makes possible the positive development of productive activity not by abolishing the property determinations excluding labour-power from its possession of the means of production but by re-establishing this unity *within* the private property relationship itself.

The important thing about the dialectic of private property is that the affirmative mediating process of objectification is now undercut by the estrangement of each side from the other; subject and object are condensed out as abstractly opposed spheres. The attempt to mediate these pure extremes, labour and capital, which 'mutually exclude each other', results, says Marx, in 'hostile reciprocal opposition' which reflects their contradictory unity in the '*opposition* of each *to* itself'.[33] On the side of capitalist: he cannot accumulate capital except through appropriating labour, yet the wages paid out represent a sacrifice of his capital. On the other side: the labourer cannot gain a livelihood except by treating his labour-power as his 'capital', a resource to be alienated through commodity exchange to the owner of the means of production (see figure 3).

What precisely is the reason for this? Each side is posited purely negatively against the other as everything which it is *not*. There is no mutually supportive interpenetration of opposites (as in the positive sense the difference between the sexes has in the need of each for the other): there is mutual repulsion within the exploitative relationship of private property. The mediations that give room for this relation to develop itself (wages, profit, etc.) establish the identity of each with its other only

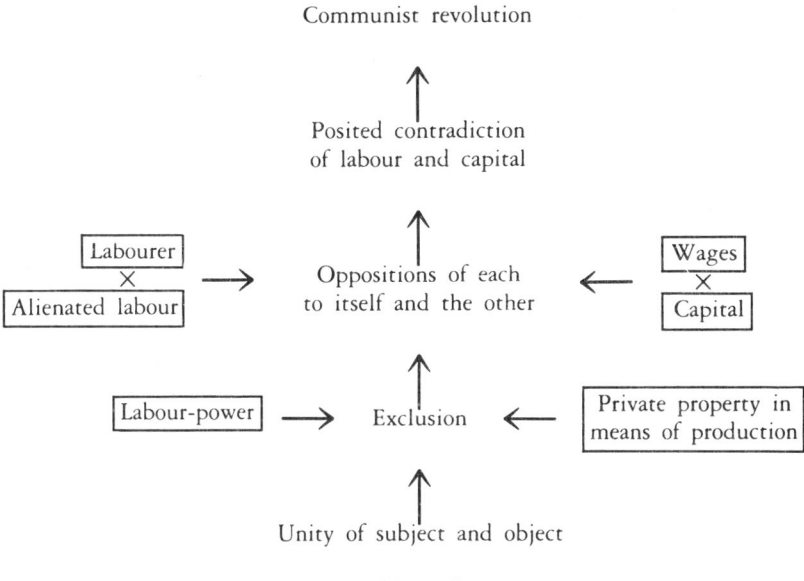

Figure 3

because each moment internalizes the contradictory unity in itself. To use the language of *Capital*: the private property relation as capital appears in the distinction between constant capital and variable capital; the private property relation as labour appears in the oppression of living labour by dead labour. In the language of 1844 Marx defines labour as 'the subjective essence of private property as exclusion of property' and capital as 'objective labour as exclusion of labour'. No matter how highly mediated the relationship of private property becomes, at bottom labour and capital remain as untransformed extremes. Hence Marx's prediction of a clash of mutual contradictions precipitating a collapse of the system.

This takes him way beyond his sources in classical political economy (even that which reflects the full development of modern industry in prioritizing *productive labour*) because such political economy mirrors the process of objectification in alienated form. When Smith traces wealth to labour, he traces the *bourgeois form* of wealth to its origin in *value-producing* labour. The first-order mediations are grasped through the prism of the estranging second-order mediation (private property).

In a very suggestive comparison, Marx, following Engels, says of Smith that he was 'the Luther of political economy'.[34] Just as Luther attacked external religiosity in the form of fetish-worshipping, priests, ritual, churches etc., in order to implant God all the more firmly in the *hearts* of the religious, so Smith mocked the mercantilists' illusions about gold and other *external* forms of property, in order to put labour as such all the more firmly under the category of property as the inner essence of wealth, that is, of value. However, this political economy cannot conceptualize the matter in a critical way because it takes property in all factors of production for granted. It therefore sees the social synthesis achieved only through money, wages and the market.

In spite of its advance from the 'being' of wealth to its 'becoming', the standpoint of classical political economy is thus not that of productive activity as such, but of this activity only as it is determined within the private property system as productive *labour* ('an activity alien to itself').

On the one hand political economy has the merit of turning the spotlight from the merely objective form of wealth to the human subject creating it. Thus Marx says that only 'the political economy which acknowledged *labour* as its principle – *Adam Smith* – and which therefore no longer looked upon private property as a mere *condition* external to man . . . has to be regarded . . . as a product . . . of the real *movement* of private property – as a product of modern *industry* . . .'.[35] On the other hand political economy, in conceptualizing labour as the subjective essence of wealth, at the same time absolutizes these alienating mediations. 'But as a result man is brought within the orbit of private property, just as with Luther he is brought within the orbit of religion', Marx points out.

> Under the semblance of recognizing man, the political economy whose principle is labour rather carries to its logical conclusion the denial of man since man himself no longer stands in an external relation of tension to the external substance of private property, but has himself become this tense essence of private property.[36]

The meaning of the shift from external tension to tense essence in political economy is easily comprehended if we remember that we developed above the real dialectic of (*a*) 'mutual exclusion'; (*b*) 'opposition of each to itself'; and (*c*) 'hostile reciprocal opposition'.

Political economy makes labour its principle, but since this labour is itself a determination of private property it is not productive activity organically united with its object and recognizing itself in its product, at home with itself in its activity; it is labour as the 'tense essence' of private property, it is an *alienating mediator* producing the product as loss of the object, activity as hateful, not as self-fulfilment but merely a source of livelihood.

Political economy capitulates to this reality because it does not problematize the private property system itself. For political economy, productive activity is necessarily labour, a determination of private property itself; hence the benefits of productive activity naturally accrue to private property. Political economy endorses this contradiction. Its principle (labour) is a category which refers us implicitly to productive activity itself, but this activity is estranged from itself, in contradiction with itself. Its principle, says Marx, is 'the principle of this rupture', hence a contradictory principle, the consequences of which ramify throughout the system.[37]

By contrast, Marx grasps the situation as one of labour's self-alienation in and through private property. Only if labour is grasped as the overriding moment in the alienated labour/private property complex can the conditions of a *real transcendence* of estrangement be established. Grounded in the alienation of labour, the immanent movement of private property necessarily produces 'its own grave diggers' (in the famous phrase of the *Communist Manifesto*). But in the dialectical opposition of private property and alienated labour the principal aspect of the contradiction then becomes the latter; hence Marx says that the fall of wage-labour and private property – 'identical'[38] expressions of estrangement – takes place 'in the *political* form of *the emancipation of the workers*'.[39]

Later in the year 1844 Marx supplements this analysis of the contradictions while composing *The Holy Family* (a critique mounted against the Young Hegelian Bruno Bauer). He argues as follows:

> Private property as private property, as wealth, is compelled to maintain *itself*, and thereby its opposite, the proletariat, in *existence* . . . The proletariat, on the contrary, is compelled as proletariat to abolish itself and thereby its opposite, private property, which determines its existence, and which makes it proletariat. It is the *negative* side of the antithesis, its restlessness within its very self, dissolved and self-dissolving private property . . . Indeed private property drives itself in its economic movement towards its own dissolution, but only through a development which does not depend on it, which is unconscious and which takes place against the will of private property by the very nature of things, only inasmuch as it produces the proletariat *as* proletariat . . . .[40]

The proletarian revolution is itself necessarily only a moment of transition. The content of the movement reveals itself as the transformation of the whole society. 'When the proletariat is victorious, it by no means becomes the absolute side of society, for it is victorious only by abolishing itself and its opposite. Then the proletariat disappears as well as the opposite which determines it, private property.'[41]

The next chapter will investigate the significance of this victory, that is to say, Marx's understanding of communism.

Summary

In and through *the private property system* labour is separated from its object. This *state of estrangement* develops into a *process of active alienation* of labour from itself, when private property becomes posited as capital, as the product of alienated labour. The condition (private property as the ground of estrangement) becomes the conditioned (private property as the result of alienated labour). The presupposition (mutual exclusion of labour and its object) of the private property relationship becomes *posited* by the dialectic of the system itself (as a *contradictory unity*).

Classical political economy grasps labour as the subjective essence of private property; but since it absolutizes the system of second-order mediation (conflating it with the first-order level) it identifies itself with the *standpoint of alienating mediation* (labour).

In Marx's view, the project of superseding alienation is grounded in the contradictory development of private property itself. It takes political form as the revolt of the proletariat against private property; but the proletariat overcomes this its other only by abolishing itself as proletariat at the same time.

3
Communism

Introduction

We have seen that Marx puts productive activity at the centre of his ontology. Man produces himself in and through this mediator; he develops new powers and new needs in the dialectic of this practice. Under the rule of private property this whole development takes place under the guise of estrangement. So, far from gaining confidence in himself and enjoying himself in his object and his activity, the producer cannot identify himself in the world he has made, his labour is the activity of alienation. It is in this light that Marx reinterprets communism. For him it is no narrowly political and juridical adjustment of existing powers and privileges. It has fundamental ontological significance as the gateway to the reappropriation by the community of the human essence, the recovery of a human meaning to production, consumption and society. This chapter is concerned with exploring Marx's concept of communism, as it is outlined at the beginning of the third manuscript.

Marx begins with the objective power of private property over the immediate producer. His investigation discloses that this alien power is the product of labour itself in its alienation. Abolition of estrangement requires the abolition of private property. But it is important to understand that Marx does not adopt a purely negative attitude to property and that he attributes a *positive meaning* to his call for the supersession of the private property system. A mere 'abstract negation' of private property would mean, he says, the negation 'of culture and civilization, the regression to the *unnatural* simplicity of the *poor*, crude man without needs, who has not only failed to go beyond private property, but has not even reached it'.[1]

Marx believes that there are good reasons why the private property system was a historically necessary stage in the development of wealth. It took the pressure of capital to awaken the slumbering powers of humanity and promote 'general industriousness'. Although this means that human productive power has taken the shape of estrangement, Marx clearly distinguishes the *ontological* necessity of objectification from the *historical* fact that it presently constitutes a world of estrangement founded on alienated labour. Overcoming estrangement through communism means the reappropriation of the 'ontological essence' of humanity which has constituted itself 'through developed industry, that is, through the mediation of private property', objectively as an external alien power.[2] This means that there is something *positive* in property, disguised by its alien form as the power of capital, namely the wealth of human self-development. Marx says: 'The meaning of private property, freed from its estrangement, is the existence of essential objects for man, both as objects of enjoyment and of activity'.[3] Previous communist doctrine, he claims, had not 'grasped the positive essence of private property'.[4] It is not a question for Marx of annulling private property and all its works, then, but of taking possession of the immensely powerful modern productive forces by society for the satisfaction on this basis of rich human needs.

Stages of Communism

When Marx considers the communist movement thrown up in opposition to the rule of the propertied classes, he distinguishes various stages in its development. The only two he treats at any length are (*a*) crude egalitarian communism and (*b*) 'communism as the *positive* supersession of private property as *human self-estrangement*, and therefore as the actual appropriation of the human essence . . .'.[5]

The first stage, 'raw communism' ('*der rohe Kommunismus*') is based on 'envy' of the propertied rather than any critical understanding of the essence of the property relationship. Its programme involves a levelling down and an attempt to impose equality through the negation of individual differences of any kind:[6] 'the category of *worker* is not done away with but extended to all men; the relationship of private property persists as the relationship of the community to the world of things.'[7] Equal wages are to be paid out by the community as a kind of 'abstract capitalist'.[8] Property is therefore not so much transcended as universalized. An expression of the 'vileness of private property trying to set itself up as the *positive* community system'[9] is the counterposing to marriage ('certainly a form of exclusive private property') of 'the community of women, where the woman becomes a piece of communal and common property'.[10] This leads Marx to the following reflections: 'The relation of man to woman reveals the extent to which *need* has become *human* need; the extent to which, therefore, the *other*, as human, has become a need, the extent to which in his individual existence he is at the same time a communal being.' It follows that 'from this relationship one can therefore judge the whole level of development of mankind'.[11] This statement of Marx's is often cited nowadays, but it is by no means original to him. Fourier argued strongly that 'the progress women make towards freedom . . . is the general principle of all social progress'.[12] In fact, Marx was reading Fourier at the time and cites a similar passage from the latter's work:

> The change in a historical epoch can always be determined by women's progress towards freedom, because, here, in the relationship of woman to man, of the weak to the strong, the victory of human nature over brutality is most evident. The degree of emancipation of women is the natural measure of general emancipation.[13]

Communism in its true form may be contrasted with crude equalitarianism by its attitude to private property. The 'abstract negation' of private property, mentioned above, treats it as 'the enemy', a malevolent power disrupting human fraternity and setting men at odds with each other. Grasped as the contradiction of alienated labour with itself, private property requires a *determinate negation* which preserves in some form the human wealth created in its history. This 'negation of the negation' takes us forwards not backwards. As Marx puts it, very generally:

> *Communism* is the *positive* supersession of *private property* as *human self-estrangement*, and hence the true *appropriation* of the *human* essence through and for man; it is the complete restoration of man to himself . . . which takes place within the entire wealth of previous periods of development.[14]

It is obvious, Marx points out, that communism understood in a historical light does not amount to a revulsion from the achievements of the epoch of private property, 'an improved regression to primitive simplicity', as he puts it,[15] but the reappropriation of mankind's historically developed essential powers through the destruction of the estranged character of this reified world in which they are embodied. In contrast to this picture of communism as a result immanent in history, crude communist ideology seeks an empirical proof for itself in isolated examples of cooperation torn from their historical context. As Marx observes, 'all it succeeds in showing is that by far the greater part of this development contradicts its assertions and that if it [communism] did once exist, then the very fact that it existed in the *past* refutes its claim to essential being [*Wesen*]'.[16] Marx is confident that communist revolution is the outcome of the movement of private property itself; it is 'the riddle of history solved',[17] he says. However, this does not mean it has the status of an 'Absolute' in his philosophy. At the end of this section he equates 'the position' of communism with 'the negation of the negation'; in so far as private property – the negation of human freedom – must itself be negated, this is a *'real* phase', necessary to the liberation and recovery of mankind. But this is not the whole story. Note Marx's conclusion: 'Communism is the necessary shape and the dynamic principle of the immediate future, but communism itself is not as such the goal of human development – the shape of human society.'[18]

Complete failure to understand this dialectic is exhibited in the identification by certain commentators of 'communism as such' with equalitarian communisms discussed earlier in Marx's chapter.[19] But those are *ideological* stages in the development of communist ideas, whereas here we are speaking of a *'real* phase'.[20] By 'communism as such' Marx clearly understands 'communism as the opposite of private property'. The communist movement develops in opposition to private property. Thus, in some sense it is even the creation of the movement of private property. But in a higher phase of development socialism stands on its own feet so to speak and 'no longer needs such mediation'.[21]

Marx illustrates the point with the example of atheism. This is a peculiar kind of humanism because it depends for its sense on first of all positing what it denies. It asserts the autonomy of man only through the negation of god. First man is negated through being reduced to a creature of god; but then the negation of the negation reasserts the essentiality of man. This humanism is thoroughly infected by the opposite through which it developed its position. This is very clear in the Sartrean man who says to himself: 'God is dead; I am abandoned; I am alone; there is no commandment; I must take complete responsibility for my destiny.' This kind of consciousness is that of the man who first believed in god and then lost his faith. It is quite different from a humanism that never knew god in the first place and hence could never feel lost without him!

In the same way socialism as 'positive humanism' stands on the ground of the essential relations of man to himself and to nature. It does not require to be perpetually mediated through its understanding of itself as the opposite of private property, although this is a historically necessary stage. Marx says that 'atheism is humanism mediated with itself through the supersession of religion, whilst communism is humanism mediated with itself through the supersession of private property'. He continues: 'only through the supersession of this mediation — which itself, however, is a necessary premise — does *positive* humanism come into being'.[22]

If 'communism as such' is not the goal, what then *is* the aim of human development? Erich Fromm has the merit of addressing this question: 'Quite clearly the aim of socialism is man', he says, 'it is to create a form of production and an organization of society . . . in which he can return to himself and grasp the world with his own powers, thus becoming one with the world.'[23] Fromm's answer is not far off the mark, as the following passage from Marx's *Grundrisse* (1857–78) shows:

> The old view, where man, in spite of his various limitations . . ., still appears as the aim of production, seems very superior to the modern world where production appears as the aim of man and wealth as the aim of production. In fact, however, when the narrow bourgeois form has been cast off, what is wealth other than the universality of needs, capacities and enjoyments, productive forces, etc. of individuals . . .? The full development of human mastery over natural forces, those of his own nature as well as those of so-called 'Nature'? The absolute working out of his creative dispositions, without any presupposition other than previous historical development . . .? Where he does not produce himself in any determined form, but produces his totality? Seeks not to remain something he has become, but is in the absolute movement of becoming?[24]

Marx's Standpoint

Let us try to identify the various levels of discussion of the problem of alienation as we have clarified them. Then we can explain Marx's standpoint with regard to the possibility of overcoming alienation.

If private property appears as the immediate cause of estrangement, two qualifications are necessary: (*a*) ontologically, productive activity is basic; private property is a second-order mediation socially relating activity, especially by specifying labourers and non-labourers; (*b*) in the movement of private property itself it comes to posit its essence as labour, the conditioned becomes the condition, and its reproduction depends on its other. Correspondingly, we can distinguish two levels of alienation; (*a*) the *state of estrangement* signified by the imposition on activity, and its object, of the determinations of private property, namely labour and capital; (*b*) the *process of alienation* whereby this labour reproduces private property, that is, its object as capital and itself as alienated labour. Finally, there are two levels of necessity for the overthrow of private property: (*a*) abstractly, there is the need to restore man to himself subsequent to the supersession of the system of estrangement; (*b*) concretely, there is the process whereby capital in its own development leaves the proletariat with no other option than to take the struggle against alienation to its conclusion through identifying the problem as capital, itself the product, expression and mediation of alienated labour.

The demonstration in Marx's *1844 Manuscripts* of the necessary relationship of proletarian politics to the dialectics of alienation is sufficient to refute those interpretations which see in this work only a general human predicament and project, to be contrasted with Marx's later stress on class war. At the same time, it must be emphasized that this does not mean that only the liberation of the proletariat is at stake, nor that only they are victims of estrangement.[25]

I have said little so far about the capitalist because I wanted to stress the impersonal character of 'the movement of private property', but of course Marx knows that the alienation of labour 'creates the relation to it of the capitalist, or whatever one chooses to call the lord of labour'.[26] With regard to the latter, Marx makes the interesting observation that 'everything which appears in the worker as an *activity* of alienation, of estrangement, appears in the non-worker as a *state* of alienation, of estrangement'.[27] Unfortunately, the first manuscript breaks off at this point. The idea later turns up in Marx's first draft of *Capital Volume One*. The capitalist is defined as the personification of capital, his rule over the worker 'is the rule of things over man, of dead labour over the living, of the product over the producer'. This 'inversion of subject and object' is 'the alienation [*Entfremdung*] of man from his own labour'. The capitalist finds his satisfaction in this alienation, it seems, because he accomplishes his purpose of appropriating surplus value. But Marx characterizes this as 'a highly impoverished and abstract content' of his activity 'which makes it plain that the capitalist is just as enslaved by the relationships of capitalism as is his opposite pole, the worker, albeit in quite a different manner'.[28]

To return to the *1844 Manuscripts*: others before Marx had observed social antagonisms and pointed to the problem of alienation; what marks *his* solution is the new standpoint adopted with regard to the supersession of these problems. As Mészáros says: 'If there is an ultimately "irreducible" element in a philosophical discourse, it is the philosopher's *"prise de position"* to the supersession of the contradictions he perceives'.[29]

As is obvious by now, the touchstone is *'labour'* – but in what sense? In spite of his praise of Hess, Marx has already gone (as he will more decisively go in the *German Ideology*) beyond the standpoint of 'true socialism', the standpoint of 'Man' rather than the proletarian struggle. (Hess, in the review mentioned earlier, objected vigorously to Stein's identification of socialism with the proletariat.) Instead of opposing capitalist estrangement, including 'labour', in the name of an ideal human society, Marx grasps socialism as a *result* immanent in the present contradiction between labour and capital. He takes the standpoint of labour, but *not* in the sense that classical political economy does when it makes labour its positive principle, identifying it with productive activity as such; *nor* in the sense that Proudhon and other egalitarians take the standpoint of labour as against capital when they demand such things as equal wages, in effect thereby staying within the determinations of private property;[30] Marx works from *a critically adopted standpoint of labour*.[31] This grasps the contradictions of private property as alienated labour's contradiction with itself, grasps the significance of alienating objectification and thus the meaning of 'the positive supersession of private property', and grasps labour as 'the negative', 'dissolved and self-dissolving private property', hence superseding itself towards 'the abolition of labour'.

Only Marx's position, taking man and his labour as the basis, can envisage as a *practical* task the overcoming of alienation. Some communists conceive of the transition to socialism as an externally structured 'final crisis' of an economic character where the working-class and its struggle is put in a secondary place. With others, as the obverse face of this, transition is the result of 'intervention' by individuals or self-proclaimed vanguards, who are mysteriously exempt from the one-dimensionality of capitalism's social consciousness. Marx himself grasps the dialectical process of self-alienation and reappropriation in the movement of living labour as the basis for a self-transcending historical practice.

Summary

The 'positive essence of private property' is its embodiment of the objectification of human productive activity. *Communism* is hence given the significance of a *'positive supersession* of private property', that is, the reappropriation of the human essence presently estranged in it.

Hence communism is 'the riddle of history solved', but it is not as such 'the goal' because its position is that of *'the negation of the negation'*, still determined by its opposite.

Marx's investigation of the private property system discloses that the estrangement of the worker from the object and the product of his activity is the presupposition and the result of *alienated labour*. Hence Marx takes the *critically adopted standpoint of labour* in conceptualizing the supersession of estrangement.

PART TWO

The Critique of Hegel

4

Marx and Hegel

Introduction

The *1844 Manuscripts* is intended by Marx as a work in the field of political economy, taking its object critically, from a socialist point of view. This is explained in the Preface; but then, abruptly, Marx states that he considers it 'absolutely necessary' to include 'a critical discussion of *Hegelian dialectic* and philosophy as a whole'.[1] This seems an odd ambition for a critical work on economics; certainly he does not explain *why* he considers it necessary to undertake this *here*. One is left to suppose that he thought it necessary to engage with the methodological concerns of his contemporaries, the Young Hegelians, who thought their philosophical inheritance allowed them to criticize anything under the sun without knowing anything about it. Marx observes pointedly that his is 'a wholly empirical analysis based on a conscientious critical study of political economy'.[2] Nevertheless, Marx had very good reason to give an important place to 'discussion of Hegelian dialectic'. We can understand why if we trace the course of his thought in the manuscripts themselves. In fact, the unhelpful 'Preface' was one of the last passages to be written; it was drafted *after* all the material on Hegel.

Why Hegel?

If we look at the manuscripts in their original order of composition, it becomes obvious that initially Marx had no intention of bringing in Hegel. There is no mention of him in the first two manuscripts. It is only in the third manuscript, in which Marx embarks on a series of discrete reflections on the topic of communism, that 'point six' begins with the remark that 'this is perhaps the place to offer, by way of explanation and justification, some considerations on Hegelian dialectic generally and especially its exposition in the *Phenomenology* and *Logic*, and also, lastly, the relation [to it] of the modern critical movement'.[3]

At first it seems there will just be a short digression, but in the remaining pages he returns twice to the question, linking the passages with his own cross-references, so that in the end we have a substantial set of notes. At this point he decides that he will pull all this material together in a 'concluding chapter' and, as we saw, he announces this when he goes on to write the Preface.[4]

The crucial question to investigate is this: what forced Marx to feel under an obligation to offer 'by way of explanation and justification' his critical discussion of Hegelian dialectic under the original sixth point? Not surprisingly, the problem is solved as soon as we refer to the last paragraph of the *fifth* point.[5] This begins with an important statement of Marx's view of *genesis*: 'since for socialist man the whole of so-called world history is nothing but the creation of man through human labour, nothing but the emergence of nature for man, so has he palpable, incontrovertible proof of his *birth* through himself, of his *genesis*.'[6]

Several problems of interpretation arise from this remarkable statement (even if one neglects Marx's belief that he therewith disposes of the religious theory of creation). It is fairly clear that Marx is not saying that man creates himself entire out of nothing. On the contrary, we have seen earlier that Marx stresses that human activity requires an object, and that labour cannot create anything, not even man himself, without nature. What Marx is summarizing here is the process whereby man, originally nothing but a part of nature, takes himself and nature as his object. At first he is 'at one' with nature, but then nature becomes '*for*' man, something he can work with, and transform. At first again this must appear as a dependence on natural conditions, but in so far as these conditions of his existence pass more and more under his own control, with the development of his productive powers, so in his existence he depends more and more on himself and his productive activity. He becomes his own product, so to speak.

Speaking thus, we inevitably recall Hegel's *Phenomenology of Spirit*, in which absolute spirit grasps itself as its own product. Its being is *self-mediated*. In his Preface Hegel emphasizes that spirit mediates itself with itself only through 'the labour of the negative', in alienation and transcendence of alienation.[7] This refers us back to Marx again; for the paragraph under discussion concludes (in an argument we considered earlier) with a definition of communism as the phase of 'negation of the negation', ushering in 'socialism as socialism', 'real life . . . no longer mediated through the abolition of private property, through communism'.[8] We can understand now that Marx 'by way of explanation and justification' has to undertake a discussion of Hegel, because friends and enemies of Hegel alike could not fail to notice these parallels and interpret the text accordingly, probably with unfortunate consequences. For example, Marx needs to show how his 'positive supersession of private property' differs from Hegelian positing through negativity.

Another problem of interpretation arising from Marx's account of human genesis is the use of the term 'labour' in 'the creation of man through human labour'. Remembering that we earlier distinguished two possible connotations of the term in the *1844 Manuscripts*, which interpretation should be adopted here? In truth, *both* interpretations are possible. This could well be a case where Marx draws attention to the ultimate consequences of the (first-order) mediatory activity constituting man for himself, and nature for man; thus 'labour' would here refer to that (ontologically fundamental) *productive activity* in and through which man becomes who he is. However, this does not exclude a narrower reading of 'labour' as 'alienated activity' along the lines of the interpretation offered earlier, if it is accepted that, in history to the present, productive activity has been *identical* with 'labour' defined in terms of the determinations of the ruling property systems. This means that human genesis proceeds by way of alienated activity. This is undoubtedly what Marx believed, and it constitutes an almost exact parallel with Hegel's view. Marx indeed gives Hegel credit for this: 'the great thing in Hegel's *Phenomenology*', he says, 'is that Hegel conceives the self-creation of man as . . . alienation and as transcendence of this alienation, that he thus grasps the essence of *labour* and comprehends objective man . . . as the result of his *own labour*'.[9] He goes on to repeat the point – this time critically noting a direct connection between Hegel's *Phenomenology* and political economy. He claims that 'Hegel's standpoint is that of modern political economy'. This is because he 'grasps *labour* as the essence . . .' In his work, just as in political economy, 'labour is man's *coming-to-be-for-himself* [*Fürsichwerden*] within *alienation* or as *alienated* man'.[10] (This last statement makes particularly clear the sense of 'labour' employed.)

Marx also give notice (in his first passage on Hegel) that he will show that Hegel's standpoint does not go beyond that of 'negation of the negation' and that this 'is not yet the *real* history of man as a previously posited subject, but simply the *act of creation*, the *history of the genesis*, of man'.[11]

The above remarks and quotations are enough to show that a number of questions arise about Marx's understanding of his relationship to

Hegel. The answers will help us at the same time to judge the significance of the claims he advances in his theory of alienation.

The problems to be investigated in the following chapters are as follows:

1. How could Marx find in Hegel's *idealist* philosophy an account of man's genesis in his own *labour*?
2. What are the similarities and differences in Marx's and Hegel's concepts of *alienation*?
3. What is Marx's opinion of Hegel's *dialectic* and why is it said to be relevant, if at all, only to the question of genesis but not to the real history of man?
4. Why does Marx equate the *standpoint* of Hegel's *Phenomenology* with that of modern political economy?

Summary

In evolving his theory of alienation, Marx realizes that, since the pattern whereby labour grasps its other (private property) as its own self, estranged from itself, and negates this negation, has obvious parallels with Hegel's *Phenomenology of Spirit*, he must explain and justify his position in relation to Hegel's dialectic. He finds both strengths and weaknesses in it, as we shall see.

5

Hegel's Phenomenology

Introduction

In his *1844 Manuscripts*, although he promises a critique of Hegel's dialectic as a whole, Marx pays most attention to Hegel's *Phenomenology of Spirit* (1807) on the ground that it is 'the true birthplace and secret of Hegelian philosophy'.[1] Marx is most interested here in trying to situate Hegel's achievement in relation to his own concept of alienated labour. Hegel's strengths and weaknesses are evaluated in this light. Hegel's strength is precisely that he gives full recognition to the problem of *estrangement*. His weakness is that, in spite of the wealth of social and historical material treated, he considers it ultimately as a problem of *consciousness*.

After Marx, whose labours remained unknown for nearly a hundred years, it is not until Georg Lukács that the problem of Hegel's *Phenomenology* is considered, first and foremost, as alienation and its overcoming.[2] It is hard for us now to realize how original Lukács was in taking up, as long ago as 1938, the question of Hegel's concept of '*Entäusserung*' (alienation),[3] albeit with the benefit of Marx's recently discovered manuscripts in front of him. The last chapter of his masterly work *The Young Hegel* is entitled '*Entäusserung* as the central philosophical concept of the *Phenomenology of Spirit*'.

A point of terminology to bear in mind is that the translators of Hegel, and of Marx, do not agree on the rendering of '*Entäusserung*' — some give 'alienation' and others give 'externalization'. I prefer, and give here, 'alienation'. Lukács notes that there is nothing novel about the terms *Entäusserung* and *Entfremdung* in themselves. 'They are', he says, 'simply German translations of the English word "alienation".'[4] The alternative to 'alienation', namely 'externalization' (the closest rendering of *Entäusserung* from a purely etymological point of view), is liable to be confused with 'objectification'. It is important to notice this because Marx explicitly *distinguishes* objectification (*Vergegenständlichung*) from alienation (*Entäusserung*). The difference, broadly, is that, while *Entäusserung* carries the sense of 'posited as objective', it also connotes relinquishment, such that an objectivity is set up from which the subject is estranged. *Entfremdung* is quite unambiguous, and may be rendered as 'estrangement'. (For further philological information, and a comparison of translations, see Appendix.)

Before embarking (in the next chapter) on Marx's critical analysis of *The Phenomenology of Spirit*, let us recall here some of the salient points about its method and results.

Phenomenological Method

In his Introduction (not to be confused with the more famous Preface), Hegel argues that traditional epistemology, worrying itself about the criterion of true knowledge, gets caught up in insoluble contradictions. It *itself* is making a claim to knowledge, and hence must either appeal to that same criterion (circularity) or to some other criterion (regress). This problem has been called 'the dilemma of epistemology'.[5] Hegel considers the possibility that we could spare ourselves the trouble of engaging in the epistemological problematic and go straight to scientific work confident that the science itself will provide its own proof of itself; but he rejects this too, because such a claim to positive knowledge, facing other claims to knowledge, as well as commonsensical views, seems helpless to prevail. It asserts itself as true – but so do they. '*One* bare assurance is worth just as much as another',[6] Hegel comments.

But it is in just such phenomena that Hegel sees the possibility of a way forward. He undertakes 'an exposition of how knowledge makes its appearance'. This is what he understands by a phenomenology. The exposition of claims to knowledge in this form seems 'not to be science' – yet Hegel believes that 'the series of configurations [*Gestaltungen*] which consciousness goes through along this road is, in reality, the detailed history of the education [*Bildung*] of consciousness itself to the standpoint of science'.[7] In his Preface Hegel likewise speaks of 'the spirit that educates itself' ('*der sich bildende Geist*').[8] 'Education' is too narrow a translation of *Bildung* if it suggests only formal training, of course; one could even speak here of 'the spirit that builds itself up'. It is apposite here also to recall the popularity in Hegel's time of the '*Bildungsroman*'. A *Bildungsroman* is a novel that presents the educative effect of the hero's experience.[9] Thus the *Phenomenology*, in a similar way, may be understood as the story of the *Bildung* of spirit.[10] Indeed, Royce argues that the *Bildungsroman* model certainly influenced Hegel's procedure in the *Phenomenology*; he cites Goethe's *Wilhelm Meisters Lehrjahre*.[11] Hyppolite says the same, but draws attention to Hegel's study of Rousseau's *Émile*.[12] Lukács prefers the epithet: 'an odyssey of spirit', but also calls attention to Goethe's work.[13]

There are some very peculiar characteristics of this *Bildungsroman* of spirit. One relates to method: Hegel's method depends, he explains, on the dialectical point that when a given claim to knowledge is to be rejected as untrue 'the exposition of the untrue consciousness in its untruth is not merely a *negative* procedure', because if the result of the argument is properly understood as a *determinate* negation of the original thesis, 'a new form has thereby immediately arisen'.[14] That is to say, to refute is not simply to deny, but to find relevant grounds for such rejection. Every claim to knowledge has its specific refutation, and this involves consciousness in a new set of commitments. Making progress in this way we generate a complete series of forms of knowledge. Validity appears here not in relation to an external measure but in accordance with what consciousness provides 'from within itself' at each stage. As Hyppolite points out, the condition of this method is the assumption that knowledge is a whole. Indeed the whole is immanent throughout the development. 'Negation is creative', he argues, 'because the posited term has been isolated and thus was itself a kind of negation.' It follows that *its* negation is in turn a step towards the restoration of the whole. According to Hyppolite, 'were it not for the immanence of the whole in consciousness, we should be unable to understand how negation can truly engender a content'.[15]

Hegel's goal is to reach 'the point where knowledge no longer needs to go beyond itself'.[16] Under what conditions could such an absolute resting place arrive? He answers that, 'in pressing forward to its true existence, consciousness will arrive at a point at which it gets rid of its semblance of being burdened with something alien'. Thus, at the point where consciousness grasps its *own* essence, this will signify 'the nature of absolute knowledge itself'.[17]

Hegel presents this progression as immanent in the phenomena themselves: for 'the necessary progression and interconnection of the forms of the unreal consciousness will by itself bring to pass the completion of the series'.[18] Consequently, 'we do not need to import criteria, or to make use of our own bright ideas and thoughts during the course of the inquiry', he says; 'it is precisely when we leave these aside that we succeed in contemplating the matter in hand as it is *in and for itself*'.[19] Hegel takes this so seriously that he says: 'all that is left for us to do is simply to look on'.[20] The book therefore takes the form, not of *Hegel's* refutations and proofs, but, as we said, of a *Bildungsroman* of spirit in which *it* develops a more and more comprehensive consciousness of itself and its world.

In the *Phenomenology* the crucial problem is that of *objectivity*. However, this is a problem primarily because of the way Hegel construes the relationship of knowledge to its object. More particularly, the problem is: how can consciousness claim to know its object (*Gegenstand*) when the latter is posited as other than it? Interesting, in view of Hegel's Swabian origins, is the information M.J. Petry provides: that in the Swabian dialect of Hegel's day '*Gegenstand*' was also synonymous with 'impediment, opposition, obstacle, resistance'.[21] Any reader of the *Phenomenology* cannot fail to be struck by the stress laid on the developing *activity* of consciousness in knowing, and the presentation of the independence of the object as an obstacle to its free movement. Nothing could be further from Locke's *tabula rasa*. As the phenomenological dialectic proceeds, the solution to the antinomy of subjectivity and objectivity emerges: consciousness becomes more and more aware that it is its own activity that constitutes the object *as* an object of knowledge. The very distinction between knowledge and its object is drawn from the point of view of consciousness and is hence to be construed as a distinction falling within consciousness itself.[22]

So, if Hegel begins with a situation in which the knowing self takes it that what stands over against it is objectivity, he overcomes this opposition through showing that every higher shape of consciousness posits the form of knowledge, and the object as it is now known, as more and more adequate to each other. The upshot is Absolute Knowing, in which knowing knows that what appears to it as its object is only itself.

Since the activity of consciousness itself in knowing becomes more and more prominent in the development, it is clear that *self*-consciousness becomes centrally involved. Equally, if the self is to make itself an object of consciousness, it can only do so (i.e. become known to itself as what it really is) through its own activity, its self-realization. Thus Hegel's discussion imperceptibly slides into terrain unknown to epistemology. The progress of critical reflection upon the adequacy of knowledge to its object becomes a progress in the history of *Geist* (spirit or mind). Spirit learns what it truly is (and its relationship to the world of objectivity) at the same time, and in exact proportion, as it *becomes* what it truly is through manifesting itself in objective form (in morality, in bourgeois life, in the state, in religion), and in so doing it eventually ends its estrangement from its world through identifying itself in it. The relationship of this history to real history is an extremely difficult and controversial topic in Hegelian scholarship; nevertheless, it is clear from the wealth of obvious allusions that Hegel wishes us to bear this connection in mind.

Engels characterizes the *Phenomenology of Spirit* as 'the embryology and paleontology of the mind, a development of individual consciousness through its different stages, set in the form of an abbreviated reproduction of the stages through which the consciousness of man has passed in the course of history'.[23] In answer to those readers who find the historical points of reference appear in a jumble, Lukács points out that these moments occur in their correct historical sequence, but that this sequence is traversed *three* times.[24] Hegel's point of departure is the natural consciousness existing as an individual to which objective reality presents itself as given even where socio-historical determinations underly the developing shapes of consciousness. The acquisition of reason makes possible the perception of society and history as the product of activity. With this, the conscious individual enters the second cycle and must traverse the whole path again, understood now in the shape of explicitly *social* forms of experience. In the 'absolute' stage consciousness looks back over the panorama of the whole history of its experience, and by recognizing, recollecting and ordering those moments, spirit grasps the significance of the whole. However, this knowledge too is not just an abstract truth, but is acquired in the dialectic of a specific domain. Thus the third stage once again recapitulates the past in its entirety but on this occasion we no longer find the actual series of moments, but a summary of mankind's efforts to comprehend reality. The last chapter, on absolute knowing, contains a compressed history of modern philosophy, for example. In it Hegel equates his own philosophy with fully developed absolute knowledge – knowledge as science.

Alienation

Absolute knowledge comprehends that 'objectivity', standing over against the 'subjectivity' estranged from it, is brought forth only within the self-alienating movement of spirit. Lukács is quite correct, therefore, to see *Entäusserung* (alienation) as the central philosophical concept of the *Phenomenology*. Marx points us to the following crucial passage from Hegel's last chapter in which he employs this term in summarizing his conclusions:

> Surmounting the object of consciousness is not to be taken one-sidedly to mean that the object showed itself as returning into the self . . . but rather that it is the alienation [*Entäusserung*] of self-

consciousness that posits thinghood [*die Dingheit*] and that this alienation has not merely a negative but a positive meaning . . . for self-consciousness . . . for in this alienation it posits *itself* as object, or the object as itself . . . This positing at the same time contains the other moment, that self-consciousness has equally sublated [*aufgehoben*] this alienation and objectivity too and taken it back into itself so that it is at home with itself in *its* otherness as such [*in seinem Andersseyn als solchem bey sich ist*].[25]

Of great service to Hegel in preserving, while supposedly overcoming, objectivity as a moment in the absolute, is his dialectical category of '*Aufhebung*' (sublation). In his *Logic* Hegel tells us that in ordinary language *Aufheben* means not only to abolish but also to preserve, and that he intends to take advantage of this double meaning. In his criticism of Hegel Marx comments that '*Aufheben*' plays 'a peculiar role' in Hegel's system. In it, affirmation and negation are brought together; thus, in spite of their 'sublation' in the course of Hegel's *Philosophy of Right*, property, the family, civil society, etc. 'continue to exist', he points out, 'but have become *moments* . . . which mutually dissolve and engender one another, moments of movement'.[26] In the *Phenomenology*, likewise, '*Aufhebung*' preserves alienation in the very moment of retracting it.

How does self-consciousness 'surmount the object of consciousness' and 'take it back into itself'? Very schematically, one could say that, in collecting together the various determinations taken on by the object of consciousness as it is experienced throughout the path traversed by spirit, the totality of these determinations is grasped by spirit as its own *self*-determination. This comprehension Hegel characterizes as a recollection (*Erinnerung*). Here we must return to our philological apparatus again, because the second time this term occurs in the final paragraph of the *Phenomenology* Hegel takes the opportunity to bring out the etymological possibility of characterizing this as an *Er-Innerung*, an *inwardizing* movement – the appropriate counter-movement to an 'externalization' (one of the meanings of '*Entäusserung*'). He says: '*die* Er-Innerung *hat sie aufbewahrt* . . .' – 'the *internalization* has preserved it'.[27]

Lukács thinks this passage is so important that he quotes it *three* times.[28] For example: if spirit has created the real objects of the world in the process of '*Entäusserung*', 'it is only logical', he says, 'for the reverse process of "*Er-Innerung*" to be nothing other than the sublation of the forms of objective reality so created, and their reintegration into the subject'.[29] He points out that, consistently with this, the standpoint of absolute knowledge does not give us any *new content*: 'all the contents available', he says, 'arise not from philosophy itself, but from . . . the historical process of the self-positing of spirit . . . now . . . illuminated by the light of absolute knowledge'.[30]

It follows from this that the estranged forms taken on by spirit when it posits itself as objective remain as they are. The novelty consists solely in the reconciliation philosophy affords, whereby spirit can feel at home, notwithstanding this estrangement, because, in it, it is in its *own* other. Indeed, the alienation of self-consciousness is given a positive significance above in that it posits the self as objective. Accordingly Hegel stresses, in another crucial passage, that there is no need to be afraid of such objectification.

'Spirit', he recalls, 'has shown itself to us to be neither merely the withdrawal of self-consciousness into its pure inwardness, nor the mere submergence of self-consciousness into substance.' Using the language of 'subject' and 'substance', he explains that 'spirit is *this movement* of the self which empties [*entäussert*] itself of itself and sinks into its substance, and also, as subject, has gone out of that substance into itself'. He goes on: 'that first reflection out of immediacy is the subject's differentiation of itself from its substance . . . the withdrawal into itself and the becoming of the pure "I" . . .'. *But* — and this is the important point — 'neither has the "I" to cling to itself in the *form* of *self-consciousness* as against the form of substantiality and objectivity, as if it were afraid of its alienation; the power of spirit lies rather in remaining the self-same spirit in its alienation and, as that which is both *in itself* and *for itself*, in making its being-for-itself no less merely a moment than its in itself . . .'.[31]

Thus, because spirit must posit itself in objective form, the objectivity consciousness opposes to itself cannot merely be subsumed away through the inwardizing movement of recollection; its problematical character must be resolved by comprehending it in all the immediacy of its otherness at the same time. Therefore, one must understand the phenomenological odyssey not merely as spirit's struggle to negate an alien objectivity, but also as the story of its gaining an objective existence, a story understood as such by spirit *itself* only in recollection when it achieves absolute knowledge, but a story whose meaning is understood from the outset by Hegel and ourselves who 'look on'[32] this development precisely from that standpoint. In the middle part of the *Phenomenology* masses of concrete historical material, including actual estranged spheres of existence (religion, the state, bourgeois life and so forth) are brought within this framework.

The objective shapes given in consciousness as it moves towards self-consciousness and absolute knowing are to be understood as shapes of the existence of spirit itself and hence its positive achievement. This explains why Hegel says that alienation has a positive meaning for self-consciousness in so far as it posits itself as objective, and becomes being-for-itself. It explains also why, whether one looks at the *Phenomenology* or the *Encyclopaedia*, one finds that Objective Spirit always occupies a higher place then Subjective Spirit. In both these systematic works the creation of a wealth of spiritual forms, for example, the state, religion and so on, is seen as a positive achievement of spirit as well as entangling it in estrangement. The 'sublation' of estrangement consists in stripping the spiritual forms of their 'external' character, not abolishing them outright, that is to say, in recognizing them precisely as spirit's own work.

Spirit in the form of substance gives us the phase of consciousness as consciousness of an objectivity standing over against it; consciousness turned inwards achieves certainty of self and becomes subject; then in the final dialectic the self recognizes that its negative attitude towards objectivity must in turn be superseded through a recognition of the necessity of this self-alienation. In this way we have a *positing through negating*. Hegel explains this movement thus: if 'self-consciousness enriches itself till . . . it has absorbed into itself the entire structure of the essentialities of substance', then 'since this negative attitude to objectivity is just as much positive, it is a positing'. It has both 'produced them out of itself', and in so doing 'has at the same time restored them for consciousness'. He goes on to explain that 'in the concept that knows itself as concept, the moments thus appear earlier than the whole in its fulfilment; the movement of these moments is the process by which the whole comes to be'. In consciousness, by contrast, 'the whole, though uncomprehended, is prior to the moments'.[33]

In his Preface Hegel explains that the exposition will show that truth is not only 'substance' – something 'out there' to appropriated by the consciousness of the subject – but it is equally 'subject' – the activity that *produces* the true. There follows the famous passage:

> Further, the living substance is being which is in truth subject, or, which is the same, is in truth actual only in so far as it is the movement of positing itself, or the mediation of its becoming-other with its own self. As subject it is pure simple *negativity* and thus the bifurcation of the simple; it is the doubling which sets up opposition, and then again the negation of . . . opposition. Only this self-restoring sameness, or this reflection in otherness within itself – not an *original* or *immediate* unity as such – is the true. It is the process of its own becoming, the circle that presupposes its end as its goal, having its end also for its beginning and only by being worked out to its end, is it actual.[34]

'Thus', he goes on, 'the life of God and divine cognition can be spoken of as love playing with itself.' But he immediately qualifies this edifying notion: if, in itself, the divine life is one of untroubled unity with itself in itself, 'for which otherness and estrangement and the overcoming of estrangement are not serious matters', this leaves out the fact that its actualization in developed form is necessarily marked by 'the seriousness, the suffering, the patience and the labour of the negative'.[35]

In the last chapter he explains that spirit needs *time* to do this: hence 'the movement of carrying forward the form of its self-knowledge is the labour which it accomplishes as actual history'.[36] The conclusion of the *Phenomenology* is that 'comprehended history' is the realm of absolute spirit, 'the actuality, truth, and certainty of its throne, without which it would be lifeless and alone'.[37]

If 'the immediate existence of spirit, *consciousness*, contains the two moments of knowing and the objectivity negative to knowing',[38] in the absolute these are united and their difference is mediated in the act of 'pure negativity'.[39] 'Our own act here', says Hegel, 'has been simply to gather together the separate moments . . .'[40]

However, there may be more to it than this, as far as Hegel's 'own act' is concerned. For in the final chapter of the *Phenomenology* there is a merger between the standpoint that 'looks on' and grasps the nature of the necessity in the transitions as it is known 'to us' (rather than in the experience of consciousness itself at that stage) and the standpoint of self-consciousness itself at each stage. This may well mean that Hegel's 'absolute' philosophy represents an arrogant claim, not merely to the discovery of truth, but to the instantiation of it. From Feuerbach[41] onwards critics have charged Hegel with representing his philosophy *as* 'the absolute'. A recent example is Peter Singer who says that, in Hegel's view, spirit comes to its final resting-place when he, Hegel, understands the nature of reality. The momentous conclusion follows that 'the closing pages of the *Phenomenology* . . . are no mere *description* of the culmination of all human history: they *are* that culmination'.[42]

This point, among others, will be taken up in the consideration of Marx's critique in the following chapters.

Summary

Hegel's *Phenomenology* undertakes an exposition of how knowledge makes its appearance, through a sequence of determinate negations. Absolute knowing knows that what appears as its object is itself. But this requires spirit to know itself through producing itself as alienation (*Entäusserung*) and then sublating this alienation, such that 'it is at home with itself in its otherness as such'. Thus the truth of spirit is actual when posited through the negation of the negation. This labour of the negative is at work in the movement of history.

6

Marx's Criticism

Introduction

It is useful in interpreting Marx's commentary on Hegel's *Phenomenology*, both when it finds cause for praise and when it damns, to remember that it is composed under the influence of Ludwig Feuerbach; it is a continuation, therefore, of a certain tradition of critical appropriation of Hegel by the Young Hegelian movement. This tradition refuses to take Hegel at face value, so to speak, and instead claims to find truth in Hegel in disguised form. In the present case the most important single influence on Marx is Feuerbach's 'inversion' of the terms of Hegel's philosophy. Of course, as with Feuerbach, Marx's claim is that *Hegel* is guilty of 'inversion'; so it is a question of putting him right side up.[1] Feuerbach, according to Marx, resolved Hegel's 'absolute spirit' into *'real man on the basis of nature'*.[2] What Marx has in mind in his own work, therefore, is the possibility of reading in the *Phenomenology* not a *Bildungsroman* of *spirit* but of *man*. Thus he says at one point that we must 'abstract from Hegel's abstraction . . . and talk . . . instead . . . of man'.[3] Correspondingly, spiritual activity he reads as material activity, primarily labour. Thus, although he complains that in the *Phenomenology* 'man appears only in the form of spirit', he also finds that in this form 'it grasps the *estrangement* of man'.[4]

What really excited Marx was the 'producing principle' in Hegel's work. He says:

> The great thing in Hegel's *Phenomenology* and its final result — the dialectic of negativity as the moving and producing principle — is that Hegel conceives the self-creation of man as a process, objectification [*Vergegenständlichung*] as loss of object [*Entgegenständlichung*],

as alienation [*Entäusserung*] and as sublation of this alienation; that he therefore grasps the nature of *labour* and conceives objective man ... as the result of his *own labour*.⁵

As far as the 'producing principle' is concerned, Marx is impressed by the dialectic of spirit's actualization of itself through positing itself in the form of objectivity as the negative of itself and then negating this negation. Marx sees in this the philosophical reflection of the material process whereby man produces himself through his own labour. Marx amplifies his 'humanist' reading of Hegel as follows: 'the *real active* relation of man to himself', he says, 'is only possible if he really employs all his *species powers* – which again is only possible through the cooperation of mankind and as a result of history – and treats them as objects, which is at first only possible in the form of estrangement'.⁶

Be it noted that both in Hegel and Marx 'the producing principle' involves the moment of estrangement and its overcoming. Nevertheless, in Hegel, a heavy price is exacted by the mystified form of his insight. Thus Marx immediately embarks on a multi-layered critique of the *Phenomenology* even at its strongest points, namely, the 'producing principle' and the acknowledgement of estrangement. His most detailed discussion is on the closing chapter, 'Absolute Knowledge', which, he says, 'contains the concentrated essence of the *Phenomenology*, its relation to the dialectic, and Hegel's *consciousness* of both and their interrelations'.⁷ (We shall follow Marx in this, reserving discussion of other parts of the *Phenomenology* to the next chapter.)

Marx's notes, being unrevised, are thus not organized in any way. Here we shall distinguish four threads in his criticism and discuss them separately before relating them. To give the reader advance notice, these are the four mistakes Marx finds in Hegel: (*a*) the reduction of man to self-consciousness and activity to spiritual labour; (*b*) the identification of objectivity with estrangement; (*c*) the claim that spirit (read 'man') is 'at home in its other-being as such'; (*d*) the failure to go beyond 'negation of the negation' to the self-sustaining positive.

Labour: Material and Spiritual

Marx praises Hegel for grasping the nature of labour, and, more particularly, for conceiving man as the result of his own labour. As we have seen, Marx can say this sort of thing only by reading into the labour of spirit, at work in the *Phenomenology*, the work of man, that is to say, primarily material labour. We must not, therefore, take Marx's praise too literally. The activity of Hegel's 'spirit' is, naturally, primarily ideal in character, because it is the activity of consciousness and self-consciousness.[8] Consequently, Marx immediately adds to the above-mentioned praise of Hegel, for grasping the nature of labour, the qualification that he knows only 'abstract spiritual labour'.[9] In fact, Hegel reverses the terms of the real relations within his philosophical reflection on the problem of estrangement. Consistently with his idealism, he identifies the human essence with self-consciousness, according to Marx, and this has the result that, in his work, 'all estrangement of human nature is therefore *nothing but estrangement of self-consciousness*'. Furthermore, this means that the estrangement of self-consciousness 'is not regarded as the *expression* . . . of *real* estrangement', but, instead, *actual* estrangement 'is in its innermost essence — which philosophy first brings to light — nothing more than the *appearance* of the estrangement of . . . self-consciousness'. Marx finds it entirely appropriate that the science comprehending this is thus called 'phenomenology'.[10]

Despite the wealth of content in the *Phenomenology* everything is treated under the form of consciousness or self-consciousness. This makes a big difference to the manner in which estrangement is to be superseded. To begin with, Marx points out that a natural being endowed with material powers works upon real objects and in its alienation produces in this process a real world of estrangement; but, he goes on, ' a self-consciousness, through its alienation, can posit only 'thinghood' [*"die Dingheit"*]',[11] an abstraction, a mere postulate of self-consciousness. We saw that in his final chapter Hegel declares that 'it is the alienation of self-consciousness that posits thinghood', but then it 'takes it back into itself'. It is clear 'thinghood' has no independent being and as a postulate of self-consciousness is at the mercy of a retraction by the self-consciousness that postulated it. Hence a *change in attitude* abolishes the consciousness of estrangement because estrangement itself is understood only as an attitude to the world adopted by consciousness. This 'reconciliation', as Hegel calls it, leaves things as they are. As Lukács points out, this reverse movement of *'Er-Innerung'*, this supersession of 'externalization', is 'not an internal movement of objective reality at all, but merely something he has invented in order to bring his philosophy to a conclusion'.[12] This means that no radical critique of the real world of estrangement can be undertaken, much less a practical *objective* transformation.

Marx complains that when 'Hegel conceives wealth, the power of the state, etc., as entities estranged from the being of man, he conceives them only in their thought form'; with the consequence that 'the appropriation of man's objectified and estranged essential powers is therefore only an appropriation which takes place in consciousness, in pure thought, i.e. in abstraction'. That overcoming estrangement is achieved, for Hegel, by a change in consciousness alone is at the root of his conservatism, Marx believes. He sums up the matter thus:

> In the *Phenomenology*, therefore, despite the thoroughly negative and critical appearance and despite the fact that its criticism is genuine and often well ahead of its time, the uncritical positivism and equally uncritical idealism of Hegel's later works, the philosophical dissolution and restoration of the empirical world, is already to be found in latent form.[13]

In a part of the manuscript that has been damaged it is possible to reconstruct an argument whereby Marx compares a real historical solution to the problem of estrangement with the typically idealist Hegelian solution. If one wanted to overcome private property in the manner of Hegel's *Phenomenology*, he apparently argues, one might be satisfied with the *consciousness* that private property is the estranged essence of social man and believe that thereby it is finished as a 'conquered moment'. But in fact 'real estrangement remains and remains all the more, the more one is conscious of it as such'; hence the abolition of estrangement requires a practical solution. Marx concludes: 'in order to abolish the *idea* of private property the *idea* of communism is quite sufficient; it takes *actual* communist action to abolish actual private property.'[14]

In Hegel, estrangement is posited as overcome, not through historical practice but through a philosophical reinterpretation of this world which can only result in the sublation of its otherness through the recognition of this otherness as spirit's own other, and hence its reconciliation with private property, the state, religion and so forth. In Marx, revolutionary practice, not speculative reconciliation, reconstitutes reality through objective reappropriation of the estranged object, thereby producing a new objectivity free of estrangement from its producers.

Objectivity and Estrangement

According to Lukács, Marx finds two errors in Hegel's theory of estrangement: 'on the subjective side, there is the mistaken identification of man and self-consciousness'; while 'on the objective side, there is the equation of estrangement [*Entfremdung*] and objectivity [*Gegenständlichkeit*] in general'.[15]

I dealt just now with the point about the reduction of the problem to the phenomenology of consciousness. What are the consequences for the status of objectivity? Marx argues that Hegel interprets the standpoint of absolute knowledge to be that the object is comprehended only as an objectified self-consciousness; that it is therefore a matter for Hegel of sublating objectivity as such in so far as the relationship to objectivity on the part of a consciousness can only be to view it as other than itself; 'consciousness is offended not by estranged objectivity but by objectivity as such',[16] he says. Thus, since 'objectivity as such is seen as an *estranged* human relationship', it follows that 'the reappropriation of the objective essence of man, produced in the form of estrangement as something alien, therefore means sublating not only *estrangement* but also *objectivity*';[17] for it is precisely 'its *objective* character which constitutes the offence and the estrangement as far as self-consciousness is concerned',[18] Marx claims.

In illustrating this criticism, Marx relies on the passage (quoted earlier) from the beginning of the last chapter of the *Phenomenology*. We saw that Hegel there speaks of self-consciousness sublating 'this alienation *and objectivity too*' (my emphasis). For Marx, objectivity as such is unproblematic; it is only an objectivity established through reification or pervaded by alienation that requires supersession; whereas, if Hegel's 'spirit' requires the sublation of a relationship of estrangement between consciousness and the objectivity posited by it as its other, in effect it requires the sublation in self-consciousness of objectivity as such.

Marx then takes up the Feuerbachian theme that objectivity is an essential framework for the existence and activity of a natural being, and, however much Hegel might go on about self-consciousness, man *is* a natural being; that is to say, an objective being. Such a being takes natural objects 'as the object of his being' and expresses his life in such objects, in acting on them. Marx brings home his polemic against Hegel by arguing, in the light of this, that without objective relationships to objects outside itself a being has no objective existence; hence to construe the surmounting of estrangement as the sublation of objectivity implies the lack of objective being of consciousness itself, and a 'non-objective being is a non-being'.[19] As I shall argue shortly, Hegel recognizes that absolute spirit must become objective to itself if it is to actualize its idea. It is because there can be nothing outside such an absolute that there is a problem about this. Spirit requires another in which to find itself reflected, while at the same time requiring that there is nothing that is not it; that it is a self-identical totality. Hence the ambiguousness, in this absolute science, towards objectivity and objective relationships. Spirit mediates itself with *itself*. As we saw earlier (in the passage on substance as subject) in the movement of the *Phenomenology* we see spirit playing with itself, so to speak, not objective human intercourse with nature.[20]

Objectification and Alienation

The identification, within the totality of spirit, of objectivity as a problem implies that for Hegel estrangement arises from objectification as such rather than from a particular alienating mode of objectification. Marx complains of Hegel: 'it is not that the human essence *objectifies* itself inhumanly, in opposition to itself, but that it *objectifies* itself in *distinction* from and in *opposition* to abstract thought, which constitutes [for him] the essence of estrangement'.[21]

In other words, the charge now is that Hegel identifies objectification with alienation. It is necessary to distinguish this charge from the error of identifying objectivity and estrangement. Unfortunately previous commentators have not done so – not even Lukács. It is very striking in *The Young Hegel* that, immediately after the paragraph quoted earlier, pointing to the equation of estrangement and objectivity, Lukács goes on to say that Marx distinguishes 'objectification in work in general and the estrangement of subject and object in the *capitalist form* of work'; and, thus armed, 'he can expose Hegel's erroneous equation'.[22] Likewise, when he says that Marx's theory of alienated labour implies 'a fundamental critique of Hegel's philosophy' this is said to be because in Marx's work 'estrangement is sharply distinguished from objectivity itself, from objectification in the act of labour'[23] (as if these were the same thing).

Lukács goes on to explain that objectification is 'a characteristic of work in general and of the relation of human practice to the objects of the external world', whereas estrangement is a 'consequence of the social division of labour under capitalism'. By contrast, Hegel fails to make such distinctions:[24] he equates objectification and alienation. This is the charge Lukács brings,[25] and which he says is to be found in Marx (utilizing the passage quoted above).

Why cannot this charge be reduced to the one treated in the previous section above, namely that Hegel equates objectivity and estrangement? The answer is that the latter equation is simply a mistake, from Marx's point of view. It can never be the case that estrangement is due to the *presence of objectivity* (albeit that for Marx estrangement is *objectively present* in our experience). The former equation, the identification of objectification with alienation, is not such a simple error and requires a much more demanding analysis to identify exactly what goes wrong, as we shall see.

To begin with, let us note that Marx begins by *praising* Hegel for grasping objectification as 'alienation and sublation of this alienation'! As we saw in the passage quoted above, this is part of 'the great thing' in Hegel's work. Why should Marx say this? There are two reasons for it.

One is that Hegel reflects the historical experience of humanity here. It has really been the case that up to now the process of objectification has resulted in estrangement. Thus Marx says that the *Phenomenology* 'grasps the estrangement of man', and that 'all the elements of criticism are concealed within it': it contains 'the critical elements – but still in estranged form – of entire spheres, such as religion, the state, bourgeois life and so forth'.[26]

As matter of fact, it is quite difficult to find a statement by Marx saying that Hegel wrongly sees in objectification nothing but alienation. What Marx *does* say is that Hegel quite rightly sees that alienation has the positive significance of objectification.[27] This is the second reason for his praise. It will be recalled that Hegel in his Preface emphasizes that within spirit's self-mediation there remains the moment of 'the labour of the negative'.

This means, as Marx understands, that Hegel is not *opposed* to objectification on the grounds that it leads to estrangement. He certainly thinks that it *does* lead to estrangement; but this does not mean that he thinks spirit should rest content in itself and avoid the misfortune of estrangement from itself in its objectification, because he sees it as necessary to spirit's actualization of itself that it embark on the 'labour of the negative'.

This is what Marx seizes on as 'the positive moment of the Hegelian dialectic'. This insight of Hegel's 'into the *appropriation* of objective being through the supersession of its estrangement' is important because, though in mystified form, it models 'the *real objectification* of man . . . the real appropriation of his objective essence through the annihilation of the *estranged* character of the objective world'. In this way 'Hegel grasps man's self-estrangement . . . as self-discovery, objectification and realization', concludes Marx.[28]

The difference between these thinkers, and the necessity for Marx to criticize Hegel on alienation, lies in their diagnoses and prognoses. Marx, rooting his understanding of the problematic of alienation in wage-labour, envisages a historical stage beyond estrangement. Hegel sublates estrangement by declaring it nothing other than spirit's interior diremption; it is necessary that this moment of estrangement be preserved *as such* because spirit does not inhabit an objective world; thus to become objective it must posit itself as such on its own account, which can be done only in and through its self-alienation. In order to know itself as what it is spirit must express itself in a medium other than itself – hence it must posit itself in the form of otherness. This negation of itself is subsequently negated in its turn, when spirit recognizes itself in these objective shapes, but this cycle of negations is eternally necessary. Spirit can come to itself only *as* the negation of the negation. Hegel, therefore, has no solution to offer other than this pseudo-movement which preserves the realm of estrangement as a moment. As he puts it, spirit is 'at home with itself in its otherness as such'. Simultaneously, spirit overcomes its estrangement from its world through knowing it as its own work, while preserving that world of estrangement in all the immediacy of its otherness.

Marx is pretty bitter about this neat trick: 'so reason is at home in unreason as unreason', he says. It seems that man 'leads his true human life in this alienated life as such'. Therefore, Marx concludes, this amounts to a substantial compromise on Hegel's part with religion, the state and so forth.[29] In Hegel, estrangement is posited as overcome, not through historical practice, but through a philosophical reinterpretation of this world, which can only result in the sublation of its otherness through the recognition of this otherness as spirit's own other, and its reconciliation with private property, the state and religion.

Nowadays it is commonplace to assert that Hegel equates alienation and objectification.[30] Accepting that Marx's commentary on Hegel's *Phenomenology* revolves around these concepts, as we have seen, we none the less find ourselves with a problem: despite Herbert Marcuse, and others, speaking of 'Hegel's category of objectification',[31] in not one line of one page of the *Phenomenology* does Hegel use the term 'objectification'[32] (*Vergegenständlichung*). What we *do* find in a central place in the text, as we have seen, is the term '*Entäusserung*'. To say that objectification is conceived by Hegel only as alienation is to point to the absence of Marx's category of 'objectification' (in the affirmative sense of the establishment by an objective being of its essential relationships in, and through, labour upon the objective world) and its replacement in Hegel's problematic by a significantly different term, *Entäusserung*. This, like *Vergegenständlichung*, has connotations of 'positing as objective' but also carries a sense of relinquishment, renunciation, of what is manifested, thus constituting the latter's actualization as an alienation. As Marx says, 'estrangement [*Entfremdung*] constitutes the real interest of this alienation/externalization [*Entäusserung*]'.[33]

If we do not find the term 'objectification', we *do* find the term 'objectivity' (*Gegenständlichkeit*). Now Hegel cannot conceive of objectivity as such except as estrangement; hence the replacement of the category of 'objectification' with that of 'alienation'. Moreover, this identification (of objectivity with estrangement) allows Hegel to interpret *actual* estrangement as arising exclusively from objectification *in general* and not a particular historically conditioned *mode* of objectification. Consequently, instead of real historical solutions Hegel displaces the problem into general philosphical reflection issuing in a solution posed exclusively within philosophy, as we saw earlier.

For Marx the realization of the human essence involves objective appropriation of the 'other', namely the object of labour, through working it up and making it part of a humanized world. This dialectic of objectification passes through a phase of alienation, but Marx's analysis culminates in the call for the practical overthrow of estrangement and the reappropriation of the estranged essence.

For Hegel the human essence is self-consciousness and Marx argues that, since something comes to exist for consciousness in so far as it knows that something, its only objective relationship is knowing. What absolute knowing realizes is that its 'other' is posited as such only through self-alienation, and is reappropriated through an inwardizing movement of thought, which is forced, in so far as consciousness must *have* an object, to preserve estrangement as a moment of consciousness (and, of course, the *consciousness* of estrangement is all this problematic knows!). In the middle part of the *Phenomenology* masses of concrete historical material, involving actual estranged spheres of existence, are brought within this framework, and the practical problems are provided with a pseudo-solution when philosophy reconciles itself, both with objectivity in general and with historically created objective estrangement in particular. Hegel appears as a radical critic of all objectivity, charging it with being estrangement; but he ends by accepting uncritically both the genuine and reified objectivities, in so far as their character as objective is granted the necessity of a moment in spirit's self-positing movement in its other as its estranged self. To the extent that Hegel accepts the necessity for such alienating objectification he becomes uncritical of the sphere of estrangement brought to life within spirit's self-actualization. In this way the positive achievement of history hidden within estrangement is equated with that estrangement itself. Objectification and alienation are one. Marx speaks, therefore, of 'Hegel's *false* positivism' or 'his merely *apparent* criticism'.[34]

Hegel's greatness as a philosopher is that he is sensitive to the complexities of the system of alienation in which we live, and, although in a mystified way, he understands that it must be the result of the manner in which human self-objectification has been actualized. His misfortune is that he is unable to see the possibility of a historical reappropriation by man of his alienated powers. Instead, the historically conditioned problem is interpreted by him as a general ontological problem of existence. Hence, to posit the possibility of a solution the fatal option of idealism was taken up, whereby the world of real objective estrangement was grasped only from the point of view of the consciousness of it as other than consciousness, that is objectivity, and thus a solution could be posited at that level in so far as reason could penetrate objectivity. Historically, Hegel cannot see beyond the horizon of capitalism. What happens, therefore, is that real alienation is conceptualized in such a thinned-out manner that this *'Entäusserung'* can be overcome in the recollection of its origins. He is too realistic to opt for utopianism in his social theory. But, in the words of Lukács, 'the idealist dialectic transforms the entire history of man into a great philosophical utopia; into the philosphical dream that "alienation" can be overcome in the subject, that substance can be transformed into subject'.[35]

Hegel's tragedy is that, though objectification and alienation are conceptually distinct, and are distinguished brilliantly by Marx, Hegel cannot grasp this possibility, for it depends upon a historical potential beyond the limits of his bourgeois standpoint. Thus he collapses them together so that the necessity of spirit's odyssey of self-objectification becomes at the same time its self-estrangement, and scientific criticism is powerless to do more than point to the content hidden behind the forms of estrangement and pass off this insight as their sublation. But as Marx mercilessly demonstrates, this still leaves real objective estrangement intact.

The Standpoint of Political Economy

As we know, Marx is interested in seeing how far Hegel's category of alienating objectification models his own category of labour. We saw that he finds the great thing in the *Phenomenology* to be precisely that Hegel conceives man as the result of his own labour. Nevertheless, Marx immediately goes on to say that Hegel's account is 'one-sided' and 'limited'. Before devoting himself to detailed analysis of the closing chapter of the *Phenomenology* to demonstrate this, Marx makes two preliminary general points. These stand right next to each other, without the least transition, in the same paragraph.

> For the moment, let us say this much in advance: Hegel adopts the standpoint of modern political economy. He grasps *labour* as the *essence*, as the self-confirming essence, of man; he sees only the positive side of labour, not its negative side. Labour is man's *coming to be for himself* within *alienation* or as *alienated* man. The only labour Hegel knows and recognizes is *abstract mental* labour.[36]

What should be noticed particularly is that the first three sentences constitute a criticism of Hegel parallel to Marx's diagnosis of the failings of political economy. Then Marx switches abruptly to a different criticism to do with Hegel's idealism (which we have already covered). In truth, these criticisms are related; but the reader must not be tempted to seize gratefully on the second criticism recognizing in it the familiar battle between materialism and idealism, and neglecting thereby the first criticism. The first criticism qualifies the previous paragraph in praise of Hegel in just as important a way as the more obvious second criticism does. What Marx says here is that Hegel, when he sees 'man' ('spirit' in Hegel) as the result of his own labour, shares in this perspective the limited one-sided view of political economy: he sees only the positive and not the negative side of labour. Just as spirit comes to know its own power in the shapes of its substance, so modern political economy has seen through the reified world of mercantilism and understood the enormous productive power of labour, truly the source of 'the wealth of nations'. What political economy avoids is 'the negative side of labour'. As Marx earlier pointedly remarks: 'political economy conceals the estrangement inherent in the nature of labour by ignoring the *immediate* relationship between the *worker* (labour) *and production*'. The truth is, he claims, that 'labour produces marvels for the rich, but it produces privation for the worker; it produces palaces, but hovels for the worker; it produces beauty, but deformity for the worker'. And so on. Machinery does not lighten labour but turns the workers themselves into cogs in the machine. There is intelligence in machines, but cretinism in labour.[37]

So the man who results from his own labour is the victim of his own self-estrangement, the wealth he creates stands over against him as an alien power. 'Labour is man's coming to be for himself within alienation or as aliented man', Marx reminds us. Thus to attribute to Hegel the standpoint of political economy is a damaging criticism indeed. It is to charge Hegel with concealing the estrangement inherent in 'labour' and identifying this alienating mediator with productive activity itself.

This seems unfair because, after all, Hegel is rightly credited by Marx with having understood that man objectifies himself in and through 'alienation and the supersession of alienation'. But we have also seen that, just because Hegel follows the labour of *spirit* in this dialectic, reappropriation takes place only within self-consciousness. We have argued that this leaves real objective estrangement intact. If such labour is posited as the essence, then, just as with political economy, the estrangement inherent in labour is overlooked or even endorsed as ontologically necessary to human existence.

In truth, Hegel's equation of objectification and alienation makes him uncritical of the estrangement brought to life in spirit's self-actualization. Hegel, in common with modern political economy, grasps labour (spiritual labour in his case) as the essence of human achievement; he even grasps it as alienating activity; but if (like Hegel and Smith) one is unable to identify a genuine historical supersession of estrangement, the existing conditions become the horizon that blocks off access to a *critically adopted* standpoint of labour. It is rather the case that these conditions that twist and distort the objectification of man in and through productive activity are endorsed as the necessary framework within which the becoming of man for himself must occur. Thus Marx can conclude that 'Hegel sees . . . self-objectification in the form of self-alienation and self-estrangement as the absolute, and hence final, expression of human life, which . . . has attained its own essential nature'.[38]

The standpoint of Hegel is that of modern political economy, namely, the *uncritically adopted* standpoint of labour, labour that is a determination of the private property system, an alienating mediator, falsely absolutized.

An important parallel here is that Hegel's account of subjectivity, thrown back into itself in the face of alien objectivity, maps philosophically the experience of labour-power as a subjectivity thrown back into itself in the face of the determination of its object as alien private property. Furthermore, the activity of Hegel's spirit, in overcoming the dichotomy in such a manner that it takes objectivity (= estrangement) back into itself while yet preserving its otherness, maps the standpoint of political economy when it proves that productive labour is the source of wealth, but 'gives everything to private property' (in Marx's words). In both cases an alienating mediator reproduces the totality, preserving rather than abolishing the estrangement of subject and object.

The Dialectic of Negativity

We have seen that Hegel's mediator is the negating action of consciousness. We found that Marx praises 'the great thing' in Hegel's book, namely, 'the dialectic of negativity as the moving and producing principle'. But there are certain problems with Hegel's dialectic: it is abstract; it is conservative; and it is stuck at the stage of negation of negation.

In presenting the activity of spirit as *pure* negativity Hegel abstracts from all determinate content. Real alienation is subsumed in the logical category of 'the negative' and its supersession is naturally another logical operation, 'the negation of the negation'. Marx complains that 'the inexhaustible, vital, sensuous, concrete activity of self-objectification is therefore reduced to its mere abstraction, absolute negativity, an abstraction which is then given permanent form as such and conceived as . . . activity itself'.[39]

Furthermore, the incorporation of the problematic of estrangement within the conceptual framework of *absolute* negativity means that Hegel's critical apparatus is unable to identify the specific historical origins of alienation, or the concrete historical conditions of its supersession. In effect, he endorses the moment of estrangement as an ontological necessity, instead of grasping it as brought about through specific material processes in the history of mankind's emergence, and as subject to radical abolition, through a revolution which is the outcome of changed historical conditions.

So, while Marx allows that 'in grasping the positive significance of the negation which has reference to itself'[40] Hegel grasps self-alienation as self-objectification, at the same time, 'since this negation of the negation is itself still trapped in estrangement, what this amounts to is a failure to move beyond the final stage, the stage of self-reference in alienation'.[41] Spirit knows itself in its negation, but posits itself only in the negation of the negation. Thus, this negation of the negation does not give rise, in a practical transformation of the entire structure of labour, to the 'self-sustaining positive'. As we have seen, for Marx communism is the *positive* supersession of private property as human self-estrangement. We have seen also that he characterizes communist revolution (because of its character as the negation of the negation, as the reappropriation of the human essence through the negation of private property) 'as being not yet the true, self-originating position but rather a position originating from private property'.[42] He concludes that 'only when we have superseded this mediation – which, however, is a necessary precondition – will *positive* humanism, positively originating in itself, come into being'.[43]

This is the crucial difference between Hegel and Marx: Hegel stays within the circle of circles of his absolute, while Marx wants to open out a new historical perspective subsequent to the supersession of alienation. Marx sums up the relation of Hegel's philosophy to real history in two propositions: (*a*) 'Hegel has merely discovered the *abstract*, *logical*, *speculative* expression of the movement of history'; (*b*) 'This movement of history is not yet the *real* history of man . . . it is simply the *process of his creation*, the *history of his emergence*'.[44]

The first point is that the abstract expression of the process of man's creation of himself, through labour and its alienation, is given in Hegel under the concept of 'absolute negativity', an abstract speculative version of activity which is empty of content and can be supplied with any content accordingly. The other point is that in the cycle of negation, and the negation of the negation, Hegel states as an absolute what is in real history relative only to the process of emergence which culminates in communist revolution; but 'communism as such is not the goal of human development'. The point here is that, though Hegel's treatment of positing through double negation is abstract, this abstraction is taken from real history, namely the genesis of objective powers of production in the shape of estrangement from the immediate producer, and the potential to reappropriate this estranged essence. But in Hegel, precisely because of his ambivalent attitude to objectivity in the dialectic of spirit, the abstract treatment is subject to the further limitation that self-recognition in estrangement is preserved as a moment within the absolute. A radical transcendence, a positive supersession, of estranged objectivity cannot be thought.

Conclusion

For an idealist to take offence at objective reality and to deny its independence would not in itself have any interest. What strikes Marx as very interesting, and serves as the point of departure for both his praise and his criticism of Hegel, is that Hegel's definition of alienation has a positive connotation just in so far as it posits objectivity. Hegel clearly distinguishes his position from that of subjective idealism in so far as the moment of objectivity is granted its necessity; consciousness must be conscious of *something*. At the same time, the identification of objectivity with estrangement poses a problem. Again, unlike Stoicism for example, Hegel's philosophy does not attempt a solution through a retreat into the inner life and a denial of the effectivity of objective reality in the subject's freedom of thought. Rather, Hegel insists that estrangement can be overcome precisely when self-consciousness appropriates objectivity and finds itself at home in this its other. This is achieved when spirit understands that the object is nothing but its own self-alienation.

Marx's objections to Hegel's idealist construction he sums up for himself at the beginning of a notebook started in November 1844 (the *1844 Manuscripts* themselves are dated April to August). He makes the following four points. First: Hegel puts 'self-consciousness instead of man'; second: 'the differences of things are unimportant, because substance is conceived as self-distinction', although it is granted that Hegel makes distinctions that 'grasp the vital point'; third: 'abolition of *estrangement* is identified with abolition of *objectivity*'; fourth: supersession of 'the object as object of consciousness is identified with real abolition' of alienation.[45]

These points are connected in the following way: given that Hegel expounds the phenomenology of knowing subjectivity, all human relations are brought within this framework; distinctions between man and the objects of his activity are hence rendered as self-distinctions produced in the negating action of consciousness; objectivity equals estrangement for such a subjectivity until the estrangement is overcome in the final revolution of spirit's progressive self-realization as a self-identical totality; this is confused with real objective abolition because of the treatment of objects as objects of consciousness simply.

It might be objected that to say nothing is really changed when absolute knowledge recollects and recognizes the determinations of substance as spirit's self-determination fails to notice that this itself counts as a change given the framework of Hegel's speculative problematic. A new shape of consciousness is born.

The answer to this would be that, although earlier stages of self-development of spirit are associated by Hegel with objective historical transformations, the development after the culmination of this in the stage of 'self-estranged spirit' leaves the ground of objective social relationships and moves in increasingly interiorized shapes of spirit: art, revealed religion and philosophy. In this way philosophy reconciles itself with the forms of social objectivity (the economy, the state) previously experienced as alienated. Marx can legitimately complain that the underlying objective relationships remain untransformed and preserve their effectivity in everyday experience. After all, the mass of people cannot become Hegelian dialecticians! In any case, it is not that his philosophy abolishes estrangement – it merely abstracts from it.

It is interesting that in the November summary there is no praise of Hegel's 'dialectic of negativity as the producing principle'. Perhaps Marx by this time had decided that the abstract character of this negativity rendered it so vacuous that there was no point in discussing it. None the less, it was precisely on that issue that Marx earlier felt it necessary to comment in order to distinguish his own position on 'communism as the negation of the negation' from any confusion with Hegelian positing through double negation. In spite of the work already produced by Feuerbach in criticism of this Hegelian dialectic – work extravagantly praised by Marx – he found when working through his critique that it would be necessary to put together a special chapter on Hegel in which the 'positive moments' (clearly stimulating Marx's own thought) could be noted along with the reproduction of the Feuerbachian critique. This, in turn, raises questions about Marx's relation to Feuerbach at this date. Such a discussion is postponed in this book to Part Three, until after we have completed our study of the relationship of Marx and Hegel by looking at some especially significant sections of Hegel's *Phenomenology*.

The Appendix to this chapter is concerned with relevant recent secondary literature on the reading of Hegel.

Summary

Although Marx criticizes Hegel for reducing man to self-consciousness and activity to spiritual labour, he nevertheless finds that in this guise Hegel 'grasps the nature of labour' and sees man 'as the result of his own labour'. Yet Hegel shares with political economy the *uncritically* adopted standpoint of labour, in conflating objectification and alienation, hence absolutizing estrangement. Marx protests against Hegel's claim that spirit is at home in its otherness once it recollects that the latter is its own alienating objectification. Marx accepts that the negation of the negation is the pattern of human genesis through alienation and its supersession. But where Hegel idealizes and absolutizes 'the labour of the negative', Marx looks to a radical objective supersession of estrangement through practical, material, and historical, revolution.

Appendix

Is Marx Fair to Hegel?

My concern with Hegel in this book is primarily with Hegel as the dialectically surpassed predecessor of Marx. From this point of view what is important is Marx's reading of Hegel; what he saw, or thought he saw, that was useful to him, and what he saw, or thought he saw, a need to depart from. It would be possible to challenge that reading of course. This has indeed happened.[46] I do not intend here to defend Marx's reading of Hegel. I believe that its general thrust is correct, despite the fact that Hegel is somewhat caricatured on occasion in the heat of the polemic.

At this point, nevertheless, for the benefit of those interested, I indicate the most interesting possible criticism. Gillian Rose, in her novel reading of Hegel, complains in passing that the *Phenomenology* has 'frequently been misread in Fichtean terms according to which the "experience" of consciousness is . . . understood . . . as a change in perspective which sees the non-ego as the ego's own alienated exteriorization, recaptures it by an act of will, and becomes absolute'.[47] Marx, and the Marxist tradition, are cited in this connection. Likewise, later on she complains that 'Marx produces a Fichtean reading of Hegel's system as the unconditioned absolute idea which pours forth nature, which does not recognize but creates determination'.[48]

If we turn to Marx's own account of Hegel's relation to his predecessors we find that he sees three elements in Hegel: Spinoza's substance; Fichte's self-consciousness; 'and Hegel's necessarily antagonistic *unity* of the two, the *Absolute Spirit*'.[49] This view of Hegel sees him trying to have it both ways. Spirit both recognizes and creates determination. An interpreter of Hegel as sympathetic as Richard Norman concedes that absolute spirit looks pretty much like God, as traditionally conceived, in certain passages, particularly in the Preface. (Then again, one should bear in mind that Hegel later remarked that in the Preface the *abstract* absolute dominates.)[50] M. Rosen goes so far as to say that the way the self-movement of the notion produces its content out of itself corresponds to the theological problematic of *creatio ex nihilo*.[51] As for Marx: he finds in Hegel 'a mystical subject – object'.[52]

A curious feature of Rose's subsequent argument is the use she makes of the following statement by Marx:

> For this third object I am thus an *other actuality* than it, that is, *its* object. To assume a being which is not the object of another is thus to suppose that *no* objective being exists.[53]

This is said by Rose to be a place where Marx's thought does not rely on abstract dichotomies, but 'captures what Hegel means by actuality or spirit'.[54] The curious thing about this is that Marx's intention in the passage at issue is to *criticize* Hegel's absolute spirit. It forms part of a discussion of Hegel's statement that it is the alienation of self-consciousness which posits thinghood. At the same time, leaving aside Marx's *intention*, it could be argued that when he says that a being with no object would exist 'solitary and alone' ('*einsam und allein*')[55] this reminds us immediately of the end of the *Phenomenology* where comprehended history is the actuality of absolute spirit without which it would be 'lifeless and alone' ('*das leblose Einsam*' in Hegel's curious phrase).[56]

None the less, Marx's point is that where the absolute is concerned, the relation to the object is grasped by Hegel ultimately as not a really objective relation. Likewise, in his *Logic*, Hegel defines being *determinate* as being for another; but again, in parallel with the *Phenomenology*, the *absolute* idea absorbs all available content, it 'contemplates its contents as its own self'.[57]

In truth, Marx's argument at this point does bear traces of the presence of Fichte. Thinghood (*Dingheit*) is said by Marx to be something *posited* by the Hegelian self-consciousness. 'And what is posited, instead of confirming itself, is but the confirmation of the act of positing which for a moment fixes its energy as the product, and gives it the *semblance* – but only for a moment – of an independent, real substance.' Marx goes on to argue against this that man 'creates or posits objects' because he is himself objectively posited. 'In the act of positing, therefore, this objective being does not fall from his state of "pure activity" into a *creating* of the *object*; on the contrary, his *objective* product only confirms his objective activity.'[58] (This is equally so in alienating objectification of course.)

Hegel, however, does not talk of 'pure activity' on the relevant pages, but this phrase *is* very reminiscent of Fichte.[59] In Fichte's *Science of Knowledge* (1794), it is argued that 'the pure activity of the self' is presupposed by 'objective activity'; it is a 'condition of any activity that posits an object' even though 'pure activity originally relates to no object at all'.[60] (Earlier, where 'the act of positing' is shown to entail 'the activity of alienation', there is also a nice definition of the object created: 'the activity of alienation', he says, 'must have a passivity opposed to it; and such there is, indeed, in that a portion of absolute totality *is* alienated; *is* posited as not posited.'[61])

A related point brought forward by Rose is the role of alienation in Hegel's *Phenomenology*. She argues that the *Phenomenology* is *not* 'the experience of consciousness recapturing its alienated existence' and that the experience of alienation is restricted to a historically specific period, namely pre-bourgeois society.[62] As we earlier said, there are two German terms used by Hegel that translate as 'alienation', namely '*Entäusserung*' and '*Entfremdung*'. There is no doubt at all that the former plays the role attributed to it by Marx at the level of the upshot of the whole *Phenomenology*. This may be confirmed by examining the last chapter.[63] Rose's reference to a historically specific period (i.e. the period covered in '*Der sich Entfremdete Geist*'), suggests that she may wish to restrict the reference to the term '*Entfremdung*'. However, Hegel's Preface employs this expression in several places: for example, the experience of consciousness is said to be a movement 'in which the immediate, the unexperienced, i.e. the abstract, whether it be of sensuous being, or only thought of as simple becomes alienated [*entfremdet*] from itself and then returns to itself from this alienation [*Entfremdung*] . . .'[64]

7

The Influence of the Phenomenology

Introduction

The fact that Marx hangs his criticism of Hegel largely on a passage from the last chapter of the *Phenomemology* warrants the inference that the main influence of the work on him is its dialectic *in general*. However, there is no doubt that Marx could not have been so interested in it if he had only acquainted himself with the rather abstract formulations in the conclusion and the Preface. Clearly the way Hegel works through historical material in the concrete to flesh out the dialectic of consciousness and self-consciousness must have impressed Marx.

Accordingly, this chapter is devoted to a discussion of some of the materials concerned. In relation to this, there is first a myth to be refuted.[1]

Lordship and Bondage

There is a widely held view that Marx was profoundly influenced by the master – servant (*'Herrschaft und Knechtschaft'*) dialectic in Hegel's *Phenomenology of Spirit*. This view was first popularized by Jean-Paul Sartre, who refers in his *Being and Nothingness* (1943) to 'the famous "Master – Slave" relation which so profoundly influenced Marx'; Sartre does not explain how he knows this.[2] Probably this remark reflects the pervasive influence of Alexandre Kojève's lectures on Hegel in the 1930s. Kojève presents a reading of the *Phenomenology* that centralizes the place of the master – servant dialectic in it, in a quasi-Marxist interpretation. Kojève may have assumed that Marx himself read it in the same way. However, it is one thing to read Marxism back into Hegel, it is another to generate it *out* of Hegel. Three years after Sartre we find Jean Hyppolite again saying that the dialectic of domination and servitude is the best-known section of the *Phenomenology* because of 'the influence it has had on the political and social philosophy of Hegel's successors, especially Marx'.[3]

As a matter of fact, despite the assertions of numerous commentators to the contrary, Sartre and Hyppolite did *not* attend Kojève's lectures. The myth that they sat at the feet of the 'unknown superior' is now well-established. Thus Wilfred Desan says that the audience included Sartre, Merleau-Ponty and Hyppolite; and, more specifically, 'Sartre learned to study Hegel in the classes of Kojève just before W.W.II'; but he does not give any evidence for it.[4] Let us turn then to first-hand accounts. Kojève's disciple Raymond Queneau, who was responsible for collecting and publishing Kojève's lectures in 1947, has given a list of participants that does not include Sartre or Hyppolite.[5] As far as Hyppolite is concerned, we have the additional testimony of Madame Hyppolite that he did not attend 'for fear of being influenced'.[6]

However that may be, by the time Sartre and Hyppolite made their equations between Hegel and Marx, a crucial document of Kojève's was already in the public domain. In the issue of *Mesures* for 14 January 1939 Kojève published a free translation, with interpolated glosses, of the section of the *Phenomenology* entitled 'Autonomy and Dependence of Self-Consciousness: Mastery and Servitude'.[7] Still more interesting for our purposes is that Kojève includes as an epigraph the following words of Marx: '*Hegel . . . erfasst die* Arbeit *als das* Wesen, *als das sich bewährende Wesen des Menschen.*' ('Hegel . . . grasps *labour* as the *essence*, as the self-confirming essence of man.') No reference is given, but in fact this is quoted from Marx's *1844 Manuscripts*, which remained unpublished until the 1930s. Kojève, therefore, was one of the first to make a direct connection between this judgement of Marx's on Hegel and the master – servant dialectic in the *Phenomenology*.

Today it is dogmatically asserted in numerous books that Marx was inspired by Hegel's analysis of the labour of servitude.[8] This view is false. Here I will attempt to show that this is so in the light of the account above of the real significance of Marx's critical appropriation of the *Phenomenology*.

If we are to examine the influence of Hegel's *Phenomenology* on Marx, the crucial text to consider has to be the *1844 Manuscripts*. As we have seen, Marx praises Hegel there for having grasped man as the result of his own labour. Nearly all commentators, innocently assuming that *material* labour is meant here, turn to the *Phenomenology* and find that there is indeed a fascinating discussion in the 'master – servant' section of the significance of material labour, in and through which the servant 'finds himself. Furthermore, the fact that this labour is seen by Hegel as actualized in the context of servitude leads some commentators to make the more extravagant claim that in his theory of alienation Marx draws on this same section. Herbert Marcuse was probably the first to do so; he says in his *Reason and Revolution* (1941) that Marx 'described the "alienation" of labour in the terms of Hegel's discussion of master and servant'.[9]

The only difficulty with these presuppositions of the secondary literature is that Marx *never refers* to this section of the *Phenomenology* – never mind giving it any importance! – when, in his *1844 Manuscripts*, he embarks on a 'critique of Hegel's dialectic'.[10] He discusses the *Phenomenology* as a whole and draws attention to its last chapter especially; he singles out three other sections for praise; but none of them is on the master – servant dialectic. This should make us suspicious, therefore, of the claims made for the '*Herrschaft und Knechtschaft*' section. (Incidentally, although it is popularly nominated the 'master–slave', the correct translation of '*Knecht*' is 'servant' or 'bondsman'. That this choice of terminology is deliberate is seen when we find that in his 1825 Berlin lecture on *Herrschaft und Knechtschaft* Hegel draws a *distinction* between *der Sklave* and *der Knecht*.[11])

Let us now rehearse the dialectic of lordship and bondage. This section occurs early in the *Phenomenology* at the point where consciousness is to turn into self-consciousness. Hegel believes that the self can become conscious of itself only in and through the mediation of another self-consciousness. The first stable relationship that emerges in Hegel's dialectical development of this topic is that of lordship and bondage. The master is acknowledged as such by his servant, and he achieves immediate satisfaction of his desires through goods and services provided by the servant's labour. The dialectic moves forwards precisely through the servant, however, because 'through work . . . the bondsman becomes conscious of what he truly is'. Work forms and shapes the thing; and through this formative activity the consciousness of the servant now, in the work outside it, acquires 'an element of permanence'; for it comes to see in the independent being of the object 'its *own* independence'.

'The shape does not become something other than himself through being made external to him', says Hegel, 'for it is precisely this shape that is his pure being-for-self.' The result of this rediscovery of himself is that, 'precisely in labour', whose meaning seemed so alien to him, the bondsman gains a sense of *himself* – 'a mind of his own' so to speak.[12] These terms are superficially comparable to Marx's in that both Hegel and Marx see work not merely in its utilitarian aspect but as a vehicle for self-realization; thus they see the servant rather than the master as the locus of a more developed human existence. Fundamental differences between

Marx and Hegel become obvious when we notice that, whereas Marx holds that only a change in the mode of production recovers for the worker his sense of self and its fulfilment, Hegel thinks that the educative effect of work, even within an exploitative relation of production, is sufficient for the worker to manifest to himself his own 'meaning' in his product. Furthermore, at this stage in the phenomenological dialectic, as we shall see below, the condition of 'fear and service' is stipulated as necessary to this end; that is, to the servant's becoming objective to himself.

Remembering now the crucial passage in Marx's complex discussion of the *Phenomenology*, in which Marx praises Hegel for grasping the importance of labour: does such a judgement (as Kojève insinuates and so many later writers boldly assert) rest on Hegel's discussion of the labour of servitude? The first thing that should give us pause is that immediately after this praise Marx qualifies it by complaining that 'the only labour Hegel knows and recognizes is *abstract mental* labour'. The servant's labour is clearly *material*, so this remark seems to show that not only has Marx not drawn on that analysis, but he has actually forgotten about it and done Hegel an injustice![13]

What Marx does refer us to is 'the dialectic of negativity as the moving and producing principle'. Spirit comes to know itself through producing itself, in the first instance as something alien standing over against it. In the final chapter, as we have seen, the world of estrangement thus brought to life is overcome, or negated, in a peculiar way in that — as Hegel puts it — 'self-consciousness has sublated this alienation and objectivity . . . so that it is at home with itself in its otherness as such'. When Marx refers to the final result of the *Phenomenology* being 'the dialectic of negativity as the moving and producing principle' it is to this entire labour of spirit in the *Phenomenology* that he refers. Of course, in Marx's view, man produces himself through material labour. It would be a mistake, however, to assume therefrom that he praises Hegel for what he says about material labour, such as that of the servant. When Marx says Hegel grasps labour as the essence he is talking not about what Hegel actually says about material labour (hence the lack of reference to 'Lordship and Bondage') but about the esoteric significance of the dialectic of negativity in spirit's entire self-positing movement (hence Marx's claim that the only labour Hegel knows is spiritual labour). Marx sees in Hegel's dialectic of negativity the hypostatization of the abstract reflection in philosophy of the material process whereby man produces himself through his own labour, a process which (Marx concurs with Hegel) must pass through a stage of estrangement.

Nevertheless, Marx holds that Hegel's discussion of the problematics of alienation is embedded in speculative illusions, and because of this it is a 'merely apparent criticism', shading over into uncritical positivism. In this connection one must draw attention to the sophisticated use of quotation by Kojève in the above-mentioned epigraph to the effect that Hegel grasps labour as the essence. The passage from which Kojève quotes is as follows — with Kojève's 'quote' stressed:

> *Hegel* adopts the standpoint of modern political economy. He *grasps labour as the essence, the self-confirming essence of man*; he sees only the positive and not the negative side of labour. Labour is man's coming to be for himself within alienation or as alienated man.[14]

This passage is not so much praise, as criticism, of Hegel. It is praise only in a paradoxical sense. As we have seen, in adopting the standpoint of labour, both Hegel and political economy achieve an understanding, in different ways, of the genesis, not merely of wealth, but of human being itself. But, just because labour is identical with alienating activity, the result is 'man's coming to be as *alienated* man'. Marx takes the *critically* adopted standpoint of labour, the standpoint of the critique of labour as alienating; he projects the abolition of labour, its transformation into free productive activity.

As we have seen, a crucial move Hegel makes is to transform labour into spiritual activity; and hence to project the overcoming of alienation as a revolution in consciousness, namely, spirit's achievement of absolute knowledge of itself and all its works. It is necessary to locate the 'master – slave' dialectic within this perspective of spirit's development of its self-awareness. As we have already noted, and now stress, it is an early moment in the story of spirit's recovery of itself. It is much less 'concrete' (in Hegel's terms) than cultural achievements such as law, art, religion and philosophy. None the less, it is located at a turning point of some importance, for the problem Hegel faces is how to develop dialectically *self*-consciousness out of the mere consciousness of external objects. Consciousness cannot grasp *itself* in things. It must distinguish itself absolutely from them through their radical negation. The consumption of objects of *desire* accomplishes this in an evanescent way. To risk one's life in forcing another consciousness to grant one *recognition* represents a more promising mediation. But the master finds himself frustrated in reducing the vanquished to his servant, his *thing*. Self-consciousness can only gain proper recognition through mutual respect such as that accorded to individuals constituted in the legal and ethical relations Hegel develops later in the story. At this stage Hegel is not really discussing *individuality*, and *a fortiori*, not social relationships. (Hence there is no discussion of master – master or slave – slave relationships.) We are concerned here with the most primitive level of self-consciousness, that of self-consciousness *in general* as against consciousness of objects.

In a neat reversal, the dialectic advances now through the despised servant. As we have seen, he 'finds himself' through the negating action of work on things. Hegel defines work as 'desire held in check'; that is to say, it involves putting a distance between the immediate impulses of self-will and formative activity grounded in objective principles. If you like, it is really the master who is a slave because his object is the 'unalloyed feeling of self-satisfaction': that is to say, he is a slave to his appetites; but his satisfactions are 'only fleeting', lacking the permanence of objectivity. The servant, on the other hand, in the work he creates, achieves mastery of his craft; it is he who rises to the level of universal human reason. But Hegel introduces the notion that 'fear and service' are *necessary* to induce the check to desire and to ensure that consciousness rises above self-centred goals to the freedom that comes from a consciousness of the 'universal power' of human creative activity.[15] Indeed, it is worth noting that in Hegel's *Encyclopaedia* 'Phenomenology' *no* mention is made of the worker finding himself in his product; the emphasis in the outcome of the 'master–slave' there is on 'community of need' and the idea that 'fear of the lord is the beginning of wisdom'.[16] By contrast, in the *Phenomenology* Hegel says that, 'albeit fear of the lord is the beginning of wisdom, consciousness is not therein aware of being self-existent'. But 'through labour it comes to itself'. However, it turns out that both are necessary: 'for the reflection of self into self the two moments, fear and service in general, as also that of formative activity, are necessary . . .'[17]

The real point in all this is that it brings about an advance to self-consciousness. Strictly speaking, it is not the *material* achievement that is important to provide a basis for Hegelian self-consciousness, but rather the *consciousness* of the power of labour to transform things. The servant becomes aware in this of the power of thought, of universal concepts. This does not have much in common with Marx's interest in the realization of an objective being in forming the material world, but it is of a piece with the project of the *Phenomenology* as a whole.[18] As it is a *spiritual* odyssey it is quite wrong to place special stress on this moment of material labour (as is the case with the overly 'Marxist' readings of Marcuse and Kojève), for its importance lies not in the material result but in the spiritual one. Only if one accepts this can one fail to be surprised when the next twist of the phenomenological dialectic brings us to the pure universality of thought in the attitudes Hegel identifies with Stoicism and Scepticism. The split between the lord's satisfaction in his autonomy and the negatively universal power developed on the servant's side is re-worked at this new level.

Desire and work are found wanting from the point of view of free self-consciousness; they fail to effect adequately the negation of otherness. The self's negating power cannot be enjoyed by the servant in the product, but only in itself, the power of consciousness working within itself. For the servant is not independent on his own account in the objective world, since he is dominated by the fear of the lord and subjected to his desires. Paradoxically, Hegel relies on just these 'negations' to make an advance, claiming that without this complete repression and fear consciousness would remain bogged down in particularity and servitude, that consciousness of freedom would be mere wilfulness and obstinacy. Consciousness wins its freedom when its power and knowledge are redirected inwards, when it deals with its own thought material. Now consciousness says to itself: 'In thinking *I am free*, because I am not in another, but remain simply and solely in communion with myself.'[19] This 'freedom' of inner life is compatible with any social position; as Hegel says: 'Whether on the throne or in chains . . . its aim is to be free.'[20] (It will be recalled that two prominent Stoics were the emperor Marcus Aurelius and the Slave Epictetus.)

Does Marx, as Marcuse and others claim, follow in his theory of alienation the terms of Hegel's master – servant dialectic? We have already said enough to cast doubt on this. It would certainly be strange, as well, to refer to this section to illustrate the claim that Hegel equates material labour with alienation, because here labour is a *recuperating* moment in spirit's drive to realize its freedom in the face of the blankness of objectivity. The peculiar thing about Hegel's treatment is that, as we have seen, in so far as his thematization of the servant's labour touches on the alienation involved in such activity, it is seen, on the one hand, as still *sufficiently* fulfilling for the worker to identify himself in it, and, on the other hand, even as *necessary* to impel his consciousness to the level of absolute negativity.

These points are illustrated if we ask the question: does Hegel actually *mention* alienation in this section? There are two terms to consider. The term '*Entfremdung*' does not occur; the nearest Hegel comes to it is when he says that the labour seems to have only '*fremder Sinn*'; this sentence, however, is precisely that in which the servant is said to discover himself in labour in spite of the fact that it is orientated to the master's desire. The term '*Entäusserung*' does not occur either at this point in the *Phenomenology*. But Hegel does use it in his *Encyclopaedia* when he thematizes the master – servant relationship. Here the labour-process is said to overcome 'self-will' and 'the inner immediacy of desire'; this in turn is identified as '*Entäusserung*' (translated by Wallace as 'divestment of self' and by Petry as 'privation'). The point, nevertheless, is that this is treated positively; it makes possible 'the beginning of wisdom', the transition to 'universal self-consciousness'.[21] We are very far from Marx now.

Our conclusion must be that Marx did not draw on Hegel's analysis of the labour of servitude in his theory of alienation. He fails to mention it for the simple reason that it did not strike him as important.

It remains to be noted that he does not cite this section in any other writings, early or late. What we do find in a few places are echoes of its terms. For example, in 1844 itself there is a somewhat obscure passage in his notes on James Mill.[22] However, let us close this section with an interesting quotation from Marx's *Capital* manuscripts.

> Hence the rule of the capitalist over the worker is the rule of things over man, of dead labour over the living, of the product over the producer . . . Thus at the level of material production, of the life-process in the realm of the social – for that is what the process of production is – we find the *same* situation that we find in *religion* at the ideological level, namely the inversion of subject and object. Viewed *historically* this inversion is the indispensable transition without which wealth as such, i.e. the relentless productive force of social labour, which alone can form the material base of a free human society, could not possibly be created at the expense of the majority . . . What we are confronted by here is the *alienation* [*Entfremdung*] of man from his own labour. To that extent the worker stands on a higher plane than the capitalist from the outset, since the latter has his roots in the process of alienation and finds absolute satisfaction in it whereas right from the start the worker is a victim who confronts it as a rebel and experiences it as a process of enslavement.[23]

'The Critical Elements'

Marx finds that, though in mystified form, Hegel tackles the problem of estrangement in his *Phenomenology*: 'even though man appears only as spirit, there lie concealed in it *all* the elements of criticism, already *prepared* and *elaborated* in a manner often rising far above the Hegelian standpoint'. What elements does Marx have in mind? As we have just seen, 'lordship and bondage' is not mentioned. In fact, he cites three sections: 'the unhappy consciousness', 'the honest consciousness' and 'the struggle of noble and base consciousness'. According to Marx, these separate sections contain 'the *critical* elements' of whole spheres of estrangement such as 'religion, the state, civil life, etc.'.[24] Unfortunately he gives us no analysis of these sections. These phenomenological figures will be touched on now in so far as they relate to the problem of alienated labour.

Citation of the 'unhappy consciousness' explains Marx's reference to the sphere of religion because the most obvious source for Hegel's subject matter here is traditional forms of religious experience. Hegel may well have intended to exempt Lutheranism from this category but Marx would obviously include it too. Findlay even suggests that it applies best to Kierkegaard's morbid Protestant Christianity.[25] The 'unhappy consciousness' finds itself desiring and working but in work and enjoyment it feels itself lost in superficiality; it does not identify itself *in* the world but supposes itself to belong to an unreachable *beyond*. Although it cannot help getting satisfaction from its work, it attributes every success to God and endeavours to play down earthly life in order to get closer to the absolute it supposes to lie beyond it.[26] Hegel's critique relies on the view that activity, especially work, is necessary to self-realization; and that self-consciousness must find its satisfaction there and not rely on priestly mediators to direct it towards salvation.

The 'honest consciousness' certainly seeks satisfaction in work, in keeping busy so to speak; but this figure of consciousness is presented as engaged on his enterprises as an *individual*. It turns up in a section with the curious title 'The spiritual animal kingdom'.[27] This seems to be Hegel's attempt to characterize a form of self-consciousness divorced from relations of inter-subjectivity. He deals here with an individuality that takes itself to be self-sufficient, single and specific. Hegel starts with some interesting remarks on the signficance of activity. He argues that 'consciousness must act merely in order that what it is *in itself* may become explicit *for it*'; in other words, 'an individual cannot know what he [really] is until he has made himself a reality through action'.[28] The 'work done' (*das Werk*) expresses the individual's original nature. Marx would certainly find this congruent with his own ontology, organized as it is around productive activity. However, Hegel's thematization of action soon slips towards idealism. This is not because he focuses on certain particular forms of activity. The work carried out could be material/physical or intellectual. It is rather a question of the meaning he finds in it. At this point it is valuable to cite Löwith's opinion: for Hegel, he says, 'work is not a particular economic activity, to be contrasted, say, to leisure or play, but the basic way in which man produces his life, thereby giving form to the world . . . Work is neither physical nor intellectual in a particular sense, but spiritual in the absolute ontological sense'.[29]

How, in the section under consideration, does Hegel spiritualize the work? He argues that consciousness becomes aware that it need not identify itself with any particular work, that it is universal because it is 'absolute negativity' in so far as it 'withdraws itself from any *determinate* or *particular* work'.[30] In so far as work takes its place as a determinate particular in the world it passes into an 'alien reality'. For example, the interest of other individuals in my work is something quite different from the work's original interest. Hegel does not give examples here, but one might recall the verdict of the market place on new commodities, or the way literary and artistic products are appropriated by audiences in ways quite unexpected by their authors. (Indeed one might recall that Hegel's own works have been read in many different ways!) Even in its own terms, whether the work is a success depends on 'fortune', the selection of appropriate means, and so on. Consciousness therefore takes an 'idealistic' attitude to work. The negation of the work is itself negated, and consciousness takes the true reality to be solely its own negativity. 'In this way then', says Hegel, 'consciousness is reflected out of its perishable work into itself, and preserves its concept and its certainty of what objectively exists and endures in the face of the experience of the *contingency* of action.'[31]

This form of consciousness, then, busies itself with 'the matter in hand' ('*die Sache selbst*') in abstraction from its moments – end, means and object. It is true that 'they all have this "matter in hand" as their essence', Hegel allows, 'but only in such a way that it, being their *abstract* universal, can be found in each of them, and can be a *predicate* of them'.[32]

It is at this point that Hegel identifies the 'honest consciousness'. 'Consciousness is called *honest*', he says, 'when it has . . . attained the idealism which "the matter in hand" expresses . . .'.[33] Hegel emphasizes that this engagement is independent of results. If it does not succeed in its action it has at least *willed* it, *something* was taken in hand. If everything goes wrong it still finds satisfaction 'just like naughty boys who enjoy *themselves* when they get their ears boxed because *they* are the cause of its being done'.[34] Hegel points out that it is not even necessary to *do* anything at all: if 'it should be an event of historical importance which does not really concern him, he makes it likewise his own; and an interest for which he has done nothing is, in his own eyes, a party interest which *he* has favoured or opposed, and even combated or supported'.[35] One recalls here the *pater familias* who leaves trivial matters, like the choice of schooling for the children, to his wife; while he concerns himself with important matters such as whether war should be declared on Russia.

Hegel now enters into one of his dialectical reversals. This man is not as honest as he seems. Although he keeps busy he is not really in earnest about anything, only about his own status in the matter. Others soon realize the dissimulation involved. For example, should they point out that they themselves have already accomplished the matter, or offer their help, the result is a fit of pique on the part of the consciousness, whose interest is really in its own action. The others are in turn put out by his rejection, because they were only interested in their own self-satisfaction too. Hegel says: 'a consciousness that opens up a new field soon learns that others hurry along like flies to freshly poured out milk, and want to busy themselves with it . . .'.[36]

In this whole discussion one is irresistibly reminded of the self-centredness and asocial sociality of bourgeois life. Although Hegel's discussion is quite general, most commentators assume that he has particularly in mind the intellectuals of his day, academics, specialists and artists of various kinds.[37] Obviously Marx found it amusing.

More seriously, however, what would Marx make of the final outcome? Consciousness acquires the concept of a common 'matter in hand', a work which is the concern of all and each, and in which the particularity of the individuals is dissolved. Thereby the 'matter in hand', Hegel argues, 'no longer has the character of a predicate, and loses the character of lifeless, abstract universality'.[38] It is a universal shared by all, a spiritual essence, ethical consciousness.

In trying to look at this whole dialectic from Marx's point of view, let us remember the general verdict: we have here 'all the elements of criticism' — 'but still in estranged form'.

Clearly Marx would agree with two points here: that human work has a universal character, and that bourgeois individualism needs to be transcended. Less clear is why Hegel's discussion is objectionable. Recall the following passage from Marx's critique:

> The rich, living, sensuous, concrete activity of self-objectification is therefore reduced to its mere abstraction, *absolute negativity* — an abstraction which is again fixed as such and considered as an independent activity — as sheer activity. Because this so-called negativity is nothing but the *abstract, empty* form of that real living act, its content can in consequence be merely a *formal* content produced by abstraction from all content.[39]

This seems very pertinent to the idea of absolute negativity Hegel evolves at the beginning of this discussion. Instead of the universality of activity being celebrated in the *wealth* of its content, the content vanishes in the purity of absolute negativity. But did not Hegel himself find wanting such abstract universality? Yes and no. The concept of 'absolute negativity' represents a real gain in the constitution of spirit, as is clear from its retention in the overview given in Hegel's 'Preface'. The problem at this stage of the phenomenological dialectic is that it is constituted in opposition to the real life of the individual subject. There is an 'antithesis of doing and being'. The solution arrived at is to make the *universal itself* the real individual, which makes itself identical with the entire content. The emphasis here, as in the rest of the story, prioritizes logical forms over real content.[40]

The third section mentioned by Marx, 'the struggle of noble and base consciousness', is part of an important stage of spirit's development, namely, 'self-estranged spirit' (*'Der sich entfremdete Geist'*). The historical allusions become particularly clear here; the material draws on the world of eighteenth century France up to, and including, the revolution. We are not therefore dealing with absolute spirit and the total process of its recovery of itself from alienation, but with a finite stage of its development. It deals with the individual and his alienation from society. We are at a richer, more concrete, level of development of consciousness than in the previous stages considered, in that the self knows the substance of social life as its spiritual essence, but society also faces the individual as an 'alien reality . . . in which it does not recognize itself'. The individual and its world are estranged from each other. Even though the individual knows that it belongs in that world and must find its place there, to begin with it finds social institutions face it simply as objectively given realities to which it must conform. It achieves something within its world only in alienating itself from itself, in leaving behind its natural self and moulding itself to these objective requirements. This process of mediating the extremes (nature and society) is *'Bildung'* – perhaps here to be translated as 'acculturation'. Hegel says: 'it is therefore through culture [*Bildung*] that the individual acquires standing and actuality'. In observing this development, says Hegel, we will see 'the estrangement estrange itself and, through this, return into its concept'.[41]

This second alienation needs explaining. The idea is symptomatic of Hegel's dialectic in general. Given a totality within which two moments stand in an antagonistic opposition, this can exist only through a mediating movement. If the estranged elements are not transformed and brought into harmony, the mediating movement itself must appear as an alienation. The original estrangement is sublated in a second alienation. Earlier we discussed the case of labour: given the estrangement of labour-power from its object, any reunification under the aegis of wage-labour is alienating in itself and reproduces the whole system of estrangement. Here, in Hegel, the self alienates itself from its original nature in cultivating social skills and acquiring power in society. In this way the original subject–object split is overcome, but *within* estrangement.

Rousseau's critique of his times rested in just such a diagnosis, namely that natural and civilized man were at odds. Even in his positive prescription we find a second alienation solution. Lacking the political virtues of the ever pre-given unity of the Greek *polis*, and thus beginning with 'natural' individuals, unity is to be established politically in 'the general will' through 'the total alienation of each associate . . . to the whole community'. Moreover, Rousseau stresses the fact that this involves taking away man's 'natural resources' and providing 'new ones alien to him, and incapable of being made use of without the help of other men'.[42]

Returning now to Hegel, the social order is presented as structured in terms of state power and wealth. It is in considering the possible attitudes of self-consciousness to these that the 'noble', and 'base', consciousness appear. The consciousness that takes a positive attitude towards each sphere is called *noble*. It respects public authority and is grateful for its enjoyment of wealth. The consciousness that adopts a negative relation to them is *base*. It regards sovereign power as a fetter and it obeys only with a secret malice, always on the point of revolt. It loves wealth but, conscious of its temporary and contingent enjoyment, suspects it at the same time. There are fairly obvious allusions in Hegel's discussion to the class struggles between the nobility and the third estate.

In a way similar to the master–servant dialectic, Hegel then develops each side into its other. The noble consciousness comes to see in the state and wealth the power of an alien reality on which it depends. The base consciousness learns to affirm itself even in its negative relation to them.

The dialectic advances next through the cultivated consciousness that 'sees through' all this. It knows everything to be self-alienated, and it adopts a detached and ironical attitude to social reality. Hegel says that 'the vanity of all *things* is its *own* vanity, it is itself *vain*; it is the self-centred self that knows, not only how to pass judgement on and chatter about everything, but how to give witty expression to the contradiction that is present in the solid elements of the *actual* world'. It seeks power and wealth while distancing itself from them in its consciousness. Aware of the self-disruptive nature of all relationships it achieves pure self-identity 'as self-consciousness in revolt'.[43]

It is clear that Marx was impressed by this description of the estrangement of individuals in the social institutions they themselves sustain in their activity: a culture of 'universal inversion and estrangement', as Hegel puts it.[44] State power and wealth appear as alien powers, even 'selves', standing over against the individuals.

At the same time, the general criticism Marx brings against Hegel's reduction of social forms to forms of consciousness applies with particular force here. Indeed, the following comment of Marx's must have been based on this section: 'when wealth, state power, etc., are understood by Hegel as entities estranged from the *human* being, this only happens in their form as thoughts.'[45]

Since this sort of criticism was dealt with in the previous chapter it will not be further laboured here. (The reader is also referred to Richard Norman's commentary where the application of Marx's criticism to this material is discussed with subtlety and clarity.[46]) Instead, let us pick up the reference in Hegel's discussion to 'the self-consciousness which rebels against this rejection of itself (*Empörung* = 'rebellion').[47] It will be recalled that in the passage from the *Capital* materials quoted earlier in connection with the master–servant dialectic, Marx also spoke of rebellion. But what is striking about Hegel's master–servant dialectic is the lack of any rebellion on the part of the servant. The most one can say is, with Richard Kroner, 'perhaps young Marx, reading this, found the germ of his future programme'; he explains that 'in any case, foreshadowed in these words ["mind of its own"] is the pattern for a labour movement which was to make the proletarian conscious of his existence and to grant him the knowledge of having a "mind of his own".'[48]

In Hegel's text the most one can find is a reference to mere obstinacy. Gadamer comments: 'obstinacy is only thought to confirm freedom and is, in fact, a form of rebellious dependency.'[49] In fact, to speak here of rebelliousness is already going too far. None the less, there is an interesting idea here. Hegel clearly distinguishes the exercise of freedom from undisciplined wilfulness. In a way, Marx could agree. Simple Luddism is not in itself revolutionary; but he believes the proletariat potentially embodies universal emancipation, not a merely partial standpoint. If one denies, as Hegel does, the historical supersession of bourgeois society, then of course the proletariat's rebelliousness *is* mere particularism.

However, in the dialectic of noble and base consciousness, Hegel explicitly speaks of rebelliousness. Therefore, if one is looking for a place where Hegel gives hints to Marx on rebellion it is here and not in the master–servant dialectic. As a matter of fact, Marx explicitly acknowledges this when composing *The Holy Family* later in 1844. Here is the passage:

> The propertied class and the class of the proletariat present the same human self-estrangement. But the former class feels at ease and strengthened in this self-estrangement, it recognizes estrangement as *its own power* and has in it the *semblance* of a human existence. The latter feels annihilated in estrangement; it sees in it its own

powerlessness and the reality of an inhuman existence. It is, to use an expression of Hegel's, in its abasement the *indignation* [*Empörung*] at that abasement . . .⁵⁰

It is possible, however, that Marx may not have had the *Phenomonology* in mind so much as the *Philosophy of Right*.⁵¹ In the 1833 edition Gans intercalated material from Hegel's lectures on the subject. One reads there: 'a rabble is created only when there is joined to poverty a disposition of mind, an inner indignation [*Empörung*] against the rich, against society, against the government, etc.'.⁵²

Another interesting point about the *Philosophy of Right* is that this idea of *der Pöbel* (translated by Knox as 'rabble'), a mass of rebellious paupers with no stake in the existing order, has been thought to be a source for Marx's conception of the modern proletariat, as he first defines it as a class in civil society but not of civil society.⁵³ Another source was Lorenz von Stein's book on French communism.⁵⁴

To conclude these remarks about the influence of Hegel on Marx, let us return to the comprehending consciousness of absolute knowledge. It is interesting to notice that Marx himself occasionally echoes the *Phenomenology* when he treats the standpoint of the communist movement as such a comprehending consciousness. In one place he states that the genesis of communism is rooted in 'the entire movement of history' and, therefore, it is 'for its thinking consciousness the *comprehended* and *known* process of its *becoming*'.⁵⁵ This seems to amount to the same claim Hegel makes for absolute knowledge when he says that it is 'comprehended history'.⁵⁶

None the less, in Marx the *objective* dialectic of supersession is dominant. The communist movement does not simply *know* itself to be 'the riddle of history solved', but will *actually* abolish private property through a revolutionary 'negation of the negation'. In Hegel, on the contrary, the shadowy status of absolute knowledge, as we noted earlier, leads some to identify it with Hegel's own achievement. Marx's view of this appears in *The Holy Family* in the following passage:

> Already in *Hegel* the absolute spirit of history has its material in the *mass* and finds its appropriate expression only in *philosophy*. The philosopher, however, is only the organ through which the maker of history, the absolute spirit, arrives at self-consciousness *retrospectively* after the movement has ended. The participation of the philosopher in history is reduced to this retrospective consciousness, for the real movement is accomplished by the absolute spirit *unconsciously*. Hence the philosopher appears on the scene *post festum*.⁵⁷

This is from a polemic of Marx against the Young Hegelian Bruno Bauer. Bauer 'overcomes Hegel's half-heartedness'; he 'consciously plays the part of *world spirit*' in opposition to the masses, says Marx. Doubtless Marx takes the possibility of a personal identification of the philosopher with absolute knowledge to be already implicit in Hegel's position.

Even if one insists on the objectivism of Hegel's unification of subject and substance, Dunayevskaya's verdict still has force: 'because Hegel could not conceive the *masses* as "subject" creating the new society, the Hegelian philosophy – though it had replaced the viewing of things as "things in themselves", as dead impenetrable matter – was compelled to return to Kant's idea of an *external* unifier of opposites.' She concludes: 'Hegel had destroyed all dogmatism except the dogmatism of "the backwardness of the masses".'[58]

Summary

As far as the separate sections of the *Phenomenology* are concerned, Marx does not mention, and does not draw upon, the dialectic of 'lordship and bondage'. Of the three sections he mentions as evidence for 'critical elements' in Hegel's work, the most influential is 'the struggle of noble and base consciousness'. Here Hegel treats of the estrangement of the individual from social institutions such as state power and wealth. As always, Marx finds in Hegel that the idealist exposition of such elements of criticism results in their presentation still in estranged form.

8

Hegel on Wage-labour

Introduction

The extraordinary complexity of Marx's verdict on Hegel's *Phenomenology of Spirit* is evident if we take three statements from the same (crucial) page.

1 Hegel grasps the nature of labour and conceives man as the result of his own labour.
2 Hegel's standpoint is that of political economy, namely labour (= alienation) as the essence of man.
3 Hegel knows only abstract mental labour.

It seems almost impossible at first sight to make these consistent. It seems equally impossible to take even one of them at face value. If (3) is true, how can (1) and (2) be true? But how can (3) be fair when we know about the labour of the servant and the 'honest consciousness'? As for political economy, Hegel never mentions it in the *Phenomenology*! (Somewhat bewildered, the editors of Marx's works cite in a footnote[1] two *other* works of Hegel – one of them unknown to Marx! I deal with both below.)

The exhaustive exposition of Marx's arguments so far has provided the necessary basis for endorsing all three points, properly interpreted. This interpretation requires discussion of the method at work in Marx's criticism of Hegel. The main difficulty in understanding Marx's critique is that he does not compare like with like. His own interest is in material production, and more especially the material labour of the wage-worker with its inherent alienation. But what he compares with his own discoveries is *not* what Hegel says about such labour, but Hegel's *alternative* 'producing principle', the negating action of consciousness and self-consciousness. That this must give rise to problems becomes obvious when we recall that for Marx the contradictions of consciousness are to be subsumed under the practical ones, whereas for Hegel material labour is merely one sphere in which spirit is at work.

The procedure adopted by Marx is to evaluate Hegel by reading spiritual activity as material. This is how he can praise Hegel for grasping man as his own product, and equally how he can blame Hegel for confusing productive activity with alienating activity. Hence, in Hegel, alienating activity is taken as the essence, just as the standpoint of political economy is that of (wage-)labour. As we noted earlier, Hegel's crucial misidentification is not the simple-minded castigation of objectification as alienating, but the more subtle endorsement of alienation because it is taken to be the only possible form of objectification. In fine, the parallelism is not one of content but of a homology of conceptual structure in the speculative philosophy of Hegel and the ideological presuppositions of political economy. This means that Marx can criticize both on the same grounds.

Once we grasp the character of Marx's procedure in his Hegel critique, two things follow: first, that what he says about Hegel's equation of objectification and alienation has nothing to do with anything Hegel says about material labour; second, that his failure to deal with what Hegel says about material labour, and more especially his claim that Hegel knows only abstract mental labour, might amount to an injustice to Hegel. Certainly, if anyone were to claim that Hegel thought material labour necessarily alienating, or even that he knew nothing of material labour at all, Hegelians could come flying with contrary quotations from nearly all his works. We have already mentioned the positive role labour is given in the master-servant dialectic and in the work occupying the 'honest consciousness'. Even in the chapter on 'self-estranged spirit', individual labour is seen as socially constitutive in so far as each 'in working for himself . . . is at the same time working for all and all are working for him'.[2] Indeed it would be closer to the truth to say that Hegel has a claim precedent to that of Marx to be the first to found social theory on material labour. It even has an important place in his *Science of Logic*. It appears in its greatest prominence in the Jena lectures of the early 1800s and then gradually diminishes in its significance in Hegel's thought. Yet as late as 1821 Hegel speaks almost casually, in the *Philosophy of Right*, of 'the moment of liberation intrinsic to work', as if this were obvious.[3]

Nevertheless, Marx is ultimately in the right, because the interest Hegel takes in labour is to show that it exhibits in actuality moments of consciousness, determinations of the will, or even categories of logic. In spite of the fact that he has more acute things to say about labour than any other pre-Marxist philosopher, Hegel is, after all, an idealist. Instead of objective relations of production, the ultimate reality is absolute spirit in communion with itself. For Hegel, material labour has an important role in the sphere of objective spirit but this is in turn incorporated within absolute spirit. If we are to compare Marx with Hegel in terms of content then it is instructive to compare what Marx says about wage-labour with what Hegel says. This is the objective of the present chapter. Here the *Phenomenology* is not of much help. The treatment of 'wealth' in the 'self-estranged spirit' section does not specify the relations of production involved; and if it did they would hardly be those of modern industry, given the historical background to it.

In truth, the young Hegel was a radical critic of modern industrial production. This is especially so in his writings from the Jena period (1801–6). In a manuscript known as *Hegel's First Philosophy of Spirit* (1803–4) Hegel points out that the subjugation of nature in modern industry increases the individual's dependence on outside forces because the division of labour ties the individual to a particular task (he cites Smith's account of a pin factory); that the labour becomes deadening mechanical work; and that 'the coherence of the singular kind of labour with the whole infinite mass of needs is quite unsurveyable . . . so that some far-off operation often suddenly cuts off the labour of a whole class of men . . . and makes it superfluous and useless'. Hegel adds that 'need and labour', elevated into the universality of money, create a 'monstrous system' of mutual dependence in society, 'a self-propelling life of the dead, ebbing and flowing blindly', which 'requires . . . taming like a wild beast'.[4]

Such striking passages were unknown to Marx because they remained unpublished for many years (a curious parallel to Marx's own *1844 Manuscripts*!)

Hegel's Philosophy of Right

In Hegel's mature published work, wage-labour is given its place within his system in *The Philosophy of Right* (1821). When Marx speaks in his *1844 Manuscripts* of the conservatism of Hegel's later work, this text is foremost in his mind. Here Hegel endorses private property and wage-labour. He claims that the subsequent socio-economic contradictions can be reconciled within the framework of a suitably constituted modern state. We shall see that Hegel's apology for wage-labour is effected through his idealist method.[5]

The central organizing idea of Hegel's *Philosophy of Right* is *freedom*; the book is designed to show that it is actualized in the institutions of the modern state. The first part introduces the notions of personality and property. According to Hegel, the person actualizes his inherent freedom through embodying his will in an external thing, immediately different from him, thereby making it his. Property, on this account, is a substantive end in virtue of its role in giving personality objectivity. It is necessary to emphasize *mediatedness* in the development of this idea. It should not be thought, for example, that Hegel's conceptual distinction between persons endowed with purposes of their own, on the one hand, and appropriable things, on the other, *immediately* coincides with the distinction between humanity and the rest of nature. A human being has to *become* a person through the development of physical and mental powers whereby its naturally given basis is sublated; and the realm of nature becomes man's object through various processes of appropriation. For Hegel, it is absurd to suppose that man is free in the immediacy of his natural existence, within which he is tied to nature, however romanticized the presentation of this so-called 'state of nature' in which the satisfaction of everyone's simple necessities is supposed to be adequately assured:

> to be confined to mere physical needs as such and their direct satisfaction would simply be the condition in which the mental is plunged in the natural and so would be one of savagery and unfreedom, while freedom itself is to be found only in the reflection of mind into itself, in mind's distinction from nature, and in the reflex of mind in nature.[6]

For Hegel, as later for Marx, it is not a question of locating the concept of freedom in a given pre-ordained place of man in relation to nature; rather it is to be grounded on a developing subject – object problematic. In order to play a part in the actualization of human freedom, Hegel claims, natural objects have to be given a new determinateness in serving human ends as property. Natural objects as such are not property – they are reduced to immediacy for free-will in so far as they are posited as 'without ends of their own', but free-will proves its ownership only by embodying itself in them through some mediation (such as 'forming', 'marking' and so on). On this account, Joachim Ritter stresses the historical dimension of this process and says that 'the freedom of the person and the determination of nature as object of the will belong inextricably together'.[7] However, he tends to pick up only the material moments in Hegel's discussion (as if Hegel were Marx). In fact, we shall see that there is a slippage in Hegel whereby the recalcitrance of the natural object to the person's material efforts to 'prove its lack of self-subsistence' is 'overcome' by mind's 'reflection back from nature into itself', its assertion of its universality in distinction from the particularity of the object world.

Let us then look at the material content Hegel attributes to the moments of private property he describes. The positive moment is signified by 'taking possession' of the thing immediately whereby one becomes objective to oneself in a particular piece of property. This sinking into the particular inadequately realizes the universality of the will. Thus Hegel moves to the moment of negativity whereby the will distinguishes itself, through the use of the thing for its own ends, from the thing itself. Yet, lest we should be tempted to look here for a material content, Hegel reminds us that use is merely a moment in the development of the will's relation to the thing. For example, squatting is rejected thus:

> The fact that property is realized and actualized only in use floats before the minds of those who look on property as derelict and ownerless if it is not being put to any use, and who excuse its unlawful occupancy on the ground that it has not been used by its owner. But the owner's will, in accordance with which the thing is his, is the primary substantive basis of property; use is a further modification of property, secondary to that universal basis, and is only its manifestation and particular mode.[8]

In the relation of use the will is still debased by its involvement with the particularity of the things and their use-value. Hence the will must be asserted absolutely and not in connection with the particularity of its objects. This is realized in *alienation*. In the dialectic of the will's relation to the thing as property, the moment of alienation, rather than posing any problem for Hegel, is seen as the most complete actualization of ownership. It is in distinguishing myself as an owner rigorously from any particular content to this proprietorship that I become a real proprietor! Possession and use are limited, finite relations of the will to property in which its movement runs aground; but through treating things merely as exchangeable objects, in the endless cycle of acquisition and alienation, the will is reflected into its own self, without getting bogged down in the natural features of the alienated objects; in this way the dialectic progresses to contract where the will is dealing with its own other. 'This relation of will to will is the true and proper ground in which freedom is existent.'[9]

Raymond Plant points out that this is a particular case of a general pattern in Hegel's thought.[10] An advance in self-consciousness (in this case the institution of private property) requires the descent into particularity (in this case the things held as property); yet institutions allowing this differentiation develop their own pattern of integration of the particulars within an ideal totality. The form in which it is achieved in this case is that, when the autonomous persons holding various objects as private property align their wills through contractual arrangements, this means that 'one identical will can persist within the absolute difference between independent property owners'.[11] Thereby universal freedom is made possible. In sum: the overriding moment in the 'mastery of things exhibited by free-will' is that which is most removed from their useful material character, namely the process of their alienation; this pushes forward the actualization of the will to the form of contract whereby it achieves recognition in another person. Only as a proprietor among proprietors am I free!

The Alienation of Labour

Hegel considers that the relation between persons and their labour-power is one of property, and also that, as such, labour is alienable. He recognizes that there is a problem in accounting for, and justifying, such alienation because he sees that labour-power is not 'immediately external' in the sense that other alienable things are. Before taking up the question of labour's alienation then, we must review Hegel's account of bodily power. Hegel considers that men, while free 'in their concept', are not free in their immediate natural existence. Thus he speaks of 'the possession of our body and mind which we achieve through education, study, habit, etc., and which exists as an *inward property* of mind'.[12] Immediately, a bodily organism is merely 'out there' without exhibiting specifically human behaviour. 'It is only through the *development* of his own body and mind . . . that he takes possession of himself and becomes his own property and no-one else's.'[13] Thus one is to own oneself and one's bodily and mental powers. Even though the actuality of men is freedom, 'not something which they *have*, as men, but which they *are*',[14] the actualization of this idea depends upon an objective development whereby man becomes what he is implicitly in accordance with his concept.

Let us note, however, that, since the immediacy of human existence need not compel recognition of personality, slavery is feasible. According to Hegel, slavery is based on a class of un-persons being taken as 'things' suitable for holding as property, in virtue of a view of man as a 'natural entity'[15] like any other. Marx, by the way, draws our attention to the fact that, 'under slavery, according to the striking expression employed in antiquity, the worker is distinguished only as *instrumentum vocale* from an animal, which is *instrumentum semi-vocale*, and from a lifeless implement, which is *instrumentum mutum*'.[16] In truth, we find in Hegel a certain confusion. First it is said that, in virtue of their being my 'substantive characteristics' rather than 'external by nature', 'my personality as such, my universal freedom of will, my ethical life, my religion' are 'inalienable'; but then it is allowed that, inherent in 'this concept of mind as that which is what it is only through its own free causality, . . . lies *the possibility of the alienation of personality* and its substantive being, whether this alienation occurs unconsciously or intentionally'. Hegel's examples of the alienation of personality are slavery, serfdom, disqualification from holding property, and so forth. He also mentions 'alienation of intelligence and rationality . . . in ceding to someone else full power and authority to fix and prescribe what actions are to be done . . . or what duties are binding on one's conscience or what religious truth is, etc.'. It is not clear whether Hegel thinks that such practices are merely offensive to 'the idea of freedom', or whether, in view of 'the contradiction in supposing that . . . I am giving up what, so soon as I possess it, exists in essence as mine alone, and not as something external', only a *pseudoalienation* would be formally effected: for example, in the case of alienation of conscience; in so far as I am a genuine moral agent I remain responsible for accepting authority in general, and for having chosen a particular source of direction.[17]

Hegel is even prepared to say that, from the standpoint of 'man's absolute freedom', 'if a man is a slave, his own will is responsible for his slavery'. In fact, Hegel believes that the progress of history has now made explicit, and irrevocably established, the knowledge of 'man's absolute unfitness for slavery'.[18] However, although Hegel finds outright slavery repugnant, he allows the alienation of personal powers in more modern forms. He recognizes that it seems unsatisfactory to speak merely of juridical ownership and alienation of such possessions for 'there is something inward' involved. But he attempts to rationalize the situation as follows:

> Attainments, erudition, talents, and so forth, are, of course, owned by free mind and are something internal and not external to it, but even so, by expressing them it may embody them in something external and *alienate [veräussern]* them . . . and in this way they are put into the category of '*things*'. Therefore they are not immediate at the start but only acquire this character through the mediation of mind which reduces its inner possessions to immediacy and externality.[19]

As he notes in the margin with respect to the term 'alienation' here, to alienate is to hand over a possession that is already external, and this leaves aside the question of how it became external in the first place.[20] Thus it has to be shown how one's 'inner possessions' acquire the mode of externality, and whether or not this is contrary to their concept.

Leaving aside any problems that might arise with a person's products, what of alienation of personal powers themselves? The alienation of such powers ought to pose difficulties for Hegel because if I possess my labour-power only in making my body my own in such a way that its powers only exist as powers developed by my will, Hegel should find it problematic that my abilities could yet be posited through alienation as the object of another's will. As we saw, Hegel regards slavery as incompatible with the idea of freedom, but he makes an ingenious distinction between wage-labour and slavery whereby the former may be endorsed as free: I can give someone 'the use of my abilities *for a restricted period*, because, on the strength of this restriction, my abilities acquire an external relation to the totality and universality of my being'. He allows that 'by alienating the *whole* of my time, as crystallized in my work, and everything I produced, I would be making into another's property the substance of my being, my *universal* activity and actuality, my personality'. As he explains, 'it is only when use is restricted that a distinction arises between use and substance'; so here, 'the use of my powers differs from my powers and therefore from myself, only in so far as it is quantitatively restricted'. It seems then that Hegel admits that my labour-power is part of the substance of my personality, an essentially inward property in so far as I am in possession of myself. However, as he notes, it might be possible that in manifesting my powers I reduce them 'through a mediation of mind' to 'immediacy and externality'. Here, the mediation required is identified with the time limit that posits a distinction between use and substance, even though the substance of my power is nothing but 'the totality of its manifestations'. 'On the strength of this restriction', the wage-labourer remains a free agent, so to speak.[21]

The trouble with Hegel's distinction between entire alienation and alienation piece by piece – a distinction supposed to guarantee the independence of the worker's personality – is that it breaks down when one considers the possibility (which is effectively realized in the case of modern wage-labour) that, through successive piecemeal alienations of the worker's time, his *entire* labour time is appropriated by others. What is a 'thing' in pieces is all of a piece a 'thing'. It is only Hegel's instinct for the non-legal essence of possession of one's powers that prevents him from reifying them wholesale, but he capitulates to piecemeal reification. If the worker's entire labouring time is thus alienated, then his distinction from a slave is surely reduced to his legal status, while materially he is in slavery to capital.

These quantitative considerations may be left at this point; for there is a deeper, qualitative, incoherence in Hegel's endorsement of wage-slavery. Since the worker's power only exists in so far as he is 'in possession of himself and he has developed it as essentially inward property, it is not a 'thing external by nature' but is itself 'will-with-thing', so to speak. In developing his powers they become his inward possessions. The mediation through which his labour-power is yielded to the will of another, even by hire rather than outright sale, cannot consist therefore in his withdrawing his will from his body, leaving behind only an 'empty will'[22] marking his right to recover his powers. The powers of his brains, nerves and muscles only exist in so far as he is present exercising them. If they are alienated their use requires, none the less, not the exclusion of his will, but his own use of his powers, however grudgingly exercised. To exercise them in the service of another requires, therefore, the subordination of his will to the other.

There are two problems with labour's alienation that arise from this fact. One is a problem for the purchaser. How is he to appropriate the use-value of the worker's labour if it involves the subordination of the worker's will? After hiring the worker the capitalist must find ways of getting the work out of him with the desired quality and maximum quantity. This requires the effective subordination of the worker to the dictates of the capitalist labour process so that surplus labour can – in Marx's graphic phrase – 'be pumped out of him'.

The other problem arises for Hegel's apologetics. There is a contradiction implicit in his view of personal powers as, on the one hand, inward property of a free being, and, on the other hand, potentially alienable property held mediately as a 'thing'. If this second relation is realized in the alienation of labour, the will exists in contradiction with itself; for, in Hegel's general theory, the moment of alienation establishes the will as will through its *reflection* from the thing back into itself; in the contractual relation with another will, *symmetrically* mediated in the thing, it becomes identical with its other and both equally achieve objective *recognition*; but, since the thing here itself embodies the will, as we have seen, the alienating mediation presupposes an *asymmetrical* relationship at the same time, in which one will bends to the other, being thus 'refracted' rather than reflected, so to speak, in this alienation.[23] This is nothing less than self-estrangement.

It is to be noted that this contradiction between the symmetry of the wage-contract effected between autonomous, juridically equal, persons, and the asymmetry of the employer's relationship during the working day to his 'hands' (to employ the striking vernacular of capital), finds its way into Hegel from *reality*. This reality disguises the relations of personal dominance inherent in wage-slavery by reifying the personal powers of the labourer so that they become a 'factor of production' like any other, to be sold or hired on the market.

Conclusion

We have shown that Hegel thinks private property is necessary for human freedom and that he manages to justify wage-slavery at the same time. What is it about his method that allows this? The procedure is in fact stunningly simple. Instead of making the historical judgement that in this society freedom means freedom of property, he makes the philosophical judgement that the concept of freedom actualizes itself in the private property system. Hegel says of his method that in philosophical science 'the concept develops out of itself', and in a 'purely immanent process engenders its determinations'. It does not advance 'by the application of the universal to extraneous material . . . culled from elsewhere'.[24] Not withstanding this assertion, Hegel does in fact 'apply universals' to extraneous material, namely the existing property system.

What Hegel does in his philosophy is to find methodological resources that allow him to pass off the facts about wage-labour as rational, as the actualization of freedom. With regard to private property itself, its various determinations are organized in a hierarchy that makes freedom appear less real in concrete work with, and use of, one's property, but more fully actualized in relations that abstract from the determinate content involved. He does not attend to the evil consequences of the commodification of labour. Whilst acknowledging that personal powers are not 'external by nature', Hegel manages to assimilate them to property in external things (and hence properly alienable within the limit specified and criticized above) through abstracting from the specific difference involved in order to pass off the alienation of labour as free activity.

Summary

In the *1844 Manuscripts* Marx compares his theory of alienated labour with Hegel's negating action of spirit. Hence, as far as content is concerned, it might be said that he does not compare like with like. In fact Hegel has a lot to say about material labour. It is in the *Philosophy of Right* that his fullest account of wage-labour is found. He is uncritical of it, reconciling it with property, and both with freedom.

PART THREE

1844: The Turning Point

9

Marx and Feuerbach

Introduction

The turning point in Marx's intellectual development comes in 1844 with his discovery of *labour*, an event documented in his manuscripts composed in Paris that year under the impetus of his first encounter with political economy. In this chapter the process of Marx's intellectual formation is investigated with the aim of illuminating the importance of this transition, and, in particular, the way in which he appropriates, and yet rejects, Hegel, as we have already seen, and appropriates, and finally yet rejects, Hegel's most determined critic, Ludwig Feuerbach, as we shall see below.

A great deal of energy can be expended in assessing the relative influence of thinkers such as Rousseau, Hegel, Feuerbach and the 'Young Hegelians' on the formation of Marx's thought. For example, Lukács declares roundly that, methodologically, 'Marx took over *directly* from Hegel' rather than from the 'Young Hegelians', who had affinities with Fichteanism.[1] Michael Löwy replies that 'the philosophy of practice' of Fichte, Cieszowski and Hess, 'is *also* a foundation stone for Marxism, a *necessary* step in the evolution of the young Marx'.[2]

Certainly, Marx is quite properly identified at the time of his move to Paris as a member of the so-called 'Young Hegelian' movement. None the less his relationship to it was always nuanced. He was never a wholehearted disciple of any of its leading figures, except, for a few months, Feuerbach. We cannot now accept as good Marxian coin the aphorism: 'There is no other road to truth and freedom but through the brook of fire [*Feuer-bach*]'. It comes from an anonymous article of 1842, attributed to Marx by Riazanov, but now thought not to be his work.[3] None the less, it expresses very well Marx's attitude to Feuerbach in 1844. At the same time, he was always 'his own man' when participating in the movement, even when heaping praise on Feuerbach.

This chapter will show that Marx, in his *1844 Manuscripts*, advances decisively beyond the standpoint of Feuerbach. Marx's *own* genius first shows through in 1844 with his category of labour, founded on the ontologically constitutive nature of productive activity for social being. We have seen that in complex ways he relates this discovery to Hegel's speculative version of activity. It could be argued that Marx's discovery of the importance of *material* production is not unexpected in the context of the Young Hegelians' anthropological reading of Hegel. Indeed, as early as the 1830s the first of them, D.F. Strauss, delivers himself of such vague formulations as that, in the course of human history, humanity 'ever more completely subjugates nature, both within and around man, until it lies before him as the inert matter on which he exercises his active power'.[4] The idea of production as a 'species activity' is further developed by Feuerbach and by Hess. However, in the works of the 'Young Hegelians' such views have no fundamental significance. They lie alongside remarks about other human functions. Only with Marx does the social and historical theory of man as his own product emerge — and here the important source is Hegel himself!

The strange thing, none the less, is that the manuscripts are penned explicitly under the sign of Feuerbach.[5] The Preface declares that 'it is only with *Feuerbach* that *positive*, humanistic and naturalistic criticism begins'; his writings 'contain a real theoretical revolution'.[6] If for no other reason, this solidarity with Feuerbach makes it necessary to avoid reading too much 'Marxism' into the early Marx. We know that as late as 1847 he was still engaged in the process of 'self-clarification' and the effort to 'settle accounts' with the Young Hegelian heritage. Only then, in the context of polemics *against* Feuerbach, does the first outline of the materialist conception of history as a sequence of modes of production take definite shape. Given the self-affiliation of Marx to Feuerbach in 1844 it is necessary to clear up the question of the role played by Feuerbach in Marx's evolution in general, and his influence on the *1844 Manuscripts* in particular.

Young Hegelianism

Hegel died in 1831 and within a few years his followers polarized: there were conservatives, or 'Old Hegelians', and radicals, or 'Young Hegelians'.[7] This divergence is foreshadowed in internal tensions in Hegel's own philosophy. In spite of the rationalist and historical elements in

Hegel's thought, he did not give philosophy a radical role in social affairs, at least in his well-known mature works; it seemed that the role of philosophy was to reconcile thought to the present. The Young Hegelians claimed that there was, nevertheless, an esoteric radical Hegel in the exoteric conservative who compromised with the Prussian monarchy. Certainly the younger Hegel welcomed the French Revolution and its Napoleonic extension to Germany. He gave philosophy the task of herald of the new order, indeed, even its promulgator. Soon after the publication of his *Phenomenology of Spirit* Hegel wrote to a friend: 'Daily I become more convinced that theoretical work accomplishes more in the world than practical; once the realm of ideas is revolutionized, reality cannot hold out.'[8] Whether Hegel himself continued to believe this or not, the Young Hegelians certainly held such a view wholeheartedly.

We need look no further than Friedrich Engels, in the period before he joined forces with Marx, to find a typical exponent of Young Hegelianism. Although already a declared 'communist' in the early 1840s (having been converted by Hess), he held that communism followed directly from 'German Philosophy', that is, from the 'left' interpretation of Hegel. Engels makes this claim in a fascinating article he wrote in 1843 for the Owenite periodical *New Moral World*. Here he explains to his English readers that Hegel 'neglected to free himself from the prejudices of his age', notably the attachment to monarchy and religion, but that the Young Hegelians had freed the principles of his thought, little by little, from these conservative encrustations. Eventually, indeed, Hegelianism became in effect atheism, a charge Engels declared himself the first to have allowed just.[9] The reference here is to a pamphlet he had published anonymously in Germany the previous year. This was a counter-attack on Schelling's Berlin lectures directed against Hegelianism.[10] Here Engels develops at greater length the theory of Hegel's 'prejudices'. He says that Hegel's conclusions would have been different if he had proceeded from 'pure thought'; but, instead, 'positive' elements crept in because he was 'a product of his time'. 'The principles', says Engels, 'are throughout independent and free-minded, the conclusions – no one denies it – sometimes cautious, even illiberal.'[11] All that is necessary for a left wing to take form, then, is to keep to the principles and reject the conclusions. Here Engels expresses the outlook of Young Hegelianism perfectly.

But what would be the right conclusions to draw? Engels has no doubt whatever that 'the necessary consequence of New Hegelian philosophy' is communism. He informs the English socialists that 'philosophical communism may be considered for ever established in Germany'. Striking a note he will return to at the end of his life, he declares that 'our party' must prove to the Germans that they must either reject their philosophical tradition as useless, or 'they must adopt communism'.[12]

Let us turn now to the knotty problem of Marx's very different encounter with Hegelianism. Althusser says that the Hegel Marx met was *the Hegel of the neo-Hegelian movement*, a Hegel already summoned to provide German intellectuals of the 1840s with the means to think their own history and their own hopes; a Hegel already made to contradict himself, invoked against himself, in despite of himself'.[13] There is some truth in this; but Marx had his own distinctive position based on his own acute reading of Hegel. Well before Engels repeats the above commonplaces of Young Hegelianism with respect to 'principles' and 'prejudices', Marx was writing in his doctoral dissertation that it was silly for Hegel's followers to explain some feature of his system by his accommodation to existing reality;[14] even if a philosopher is consciously making some sort of accommodation, 'what he is not conscious of is the possibility that this apparent accommodation has its deepest roots in an inadequacy . . . of his principle itself'.[15]

Thus the searchlight must be turned on the principle itself to see how it makes possible the expression of conservative prejudices. This is precisely the task Marx undertakes in 1844 when he shows how Hegel's conceptualization of the problematic of alienation leads to a reconciliation of 'reason' with 'unreason' and an accommodation with religion, the state etc. This false position, Marx concludes, is founded in 'the falsehood of his principle'.[16] The Young Hegelian attempt to preserve the 'principle' from 'accommodations' on Hegel's part is therefore untenable. However, we are running ahead of our story.

Let us return to the beginning. We know that when Marx first came into contact with Hegel's philosophy at the University of Berlin its 'craggy melody' repelled him. For a time he was imbued with 'the idealism of Kant and Fichte' and wrote effusive poetry in this vein.[17] He later dismissed this poetry as marked by 'complete opposition between what is and what ought to be'.[18] A slightly later poem is of peculiar interest in exhibiting his first reaction to Hegel. In a book of verse sent to his father in the spring of 1837 we find the *Hegel Epigramme*, which are full of irony at Hegel's expense. The most piquant is the third:

Kant and Fichte soar to heavens blue
Seeking for some distant land;
I but seek to grasp profound and true
That which in the street I find.[19]

This epigram is completely misunderstood when it is thought that 'I' refers to Marx himself.[20] The 'I' is Hegel – just as it is in the previous epigram beginning 'words I teach all mixed up in a devilish muddle' – but it is Hegel forced to speak against himself by Marx. Given this, it is not the case that Marx here endorses the standpoint of Hegel against that of Kant (much less opts for materialism).[21] According to Marx's own account, in a letter to his father, it is later in 1837 that he 'arrived at the point of seeking the idea in reality itself' and found himself delivered into 'the arms of the enemy', namely Hegel.[22] As was noted in the remarks on his dissertation, Marx very soon begins to depart from Hegel, but the project of 'seeking the idea in reality itself' remains.

In departing from Hegel Marx was enormously encouraged by the work of Feuerbach. In 1843 and 1844 he works with the slogan 'real humanism', following Feuerbach's basic principle. Feuerbach wrote: 'the new principle makes *man*, together *with nature*, as the basis of man, the sole, universal and highest object of philosophy.'[23] At this time Marx is an enthusiastic partisan of Feuerbach and continually tries to interest him in new publishing projects.

The received version of events is that Marx was an Hegelian, then he was converted by Feuerbach to materialism and then he struck out on his own 'to change the world'. The true story is more complicated.

The authority of Engels has to be recognized of course, so let us begin with the account in his book *Ludwig Feuerbach and the End of Classical German Philosophy* (1888). He speaks of Feuerbach in dramatic terms: 'with one blow' Feuerbach's *Essence of Christianity* (1841) 'broke the spell' of idealism; Hegel's system was 'exploded and cast aside'; 'the liberating effect of this book' aroused 'general enthusiasm'; 'we all became at once Feuerbachians'.[24]

Engels' memory plays him false here. At first Feuerbach's book was generally taken to be an *application* of Hegelian principles rather than a *refutation*. Engels himself is testimony to this. In his anti-Schelling pamphlet of 1842, in passing he defends Hegel also against Feuerbach and opines that 'Feuerbach's critique of Christianity is a necessary complement to the speculative teaching on religion founded by Hegel'.[25] Engels also forgets to mention that as far as the critique of Hegel is concerned Feuerbach's major blows were delivered in the 1843 texts, *Preliminary Theses towards the Reform of Philosophy* and *Principles of the Philosophy of the Future*.

As for Marx, Engels goes on, 'how enthusiastically Marx greeted the new conception and how much – in spite of all critical reservations – he was influenced by it, one may read in *The Holy Family*'.[26] But this is a work written three years after *Essence of Christianity* appeared. In fact,

Marx was somewhat slow to respond to the book; there is little sign of its influence in his 1842–3 newspaper articles. In truth, the first major impact on Marx's thinking of Feuerbach is documented in his study of Hegel, written in Kreuznach in the spring and summer of 1843. The method applied is taken straight from Feuerbach's newly published *Preliminary Theses*.

It is true that at the outset Marx expresses some reservations about this work. In a letter to Ruge of March 1843 he says that Feuerbach's aphorisms refer 'too much to nature and too little to politics'; he explains that philosophy needs an alliance with politics to come true.[27]

It is a great mistake to treat this opinion as Marx's final judgement on Feuerbach, and to collate it with the critique offered in the theses *On Feuerbach* of 1845. For example, N. Rotenstreich connects the appeal to politics here with the first of the theses, in which Marx appeals to practice against Feuerbach's contemplative materialism;[28] but the practice meant there is not politics, it is a material production. At the earlier date of 1843 Marx is concluding his period as a journalist whose radicalism is clearly idealist in tendency. In taking up in his articles such questions as the law on the 'theft' of wood from forests, and the distress of the Mosel peasants, he becomes aware of the inadequacy of his knowledge. Under the impact of this practical experience in coming to terms with material interests, and of Feuerbach's 'theoretical revolution', Marx took advantage of the closure of his newspaper to undertake a materialist critique of Hegel.[29] This is inspired methodologically by Feuerbach's charge that Hegel inverts the real relations and that, therefore, the road to truth lies in a reinversion. Feuerbach has in mind, very largely, central philosophical questions about man, God and nature. Marx undertakes to remedy the one-sidedness of Feuerbach's critique by applying the latter's method to Hegel's *political* philosophy. In this study he shows how Hegel inverts the real relations of 'civil society' and 'the state'. But, in spite of his turn to 'civil society' as the 'real basis', there is as yet no properly materialist ontology grounded in production. Hence the turn from politics to economics, even to nature, in the *1844 Manuscripts* represents an *advance* over the position held at the time of the letter to Ruge of March 1843.

Given that in the 1843 study on Hegel there is no stress on productive activity, obviously Hegel cannot be praised for grasping man as his own product. The verdict on Hegel at this stage is simply that his idealism mystifies real relations. Although Marx's critique opens up a new field of inquiry, and although he goes beyond the critique of Hegelian ideology to a critique of real relations, the whole enterprise is Feuerbachian through and through. For example, one of the most striking, and oft-quoted, pronouncements is that 'knowledge is not gained by applying "the logical concept" everywhere, but in grasping the logic proper to the peculiar character of the object concerned'.[30] This is well within the scope of Feuerbach's criticism.[31] Feuerbach writes (in his *Philosophy of the Future*, 1843):

> Only those determinations are productive of *real* knowledge which *determine the object by the object itself, by its own individual* determinations; but *not* those that are *general*, as for example the logico-metaphysical determinations that, being applicable to *all objects without distinction, determine no object*.[32]

More than in the 1843 notebook study, Marx's articles *On the Jewish Question*, published in 1844, go beyond the critique of ideological inversions to criticize the real estrangement of the modern state from civil society. Marx calls for a recuperation of the sociality disrupted in the split between the atomized members of civil society and the abstract community of citizenship well described by Rousseau. Human emancipation will be achieved, Marx concludes, 'only when the real, individual man re- absorbs in himself the abstract citizen . . . only when man has recognized and organized his *"force propres"* as *social* forces, and consequently no longer separates social power from himself in the shape of *political* power'.[33]

It is at this date, that is early in 1844, that Marx for the first time nominates the proletariat as the revolutionary force in Germany, in a remarkable essay which exhibits the connection of theory and practice in the highest degree of tension.

However radical philosophical critique becomes, it remains the case, he says, 'that revolutions need a *passive* element, a *material* basis'. The theoretical revolution brought about within post-Hegelian philosophy cannot complete itself within the domain of theory. 'It is not enough that thought should strive for realization; reality must itself strive towards thought.'[34] Where then is the *material* agent of revolution? Marx answers that it must be a class which is forced to revolt under the compulsion of 'material necessity', whose revolt has a universal character 'because of its universal suffering'; it must be a class 'which is the total loss of humanity and which can therefore redeem itself only through the total redemption of humanity'. There is indeed such a class without any stake in the existing order and thrown into opposition to it – 'the proletariat'.[35]

So the proletariat is nominated as the material agent of revolutionary change. But let us look carefully at how its struggle is related by Marx to 'theoretical needs'. 'Clearly', he says, 'the weapon of criticism cannot replace the criticism of weapons, and material force must be overthrown by material force; but theory also becomes a material force once it has gripped the masses.'[36] He finishes the essay with a whole series of such propositions: 'just as philosophy finds its *material* weapons in the proletariat, so the proletariat finds its spiritual weapons in philosophy'; 'the *head* of the struggle is '*philosophy*, its *heart*, the *proletariat*'; 'philosophy cannot realize itself without . . . the proletariat' and the proletariat cannot liberate itself from its chains without 'the realization of philosophy'. These are the 'inner conditions' of revolution.[37]

It is clear from a reading of this text that Marx has broken with his erstwhile philosophical background in so far as he realizes that criticism cannot change reality. But it is equally cleat that he is simply *adding* in a mechanical way the practical needs of the proletariat to this theoretical criticism. It is a marriage of convenience, not a real union. Furthermore, in the above formulations it is still theory which is the overriding moment; it 'grips the masses'; theory is not evolved from the practical standpoint of the proletariat. Hence it retains an abstract and moralizing character. He speaks of the 'categorical imperative' to redeem humanity.[38]

The proletariat is assigned its revolutionary role because of its neediness and oppression; it is thus qualified to be the bearer of universal emancipation. This intuitive imputation is buttressed dialectically by a very bare and abstract play of the categories of universality and particularity. It is too glib. It has justly been characterized as Marx's 'Hegelian choreography'.[39] The antithesis of property and propertylessness is not yet interpreted as that of labour and capital. Furthermore, the revolutionary perspective remains an utterly vague call for 'human emancipation'.

In the Preface to the *1844 Manuscripts* Marx says that he abandoned his plan to do a critique of Hegel's political philosophy because 'the intermingling of criticism directed only against speculation with criticism of the various matters themselves proved utterly unsuitable'.[40] From this original critique of Hegel to the subtitle of *Capital* – 'Critique of Political Economy' – 'criticism', is one of Marx's favourite words. But what does it mean? Early on, in his doctoral dissertation, a purely idealist definition appears: critique 'measures the individual existence by the essence, the particular reality by the Idea'.[41] This is the guiding spirit of his articles for the *Rheinische Zeitung*. But in the 1843 Hegel study a more interesting definition emerges: 'truly philosophical criticism . . . not only shows up contradictions as existing, it *explains* them, it comprehends their genesis, their necessity'.[42]

In fact there is a hint of this idea already in the *Rheinische Zeitung* when Marx is forced to touch on communism for the first time. In 1842 his newspaper was attacked by another for 'communism'; in his reply Marx 'does not admit that communist ideas in their present form possess even *theoretical reality*', although he also says that 'the sharp-witted work of Proudhon' (*What is Property?*), and others, can be criticized only after proper study.[43] Such a study must take on board the objective fact that 'the estate that today owns nothing *demands* to share in the wealth of the middle classes'. This is 'obvious to everyone in Manchester, Paris, and Lyons'.[44] We see that already Marx is shifting the focus of attention from the ideological level to the real social forces in motion.[45] A year later, nevertheless, Marx still writes that communism is 'a dogmatic abstraction'. The interesting thing, however, is that this complaint is spelled out as an objection to its partial, one-sided realization of 'the humanistic principle', and, more explicitly, it is said to be 'still infected with its antithesis – the private system'.[46] It seems that until his studies in political economy convinced him of the dynamic potential of the struggle against capital he was inclined to regard communism as a mere reflex response to inequality, its mere contrary, ungrounded in an adequate theoretical understanding of the inner relationships of private property.

In the years 1843 and 1844 Marx's ideas are changing rapidly and the stages of development are hard to map on the texts because these stages frequently overlap each other in the same work. However, it is clear that three 'pure' stages may be disentangled from the material. First there is the criticism of private property in the light of its lack of accord with the idea of humanity, private property seen as an alien mediator; such a criticism reveals a discrepancy of real existence and supposed essence. Second there is the transference of the contradiction to reality itself, a self-criticism of society in so far as it produces the propertyless proletariat as 'the dissolution of society', forced into revolt by 'material necessity'. Finally, when the antithesis of property and propertylessness is grasped as the antithesis of labour and capital, the proletariat is seen as reappropriating its estranged powers in the positive supersession of private property.

Prior to 1844 Marx's effort to unify theory and practice remains an abstract programme because he has not yet identified productive activity as the socially constitutive axis on which all else turns. Now the way opens for an investigation of the material foundations of society and history.

Once Marx grasps labour as the central category of historical dialectic, communism takes its place as the necessary moment of transition to 'the positive supersession of private property'. Such a communism 'is the riddle of history solved and it knows itself to be this solution'.[47] Thus grounded, communism, he says later, is not an ideal to which reality has to accommodate itself: 'we call communism the *real* movement which abolishes the present state of things'.[48]

Feuerbach's Critique of Hegel

Given Marx's account of 'the great thing about Hegel', a strange thing about the *1844 Manuscripts* is that Marx gives credence in his Preface to the idea that Feuerbach comprehensively supersedes Hegel, and nowhere does he compare him unfavourably with Hegel. Marx says that 'the less noise they make, the more certain, profound, extensive, and enduring is the effect of *Feuerbach*'s writings, the only writings since Hegel's *Phenomenology* and *Logic* to contain a real theoretical revolution'.[49] The main reason Marx advances in the body of the text for holding Feuerbach in such high esteem is precisely his refutation of Hegelianism. Feuerbach, Marx holds, 'is the only one who has a *serious, critical* attitude to the Hegelian dialectic and who has made genuine discoveries in this field'. In fact, 'he is the true conqueror of the old philosophy'.[50] Of particular interest is Marx's judgement that 'a great achievement of Feuerbach is to have opposed to the negation of the negation which claims to be the absolute positive, the positive which is based upon itself and positively grounded in itself'.[51]

How did Feuerbach argue against the 'negation of the negation which claims to be the absolute positive'? Hegel holds that absolute spirit posits itself in opposition to the material world. Feuerbach does not accept the substantiality thus assigned to the mediated being, spirit, as opposed to that which is immediate, the concrete and sensuously manifest. If the natural, material and sensuous is merely the self-alienation of spirit then it is only 'something to be negated', he says, 'like nature which in theology has been poisoned by original sin'.[52] Feuerbach says that 'according to Hegel it is only the negation of the negation that constitutes the true positing'.[53] But, he argues, 'a truth that *mediates itself* is a truth that still has its opposite clinging to it'; spirit can come to itself only through its mediation in its other, the material world. Feuerbach asks rhetorically: 'Why should I not proceed directly from the concrete? Why, after all, should that which owes its truth and certainty only to itself not stand higher that that whose certainty depends on the nothingness of its opposite?'[54] 'The Hegelian philosophy', he comments, 'lacks *immediate unity, immediate certainty, immediate truth.*'[55]

Feuerbach argues at length that sensuous intuition *does* possess immediate truth. Of course, he is well aware that the *Phenomenology* begins precisely with a refutation of the standpoint of sense certainty; although sensuousness claims immediate certainty, it lacks the form of truth; it is therefore sublated in higher forms of cognition and grasped ultimately in terms of spirit's own objectification of itself, its free product constituted as an otherness to be intuited. Feuerbach responds that all that is refuted in the *Phenomenology* is the *logical* 'Here' and 'Now' – which does not touch the *real* sensuous object.[56]

The second objection to the *Phenomenology* is that it rests on the presumption of the identity of thought and being. Feuerbach argues that the circle of thought-determinations can never reach the *other* of thought and must collapse to a formal identity merely; difference is unreal where there is no *objective* ground for it. Hegel fails to produce an actual substance because it relies for its content on forms of alienation, and since these are denied their independence from spirit, this means that spirit is denied real substantiality. Feuerbach argues that 'thought which is isolated and cut off from sensuousness cannot get beyond formal identity'. For thought determinations are 'always repetitions of the self-identity of thought'. Hence the 'other', if 'posited by the idea itself, is not truly and in reality distinguished from it'.[57] Feuerbach concludes that 'the identity of thought and being expresses, therefore, only the *identity of thought with itself*: 'this means that absolute thought is *unable to cleave itself from itself, that it cannot step out of itself to be able to reach being*'.[58]

For any idealist philosophy the question of the reality of the natural world, including the human organism, clearly poses problems. The transition to 'Nature' in Hegel's *Encyclopaedia* has always been found especially problematical. The various moments of thought outlined in the *Logic* are internally connected through the self-determination of the concept in its development. The categories cannot be external to each other – they form a mediated whole. However, at the end of the *Logic* the absolute idea freely posits itself in the form of *otherness*, 'as nature'.[59] This problem Feuerbach very early identified as a crucial limitation. In relation to the vexed question of the validity of this transition he says: 'If nature did not exist, logic, this immaculate virgin, would never be able to produce it out of itself.'[60] Hegel's explanation is as follows:

> The idea, which is *for itself*, when viewed on the point of its *unity* with itself, is *intuition*: and the intuited idea is nature. But as intuition the idea is posited, through external reflection, in a one-sided determination of immediacy or negation. Enjoying, however, an absolute freedom the idea . . . resolves to let the moment of its . . . other-being, the immediate idea as its reflected image, go forth freely as nature.[61]

Marx comments on this trenchantly as follows:

> The absolute idea which . . . '*resolves* to let the moment . . . of its other-being, the *immediate idea*, as its reflection, *issue freely from itself as nature*', this whole idea, which conducts itself in such a strange and baroque fashion, and which has given the Hegelians such terrible headaches, is purely and simply . . . *abstraction* which, taught by experience and enlightened as to its own truth, resolves . . . to *relinquish itself* and . . . in place of its self-absorption, to let *nature*, which it concealed within itself as a mere abstraction, as a thing of thought, *issue freely from itself*: that is to say . . . it resolves on intuition . . . The *mystical* feeling which drives the philosopher from abstract thinking to intuition is *boredom*, the longing for a content.[62]

This follows the same line as Feuerbach's criticism. Marx follows Feuerbach too in saying that 'the abstract thinker who decides on intuition, intuits nature abstractly'; hence 'the whole of nature only repeats to him in a sensuous external form the abstractions of logic'; and it follows that '*nature as nature* . . . distinct from these abstractions . . . has no meaning, or has only the sense of an externality to be superseded . . .'.[63] This is seen when Hegel says that 'since . . . the idea is present as the negative of itself, or is *external to itself*, nature is not merely external in relation to this idea . . . but *externality* constitutes its specificity, as nature'.[64] Nature is an external world of objects externally related to its own truth. It is absolute externality because the internality to which that externality is related can only be reconstituted through the medium of *thought*.

In the final part of Hegel's *Encyclopaedia*, 'Spirit', there is a 'return out of nature'. Spirit is defined as the unity of subject and object. 'This identity is *absolute negativity* – for whereas in nature the concept has its objectivity in a completely external manner, this its alienation has been sublated.'[65] When Hegel characterizes nature as 'externality' this sounds innocent enough; but, as Marx explains, externality here should not be understood as a sensuously accessible world exposing itself to the light of day; rather, he says, 'it is to be taken in the sense of alienation, a flaw, a weakness . . .'. For Hegel it is not a question of natural objectivity of which man is a part and in and through which his existence is naturally mediated; it is a question of spirit positing the realm of nature as immediately *other*, hence being moved to idealize this actuality, since, as inherent externality, nature lacks ideality itself and must submit to its incorporation as a moment in spirit's actualization. As Marx puts it: 'For the abstract thinker nature must therefore supersede itself, since it is already posited by him as a potentially *superseded* being.'[66]

The difficulty in interpreting Marx's position arises when we see that, although he does not explicitly say so, he takes up a fundamentally different position from that of Feuerbach with respect to *materialism*; and this in turn allows Marx a deeper appreciation of Hegel's merit. The issue turns on the centrality of material labour in Marx's social ontology. For Feuerbach, whatever the qualifications he introduces, the main drift of his positive doctrine is the assertion of an immediate unity between man and nature. He seems to identify *mediation as such* with the distance *thought* introduces between man and the object and to reject it accordingly. For Marx, by contrast, the unity of man with the rest of nature is not immediate, but established by labour, and hence changes and develops with new forms of labour. The unity of man with nature is always mediated in industry and incorporates within itself equally a *struggle* to bring into human use the recalcitrant forces of nature. This gives rise to a historical dimension, which depends on changes in the mode of production. This dimension is lacking in Feuerbach. Marx finds it in Hegel, but it is raised to the level of purely philosophical reflection which has lost touch with the *real* basis of history in material labour. None the less, Hegel's philosophy contains the idea of activity, and, moreover, an activity that develops through a stage of alienation and estrangement.

Feuerbach sees Hegel's negation of the negation *only* as a contradiction of philosophy with itself: to this he counterposes the positivity of sensuous immediacy. He does not grasp the objective basis of Hegel's thematization of alienating objectification. However, Marx looks deeper into the historical content of Hegel's work, and its real achievement. He appears to follow Feuerbach in his critique of Hegel's dialectic, and he endorses Feuerbach's naturalism; but this is by no means all, because he transfers the problems of philosophy to the ground of historical practice and of revolutionary transition. For Marx it is necessary to take the speculative problematic seriously as a symptom of the real historical agenda. Feuerbach sees in Hegel's problematic of alienation only the self-delusion of a philosophy estranged from the real world, in that it refuses to abandon itself to sensuousness. For Marx, Hegel's speculative problematic is an attempt to pose, and hence to solve, *within philosophy*, a real historical problem, which Marx sees in terms of the necessity to supersede the rule of private property. Hegel's speculative solution is inadequate because the problem is not so much a theoretical as a practical one.

But Feuerbach's standpoint *too* cannot link up with practice. He interprets the problem of estrangement as the view of nature as the 'otherness' of the idea, and the logical as opposed to the human. This is interpreted again as exclusively a problem of the consciousness of theologians and philosophers. To this speculative illusion Feuerbach counterposes the immediate truths of naturalism and humanism, and he sets out to reform consciousness to this effect. This makes him an *idealist* in practical philosophy, as he himself näively confesses.[67] For Marx 'positive humanism' is a result of real historical development, a necessary sequence in the self-production of the ontological essence of man, whereas for Feuerbach it is seen in ethical terms; Feuerbach posits the 'communal essence' of man as a fixed abstraction based simply on the capacity for universal mutual recognition on the part of individuals. At best this allows for an equally abstract criticism of the perversities of theology and philosophy. In Marx the communal essence is established through production in society. Its estrangement is expressed in the development of the division of labour and the money system. Money is the mediation that both ties and separates individuals; it is the 'estranged and alienating species-essence of man';[68] a person's bond with society lies literally 'in his pocket'.[69] However, this critique is not an ethical–anthropological one, for it is grounded in an ontology which allows for the development of alienation and its supersession to be grasped as historical necessities. Thus Marx can assert 'both that *human* life needed *private property* for its realization and that it now needs the abolition of private property'.[70]

In effect, Feuerbach falls below the level of historical concreteness already attained by Hegel. One is inclined to agree with Lukács' verdict that Hegel poses the problem of estrangement as a problem of the structure of social being, and in the development of the stages of spirit the reality of the historical periods breaks through their conceptual expressions in the aprioristic framework.[71] But, although Feuerbach uses a *methodological* dialectic in evolving and situating his thought in the history of philosophy,[72] his *positive* doctrine in effect rejects objective dialectic altogether.[73] Lukács is therefore right to set Hegel above Feuerbach, because in the materialist alignment of Marx with Feuerbach we miss Hegel's great insight into the dialectical movement of history.[74]

Certainly Marx had good reason to feel much sympathy with Feuerbach's Hegel critique. He credits Feuerbach with having drawn attention to Hegel's conflation of objectivity with estrangement.[75] Much of what Marx says about the objective character of man and his world is drawn from Feuerbach. It is possible to overlook this and take as great discoveries of Marx himself things he copied wholesale from Feuerbach. As an example of the identity and difference of Marx and Feuerbach let us look at the last section of the *1844 Manuscripts* to be written – a fragment on money. It begins with the premise that 'man's feelings [*Empfindungen*], passions [*Leidenschaften*], etc., are not merely anthropological phenomena in the narrower sense, but truly *ontological* affirmations of being (of nature) and . . . are only really affirmed because their object exists for them as a sensual object'.[76] This is straight out of Feuerbach, who says that 'man's feelings have no empirical or anthropological significance in the sense of the old transcendental philosophy, they have rather, an ontological and metaphysical significance . . . .'. Significantly, however, Feuerbach's chosen example is that 'love is the true *ontological* demonstration of the existence of objects apart from our head . . . .'.[77] Marx, by contrast, chooses a different path: 'only through developed industry . . . does the ontological essence of human passion come into being'.[78]

The passage is a good illustration of how Marx goes beyond Feuerbach in the attack on idealism. The recurrence in Marx's text of words such as 'feeling', 'passion', 'ontology', etc., which come from Feuerbach, obscures the fact that Marx's ontology is very different. In Feuerbach's naturalism the emphasis is on feeling, whereas in Marx it is on productive activity. 'Feeling' (*Empfindung*) denotes a relatively low form of experience in which no distinction is drawn between subject and object; hence Feuerbach uses it to denote an indifferent immediacy, not a dialectically mediated unity. It is true that Feuerbach is capable of incorporating productive activity in the essence of man. He says in the *Essence of Christianity* that 'the idea of activity, of making, of creation, is in itself a divine idea' because 'in activity man feels himself free, unlimited, happy'; and 'the most blissful activity is that which is productive'. Hence, he concludes, 'this attribute of the species – productive activity – is assigned to God'.[79] Nevertheless, this is not with Feuerbach, as it is with Marx, a *synthesizing* category.

For Feuerbach the paradigm case of an objective relation is *love*, as we have just seen. No such thing appears in Marx's *1844 Manuscripts*. Yet Erich Fromm[80] gets excited when he reads this from Marx's pen in *The Holy Family*: 'love . . . first really teaches man to believe in the objective world outside himself'.[81] Although Fromm's reading of Marx is Feuerbachian through and through, he does not recognize the provenance of this remark in such statements as that quoted above. What happened was that Edgar Bauer, under the pretext of a book review, attacked the idea of a love object, thus covertly attacking Feuerbach. Then Marx, in his critique of the Bauer circle, reasserted the Feuerbachian view in a highly contextualized manner, within this debate. Therefore, although it is interesting that Marx expresses his solidarity with Feuerbach even on this point, it is not this that Marx finds important about Feuerbach. Certainly no great ontological significance should be attached to this isolated statement when Marx over and over again stresses production as the central mediator. For example 'species being' in the *1844 Manuscripts* has quite a different content from what it has in Feuerbach. It is not constituted in consciousness but in social production.

Feuerbach's critique of religion is often given as an important source of Marx's theory of alienation. Undoubtedly Marx was impressed by it; but it is important to notice how much more thoroughgoing is Marx's own theory. For Feuerbach, religion consists in 'the objectification of the essence of man'.[82] This means that 'the personality of God is the alienated, objectified, personality of man'.[83] Feuerbach finds 'the secret of religion' is that man 'objectifies [*Vergegenständlichkeit*] his being, and then again makes himself the *object of this objectified* being, transformed into a subject, a person'.[84] He amplifies this in an interesting note where 'religious self-objectification' is distinguished from 'that occuring in reflection and speculation'; for 'the latter is arbitrary, the former necessary – as necessary as art and language'.[85] The reference in this note to 'speculation' is explained by Feuerbach's claim that Hegel's philosophy is itself alienating! It 'estranges man from his own being and his own activity'.[86] This remark is indicative. Feuerbach's critique in truth is limited to a critique of *ideology* – worthless ideology in the case of theology and philosophy, man's lived relation to himself in the case of religion as a necessary medium of species self-awareness.

Marx, by contrast, stresses that man 'duplicates himself not only . . . in consciousness, but actively, and actually, and therefore he sees himself in the world he has created' (see p. 9). Likewise, alienation is objective.

In this light, one must enter qualifications about Marx's – genuine – enthusiasm for Feuerbach at this stage of his development. When he says Feuerbach's great achievement is to have counterposed to the negation of the negation the self-subsistent positive, he has in mind primarily the way in which Hegel uses the negation of the negation to affirm the absolute as spirit. Secondarily, Marx has in mind the way in which the idealist negation fails to move beyond the stage of self-reference in estrangement to a *positive* supersession. These two aspects of the matter are connected, of course.

On the first point, however, Feuerbach rejects objective dialectics along with idealism; while, on the second point, Marx diverges at least as far from Feuerbach as he does from Hegel, because for Feuerbach 'positive humanism' is merely a philosophical perspective produced by inverting religion and philosophy so that speculative thought is brought down to earth, while for Marx it is historically produced through the supersession of real *objective* estrangement. Marx is primarily interested in the *historical* dialectic, and he wants to root communist revolution immanently in it; hence he tries to recuperate Hegel's dialectic of negativity within a materialist conception of history. Feuerbach rejects Hegel's negation of the negation altogether because he is primarily interested in nature, which idealist dialectic reduces to the status of an 'externality' to be sublated. Here Marx is bound to go some of the way with Feuerbach. However, although the *1844 Manuscripts* contain some undigested lumps of Feuerbach's naturalism, it is already clear that Marx advances beyond Feuerbach's endorsement of the immediate unity of man and nature to pose labour as their mediation. This provides him with the ontological basis for his historical dialectic. It follows that, with Marx, alienation is read as objective alienation. The new interpretation of the world and its religious reflex provided by Feuerbach is inadequate from this point of view: the point is to *change* the world.[87]

The Changing Verdicts

The thesis of a linear development from Hegel through Feuerbach to Marx is seen to be untenable when we consider the evidence of the *1844 Manuscripts*. Marx's turn to political economy there brought the category of labour to the forefront of his thought and allowed him to make the complex connections with Hegel's *Phenomenology* we have already examined. Commentators as different as Marcuse and Althusser recognize this return to Hegel.

Marcuse points out that when, in his theses *On Feuerbach*, Marx demarcates himself from Feuerbach through the concept of human practice he thereby 'reaches back beyond Feuerbach to Hegel'; so the matter is not as simple as a straight road from Feuerbach to Marx subsequent to a rejection of Hegel; 'instead of this, Marx, at the origins of his revolutionary theory, once again appropriates the decisive achievements of Hegel on a transformed basis'.[88] Althusser speaks of 'Hegel reintroduced by force into Feuerbach'.[89]

It has to be said that Marx fails in the *1844 Manuscripts* to make his differences with Feuerbach explicit. No doubt the general enthusiasm of Marx and Engels for Feuerbach's devastating critique of theology and philosophy in the early 1840s led to an over-estimation of his contribution and a lack of interest in taking any distance from him at the outset of Marx's own development of materialist criticism. This may be why there is no trace in Marx's *1844 Manuscripts* of any recognition of the distance he has travelled from his mentor.

The first documented break comes with the theses *On Feuerbach* drafted in the spring of 1845. Nothing before this is conclusive in my view. The early letter quoted above containing a reservation on Feuerbach's naturalism is evidently retracted in practice with Marx's materialist turn. Those, like Lukács[90] and Naville,[91] who cite Marx's 1844 statement that Feuerbach sees Hegel's negation of the negation only as the contradiction of philosophy with itself, as if it were a criticism of Feuerbach, are reading too much into the text. The statement occurs in a passage summarizing and endorsing Feuerbach's counterposition to Hegel of 'positive facts'.[92] Instead of starting from positive facts Hegel engages in a positing through double negation. If such Hegelian doctrine is taken *literally*, then Marx rejects it as mystifying and anti-naturalistic. At this level Marx is in agreement with Feuerbach and the statement quoted should be read as an endorsement, or at least as a neutral report. Certainly no other remark in the *1844 Manuscripts* can be said to be critical of Feuerbach, so the balance of probability is that this is not either.

Where Marx goes beyond Feuerbach is in recognizing that Hegel's dialectic of negativity, freed from its estranged form of expression within philosophy, can be given concrete content in the pattern of historical genesis. What Marx seems to say is that past history itself can be criticized for positing through negation, but in the future socialist man knows how to start from himself as a positive fact, so to speak.

At this stage Marx does not see it as his task to point out Feuerbach's limitations with regard to the comprehension of historical dialectic. Indeed, at this stage he still entertains the hope of securing Feuerbach's collaboration. He writes to him in August 1844 to persuade him that on his own humanist principles he too should become a socialist. Marx points out that, whether he knows it or not, Feuerbach has provided 'a philosophical basis for socialism' and that 'the communists' have understood this.

> The unity of man with man, which is based on the real differences between men, the concept of the human species brought down from the heaven of abstraction to the real earth, what is this but the concept of society?[93]

Strangely enough, Feuerbach responds to this injunction. While at first reluctant to state publicly that he is a communist,[94] his reply (1845) to Stirner's criticism of his work ends in ringing tones with the declaration that, in as much as he 'places the essence of man in community alone', he is '*Kommunist*'.[95]

Rather ungratefully, Marx later writes (in the *German Ideology*) that Feuerbach 'is deceiving himself when he declares himself a communist' because his conception of 'communist' is merely a category that registers an ahistorical fact about men's need for society whereas 'in the real world' a communist is a follower of a revolutionary party bent on overthrowing the existing order:[96] 'rather ungratefully' because Marx's original letter makes such an equation between communism and 'the concept of society'. As for party affiliation: it is touching to learn that, when he was almost forgotten, Feuerbach joined the Social Democratic Party, two years before his death.[97]

However, this is to run ahead of the story. Returning to the question of Feuerbach and Hegel, we have seen that the *1844 Manuscripts* hail Feuerbach as 'the true conqueror of the old philosophy'. The only hint of a doubt in Marx's mind is revealed by a passage at the end of the Preface. He says that 'Feuerbach's discoveries about the nature of philosophy still, for their proof at least, call for a critical discussion of philosophical dialectic'.[98] Even then Marx had second thoughts and hastily crossed it through. In *The Holy Family* (1845) he still talks of Feuerbach's 'masterly criticism' of Hegel,[99] and says that 'Feuerbach was the first to describe philosophy as speculative and mystical empiricism and to prove it'.[100] But in the *German Ideology* (1846) Marx concludes that, after all, Feuerbach does *not* provide a criticism of Hegel's dialectics.[101] Before the *German Ideology* we have the well-known theses *On Feuerbach*. For the first time Marx comprehensively, and consciously, breaks with Feuerbach.

It must be remarked that this break occurs *after* the appearance of Max Stirner's scorching critique *Der Einzige und sein Eigenthum*. Although dated 1845, this came out late in 1844 and, judging by his correspondence, Marx must have read it at once.[102] All the Young Hegelians felt constrained to reply to Stirner. Feuerbach's reply was mentioned above. M. Hess (using material in a letter of Marx's) replied immediately in his *Die Letzten Philosophen*. Marx and Engels set to work late in 1845 on the *German Ideology*, by far the largest section of which is a page by page attack on Stirner's work. In this connection it should be noted that Engel's reminiscences, quoted earlier, are misleading. He lists the Young Hegelians in the order Strauss, Bauer, Stirner, Feuerbach. The uninitiated might think that Feuerbach's main works replied to Stirner. In fact, it was Stirner who came last with a book, and that included a violent attack on Feuerbach. At all events, Marx and Engels, in 1845, began to include Feuerbach with the other young Hegelians as part of their past, now superseded.

From our point of view, the most important of the theses *On Feuerbach* is the first, because in it 'materialism' (Feuerbach's explicitly included) is charged with neglect of the practical relation to objectivity; by contrast 'the *active* side was set forth abstractly by idealism'.[103] This shows how far Marx's materialism, in its concentration on practice, goes beyond the passivity of sensuous intuition presented by Feuerbach and so many others as the nub of materialism. In thus distancing himself from 'the old materialism' Marx even acknowledges once again merit in idealism (Hegel), despite the fact that it transposes real activity into the dialectic of abstractions.

It is in the *German Ideology* that Marx and Engels develop the method of historical materialism at length for the first time. However, these positive views are embedded in a critique of the Young Hegelians, including Feuerbach. According to this account, 'their polemics against Hegel and against one another are confined to this – each takes one side of the Hegelian system and turns this against the whole system as well as against the aspects chosen by the others'.[104] A rather nice example of this occurs in Feuerbach's first Hegel-critique, where he inverts Hegel's ordering of space and time, preferring 'the liberality of space' to 'the monarchical tendency of time'; but where both are still recognizably Hegel's categories.[105]

The main point, of course, is the emphasis placed by Marx and Engels on the importance of the mode of production. Feuerbach says in his *Essence of Christianity* that man is distinguished from animals by religion and by consciousness.[106] Obviously with this in mind, Marx and Engels say:

> men can be distinguished from animals by consciousness, by religion, or anything else you like. They themselves begin to distinguish themselves from animals as soon as they begin to *produce* their means of subsistence . . . This mode of production is a definite mode of life on their part . . . What they are, therefore, coincides with their production.[107]

They take Feuerbach severely to task for his abstract contemplative materialism; they point out that the cherry tree outside his window is an object of sensuous certainty for Feuerbach only as a result of world trade; nature just as 'given' exists only on a few coral islands; the progression of industry has thoroughly transformed the objective world.

The final verdict of Marx on Feuerbach is given much later on. In an obituary (of January 1865) on Proudhon, Marx remarks in passing that 'compared with Hegel, Feuerbach is exceedingly poor'. So why all the fuss? Because 'he was epoch-making *after* Hegel, since he laid stress on certain points disagreeable to Christian consciousness while important for the progress of criticism, and which Hegel had left in mystic semi-obscurity'.[108]

'Compared with Hegel, Feuerbach is exceedingly poor': this is interesting not only for Marx's opinion of Feuerbach but for a revaluation of Hegel. How does it come about that 'the conqueror of Hegel' now bears no comparison with him? What happens with Marx is that as Feuerbach's star wanes, Hegel's rises. Not at first: not in *The Holy Family* for example. Although this was composed – mostly by Marx – immediately after the *1844 Manuscripts*, there is little trace in it of the advances made there. In particular, there is no mention of any 'great thing' in Hegel; Feuerbach is the hero. Hegel is treated scornfully throughout, under such headings as 'Mystery of Speculative Construction'. Indeed, for the next ten years Marx's references to Hegel and his dialectic are almost uniformly negative: the *German Ideology* dismisses Hegel's speculative history; the *Poverty of Philosophy* (1847) makes fun of Hegel's 'strings of thoughts' in the methodology section; the dialectic of negation of the negation is attacked without reference to any virtue in it.

It is only when Marx seriously tries to get his economics into shape that there is a second return to Hegel. The first was the 1844 return to the *Phenomenology*; this time it is to the *Logic*. We have a letter (January 1858) in which Marx reports that he had been made a present of Hegel's *Logic* and found it of great service 'in the method'.[109] This influence was noted by several reviewers of *Capital* (1867), mostly with disapproval. In a letter of 1868 Marx remarks of the fashion to treat Hegel's dialectics as a dead dog that 'Feuerbach has much on his conscience in this respect'.[110] So the man who was first applauded for overthrowing Hegel's dialectic should now apologize! Again in 1870 Marx mentions how put out Lange and others are by his resurrection of Hegel – after they had long buried him![111] When the second edition of *Capital* appeared in 1873, Marx made a special point of asserting his affiliation to Hegel on the question of dialectic – unfortunately in words too cryptic to construe easily.

Summary

What this survey shows is that there is no unilinear development from Hegel through Feuerbach to a 'mature' Marxism. Moreover, in contrast to much recent talk of a 'break' in Marx's work, and the contraposition of a 'young' and 'old' Marx, Marx himself showed no inclination to reject any of his work, however early. In 1851, well after his adoption of a communist outlook, he was happy to see republished his early journalism.[112] In 1867 he re-read *The Holy Family* and reported to Engels that he 'was pleasantly surprised to find that we do not need to be ashamed of this work, although the cult of Feuerbach produces a very humorous effect upon one now'.[113]

At the same time, it is obvious that there are important developments in Marx's thought. We can mark out the following stages:

1840–3 Young Hegelianism leading to radical democratic works.

1843–4 Feuerbachian works, especially his notes on Hegel's *Philosophy of Right* applying the method of inversion of Hegel. A turn towards a practical thrust in the Introduction.

1844 The turning point. Birth of Marxism in that labour is centralized, and political economy is seen as a key science. Feuerbach is not yet rejected. The first return to Hegel in that there is praise for the 'producing principle' of the *Phenomenology*.

1844–57 Transitional works. Anti-speculative settling with philosophy, both Hegel's, in *The Holy Family* (still under the sign of Feuerbach) and Feuerbach's also, in the *Theses* and *German Ideology*. Growing concreteness of outlook, e.g. class struggle in the *Manifesto*.

1857 on Mature work on political economy and politics; the second return to Hegel, this time to the *Logic*.[114]

10

Towards an Assessment

Introduction

So far, we have concentrated largely on exegesis and clarification of Marx's ideas and their relationship to his philosophical antecedents. The remainder of this book gives some indication of their validity and their limitations.

Given that we claim Marx's theory of alienated labour has not been properly understood, it follows that most previous objections raised against it are irrelevant.[1] This chapter considers the most interesting charge, namely that Marx does not really break with Hegel's problematic as far as alienation is concerned. I reject this; but acknowledge also that there are important limitations in the ontology of the *1844 Manuscripts*. I believe this is overcome in the subsequent development of Marx's thought, and that the ambivalence in his later writings on the question of the abolition of labour flows from his appreciation of the difficulties inherent in such a perspective.

The next chapter will go on to discuss briefly the contribution to Marx's *Capital* of the ontology inaugurated in the *1844 Manuscripts*.

Marx and the 'Inversion' of Hegel

Louis Althusser holds that the *1844 Manuscripts* represent nothing but an inversion of Hegel and that consequently the dialectical form remains the same, even though activity is grasped as material rather than spiritual. Althusser holds that in Hegel we have 'the simple unity of a totality produced by the *negation of the negation* . . . a simple original unity which develops within itself by virtue of its negativity, and throughout its development only ever restores the original simplicity and unity in an ever more "concrete" totality'.[2] Again: 'the *Phenomenology* celebrates "the labour of the negative" . . . but negativity can only contain the motor principle of the dialectic . . . as a strict reflection of the Hegelian theoretical presuppositions of simplicity and origin . . . as a pure reflection of the principle of alienation itself'.[3] Althusser alleges that 'it is this "Hegelian dialectic" that reigns in glory over Marx's *1844 Manuscripts*'.[4]

Let us consider this charge that the *1844 Manuscripts*, being nothing but a materialist inversion of Hegel, are open to the objections sustainable against Hegel's dialectic. To begin with: even a cursory reading of Marx's criticism of Hegel's dialectic discloses that the self-identical totality is a main object of attack. It is linked to, but distinct from, the criticism that Hegel does not know real material labour but only the movement of mind. The attack is against the way in which Hegel uses the concepts of negation of the negation, and of '*Aufheben*', to present spirit as at home with itself in its otherness, having overcome, and yet preserved, estrangement as a moment in the absolute.

As we have seen, Marx follows Feuerbach in counterposing to Hegel's self-identical totality a view of man as an objective being constituted in and through objective relationships. There is no suggestion in the text of a subject requiring to negate objectivity as such through grasping it as its own. On the contrary, Marx carefully distinguishes objectification and objectivity as such, on the one hand, from alienation and private property as specific historical determinations, on the other. As far as Marx's concept of practice is concerned, we have seen that he pictures man as created in and through material production, but he stresses that the worker can create nothing without the sensuous external world as material for production; he speaks of the necessity for a dialogue with nature.[5]

In order to solve the problem of Marx's conceptualization of the totality within which material production goes on, it is necessary to distinguish between an '*identity*' of opposites, in which the 'other' is nothing but the self in alienation, and a *unity* of opposites in which the other is really distinct as a pole of the relationship, however transformed in it.

It is clear that Marx conceives the unity of man and the rest of nature as a unity of this latter type. The unity is *grounded* in man's natural origins ('for man is a part of nature'[6]); but the specific difference of the social must also be granted; the *synthesizing* moment is historical practice which takes up natural elements as material in the development of industry, the ontological foundation of properly human existence in society. It is clear that this work is an open-ended, always to be furthered project.

What then of Marx's appropriation of the 'negation of the negation' and of 'alienation' from Hegel? We have shown that there is a big difference between Hegel's absolutization of these moments and Marx's view that they relate only to the history of mankind's emergence, and are to be superseded in socialism positively grounded on itself. This is only possible in turn because his fundamental ontological frame of reference is the mediation of man and nature in industry, while the problem of alienation is reduced to a historically relative stage, however prolonged, by inscribing within the fundamental mediations the distorting effect of the secondary mediations: wage-labour and private property.

In this dialectic Marx is very careful to distinguish his understanding of estrangement from Hegel's precisely through inscribing it within the unsurpassable reality of objectification as a specific historical determination. Therefore, overcoming alienation does not mean, as in Hegelianism, the encompassing of all otherness; it just means 'the destruction of the estranged character of the objective world'.[7] Spirit has as its negative something which is merely *its own* other because objectification can only be brought about within the absolute movement of negativity. The negative is easily negated in its turn simply through recollection of the process of its origination. In spite of Hegel's incorporation of history within his system, his conception is ultimately ahistorical in that it requires a fixed 'end' to development, an end which always implies a *return*, however more developed, a closing of the circle. Marx's conception implies a spiral progress which is open-ended; being immanent in a self-mediating subject with objective relationships it implies a perennial 'starting over' whenever the objective room for development of a given social totality is exhausted. Marx's inquiry is into the material stages of development of human history, not the moments of movement of spirit's production of itself out of itself. In the latter case the end bends back on the beginning, which in some sense presupposes it. But Marx's inquiry into real history discloses the existence of distinct stages of development, complete in themselves, and separated by real discontinuities, by revolutionary transformations. One must distinguish transitions *within* a self-developing totality from transitions of such a more radical type, ontological *breaks* which refound the fundamental determinants of social being. In the present case the communist revolution marks a transition from 'the relative ontological continuity inherent in the unfolding of capital' (Mészáros[8]).

In the transition from capitalism to socialism the achievement of capitalism in developing the productive forces is to be appropriated and preserved, not by incorporating their existing form as private property within a higher totality, but by divesting them of their alien form through abolishing private property. It will not be the case that socialism will recognize its productive forces as marked by their origins in private property (once the transitional stage passes) even though Marx believes that the capitalist stage of their development was historically necessary.

In the dynamic contradiction of labour and private property the negation of the negation does not effect a closure then – an end of history – because this specific dialectic is inscribed, as the estrangement of social being, within the wider *intermediations* of man and nature. Hence the negation of the negation brought about through communist revolution opens out the possibility of a real human history no longer carried on under the mark of estrangement.

It is important here, therefore, not to oversimplify the dialectical movement of alienation and its supersession. When Marx speaks of 'the emergence of nature for man' this relation of difference – man for himself and nature for man – is a genuine advance beyond that state in which man is sunk in the natural, unable to perceive his own specificity as an acting subject and to grasp nature as an object of purposeful activity. At the same time this difference must maintain its necessary unity; for man depends on nature for his material reproduction. Two consequences follow; first, that, if in the estranging system of secondary mediations subject and object are opposed, they are none the less united, even though in a contradictory dynamic; second, that abolition of estrangement does not abolish this difference and restore relations of natural immediacy, but rather produces a unity in diversity, mediated through social labour, and freed from the contradictions of the estranging system of private property. The history of alienation does not go from identity to difference back to identity; rather, it goes from identity to contradictory unity in difference, on to non-antagonistic unity in difference.

Before I admit my own reservations on Marx's *1844 Manuscripts*, let us look further at criticism. Ian Hunt and Roy Swan claim that in the *Manuscripts* Marx conceives of society 'after the Hegelian manner' as taking up its origin into itself. It is worth quoting in full the difference they see between the young Marx and mature Marxism.

> In the transition from the Hegelian to the mature Marxist dialectic, the initial step is from an ideal to a material content, from the Idea to (material) labour, from Spirit to Society, which in Early Marx is conceived in its fruition as the union of humankind with nature in free, conscious self-determination.
>
> As Marxism develops, it effects no radical alteration of the materialist content, although it does render it radically more concrete. However, the developing Marxism effects a radical change in dialectical form, and later in its formulation of the dialectical process. In terms of Hegel's metaphor of the circle, there is a change

from an emphasis on the circle 'closing on itself' to an emphasis in mature Marxism on 'bursting out' of the circle, which while completing, more fundamentally brings to dissolution one process and begins another. Whereas Hegel sees a 'circle of circles', that is, every 'bursting out' as in turn a circle enclosed in the all-embracing circle of the absolute, mature Marxism see an endless progression, a spiral movement (i.e. a 'bursting out' of a circle) which does not close on itself, but is open-ended.

By an emphasis on self-enclosure we mean, to begin with, the encompassing of all otherness within the subject that is supposed to ensure the true infinitude and freedom of the subject. Thus, in early Marxism, the conclusion of social 'prehistory', itself a part of nature and natural history, is Society brought to fruition, and this is after the Hegelian manner conceived as in turn encompassing (practically and theoretically) nature and natural history. In mature Marxism society is conceived as a part of natural history which in turn does not enclose natural history.[9]

Thus Hunt and Swan. What textual support could be mobilized in support of this view?

In the *1844 Manuscripts* the description of communism as the positive supersession of private property certainly uses the imagery of 'return'. Thus it is said to be 'the complete return of man to himself as a *social*, i.e. human, being – a return accomplished consciously and embracing the entire wealth of previous development'. Furthermore, 'it is the *genuine* resolution of the conflict between man and nature and between man and man – the true resolution of the strife between existence and essence, between objectification and self-affirmation, between freedom and necessity, between individual and species'.[10] In this light, communism 'is the riddle of history solved, and knows itself to be this solution'.[11] Further on it is asserted that '*society* is the complete unity in essence of man with nature'.[12] This means that 'it is only when the objective world becomes everywhere for man in society the world of man's essential powers . . . that all *objects* become for him the *objectification* of himself, become objects that confirm and realize his individuality, become *his* objects: that is, man himself becomes the object'.[13] The key relationship here is that of industry: 'conceived as the *exoteric* revelation of man's essential powers' it realizes 'the *human* essence of nature or the *natural* essence of man'.[14]

What are we to make of all this? The charge is that Marx here conceives man, in Hegelian fashion, taking up his origin into himself such that the condition of his activity becomes its consequence. This is answered if we recall the distinction between the set of primary mediations inhering in the permanent ontological framework man–activity–nature, and the secondary mediations labour–capital inscribed within it. It is only with regard to the secondary mediations that it is plausible to speak of a radical transcendence of the objective *condition* (private property) consequent on its being posited as the *product* of labour. But such a reversal is not possible with the material aspect of private property, the objects of productive activity; for nothing can be produced without naturally given material on which to work, however much this objectivity becomes socially mediated and mediates social man. Nature remains as a condition of activity, albeit more and more a determined determinant.

Certainly the natural basis of human being which lies at the origin as a *given condition* becomes more and more the object of human *practice* with the consequence (as Marx formulates it in *Capital*) that in acting on external nature man changes himself.[15] Yet, however highly mediated, social being still presupposes transformed natural objectivity, and reproduces itself in this framework.[16]

In distinguishing Marx's 1844 dialectic from Hegel's, it is important to contrast the self-mediatedness of spirit established through absolute negativity with the self-mediatedness of human being established in and through material practice. Take this crucial passage cited by Marx from Hegel's 1830 *Encyclopaedia*:

> Spirit is nature's *truth*. In this truth nature is vanishing, and spirit has resulted as the idea which has attained being-for-itself, whose *object* as well as *subject* is the *concept*. This identity is *absolute negativity*, for whereas in nature the concept has its perfect external objectivity, its alienation has been sublated and the concept has become identical with itself. It *is* this identity *only* in that it is a return from nature.[17]

Marx charges Hegel with here characterizing the *externality* of nature as a *defect*, and with positing it as potentially superseded from the outset.[18] From this we must conclude that Marx could not simply replace the negating activity of thought with the material transformation of practice, while yet holding nature in the same contempt. If Marx insists, following Feuerbach, that man acts in the context of objective relationships, then his self-mediatedness cannot be *absolutized* in the manner of Hegel's spirit. This is because he bases himself not on the *identity* of opposites but on their *unity*, in this context. One can see now that the difference in *content* must make a difference to the general *form* of working of the dialectic when it is stood on its feet, having been grounded materialistically. In Hegel, the unity of opposites collapses to an identity, pure *self*-distinction, which allows the negation of the negation to effect a closure and reduces historical time to an organon of absolute teleology. It is the irreducible distinction between man and the objective basis of his activity, however intermediated through labour and industry, that allows us to grasp the dialectic of human practice as historical and open-ended.

Furthermore, it is not possible to say that Marx views nature as inert matter to which human activity is to give shape. In discussing the appropriation of objects Marx says that such activity must take into account the *determinate* nature of such objects: 'The *manner* in which they become *his* depends on the *nature of the objects* and on the nature of the *essential power* corresponding to *it*; for it is precisely the *determinate nature* of this relationship which shapes the particular real mode of *affirmation*.'[19]

It cannot be said, therefore, that Marx simply substitutes material labour for that of spirit in Hegel's dialectic, with the consequence that society is to *enclose* nature. The stress on *objectivity* in the text speaks too strongly against that. At the same time, it has to be allowed that there is something unsatisfactory about talk of 'a complete unity in essence of man with nature'. There is indeed something deficient in the ontology of the *1844 Manuscripts*. In my view the problem has to do less with the assimilation of Hegel than with that of Feuerbach.

The Real Problem

The defect is not a question of Marx's conceptualizing subjectivity as enclosing all otherness in the Hegelian manner. The difficulty lies rather in the unproblematized unity of subject and object conceptualized under the influence of the Feuerbachian absolute – 'man on the basis of nature'. The assumption is present that, just because man is natural, nature can be humanized through the mediation of industry. It is true that Marx (like Feuerbach) says that 'man as an objective sensuous being is therefore a *suffering* being – and because he feels that he suffers, a *passionate* being'.[20] The stress, however, lies on the *affirmative* character of appropriation of the objects satisfying particular needs. There is no real recognition of the sheer *recalcitrance* of nature to human use.

The *1844 Manuscripts* concentrates on the importance of overcoming the estrangement inherent in the private property system. Upon the reappropriation of the ontological essence of man therein alienated, it seems that man's genesis through negation of the negation is complete. Marx fails to recognize here that genesis is a continuing process because the struggle to overcome 'the realm of necessity' (as *Capital* will call it) remains ever present; the retreat of the natural boundary, as the conditions of his existence pass under his control, is always a relative matter.[21]

Instead of bringing this aspect into focus, Marx takes the rather 'phenomenological' stance that with the end of estrangement man knows he is his own creation and freely exercises his active power on nature. He does not think through the problems inherent in slogans about the unity in essence of society and nature. He does not have clearly in view the fact that nature is self-subsistent on the basis of natural interactions. Of course, if asked, he would admit that this is so, because to do otherwise would be too obviously idealist. What he does not yet realize is the consequences of this in terms of the real recalcitrance of nature to human efforts and the problems to which this gives rise. Later he becomes more aware of it, as we see in this passage from the third volume of *Capital*:

> The realm of freedom really begins only where labour determined by necessity and external expediency ends; it lies by its very nature beyond the sphere of material production proper. Just as the savage must wrestle with nature to satisfy his needs, to maintain and reproduce his life, so must civilized man, and he must do so in all forms of society and under all possible modes of production. This realm of natural necessity expands with his development, because his needs do too; but the productive forces to satisfy these expand at the same time. Freedom, in this sphere, can consist only in this, that socialized man, the associated producers, govern the human metabolism with nature in a rational way, bringing it under their collective control instead of being dominated by it as a blind power; accomplishing it with the least expenditure of energy and in conditions most worthy and appropriate for their human nature. But this always remains a realm of necessity. The true realm of freedom, the development of human powers as an end in itself, begins beyond it, though it can only flourish with this realm of necessity as its basis. The reduction of the working day is the basic prerequisite.[22]

What we find in the *1844 Manuscripts* is a peculiar synthesis of Hegel and Feuerbach. Whereas a purely Hegelian dialectic would arrive at an identity in which man incorporates his origin, Marx, having absorbed Feuerbach's critique of identity, pushes the movement of negativity back into a kind of pre-history so as to arrive, after this 'genesis' is completed with communist revolution, at a Feuerbachian 'positive, positively grounded in itself', that is, the recognition by man of his origins in and unity with nature and the reorganization of social relations on this basis so as to promote the resolution of all contradictions.

In a way, the young Marx combines both Hegel's and Feuerbach's optimisms. In hailing man's achievement in becoming aware of his self-mediatedness as the riddle of history solved, Marx is too Hegelian. In not taking the otherness of nature too seriously, once it has been retrieved from the alienated objectivity of private property and posited as the internally related object of man himself, Marx is too Feuerbachian.

After the end of alienation there must remain a dialectical process of interaction, even of opposition, as successive obstacles thrown up by nature are encountered. Negative ecological feedback cannot be supposed only a problem of capitalist anarchy, for example. The nature that is 'for man' is always a continually surprising interlocutor.

Although the unity of man with nature is insufficiently problematized in the *1844 Manuscripts* the centralization of the category 'labour' already destabilizes such Feuerbachian residues. The curious thing is that Marx does not yet seem to realize this, although he will soon attack Feuerbach precisely for neglecting the ontological importance of activity. Because Marx follows Hegel in giving priority to activity, now transposed to a materialist key, the Feuerbachian immediacy of 'man on the basis of nature' is undermined.

Marx's view is of man at the centre of a totality in which nature is 'for man', not as a passive object appropriated in a contemplative synthesis of sensuous intuition, but in a mediated unity *actively* constituted in so far as nature is posited as the object of human productive power. Inevitably, Marx soon sees that simply abolishing the status of the object as private property is not enough, that the level of development of the productive forces is also a key to emancipation. Without this, socialization of property could not have the desired consequences.[23]

The implications of such revisions in the ontological perspective are significant. For example, one cannot take seriously talk of genuine resolution of existence and essence, freedom and necessity, and so forth. If human essence is not merely species consciousness but is reproduced socially through material activity, it becomes subject to continual transformation. Any 'naturalism' of the essence must be rejected in favour of historically developing mediatedness. This means, as Mészáros says, that there cannot be 'a point in history at which we could say "now the human substance has been fully realized" . . . .'.[24]

The most interesting consequence, for our theme, is that of the future of labour.

The Abolition of Labour

It is necessary before going any further to recall the terminological point discussed in chapter 1, namely, that in the *1844 Manuscripts*. Marx uses the term 'labour' to refer to alienated productive activity carried on under the regime of private property. As was said there, failure to consider such terminological problems leads to intolerable confusion. (An example, giving rise to such problems of interpretation, is discussed in an Appendix to this chapter.) Nevertheless, this point about the differences in usage of 1844, and Marx's later work, is connected to a genuine problem. In the *1844 Manuscripts* Marx could use the term 'labour' in the way he does because he is working with a very simple dichotomy: under the regime of private property, productive activity is labour, that is, alienated activity; with the positive supersession of private property it is free activity — 'labour' is abolished.

He speaks of the abolition of labour as late as the *German Ideology* (1846). He says there also that, whereas now self-activity and material production diverge completely, with the appropriation of the existing totality of productive forces 'self-activity coincides with material life', and labour 'is transformed into self-activity'; then, the fully developed individual casts off the 'natural-grown' one.[25] With the change in ontological perspective such a simple inversion can no longer be maintained.[26] The abolition of the system of estrangement cannot amount to the abolition of the realm of necessity itself. Material production ('labour' in the revised terminology) remains subject to its imperatives. Hence in the quotation from the third volume of *Capital* given above Marx sees a permanent opposition between a realm of freedom and a realm of necessity, within which only the balance can change, in that the working day can be shortened.

Before looking further at the question of how Marx revised the oversimple perspective of his youth, it should be emphasized that when he speaks there of the abolition of labour he certainly does not mean the abolition of material productive activity itself. He has in mind rather the seizing by the workers of the instrument and object of production and the consequent abolition of vertical and horizontal stratification (self-management, end of the division of labour). At this stage in Marx's development it seems clear that his view of the potential of socialism is considerably influenced by Fourier in this respect, although his terminology is somewhat different.[27] The clearest example of Fourier's influence is the notorious passage in the *German Ideology* on the abolition of the division of labour. Then 'nobody has one exclusive sphere of activity but each can become accomplished in any branch he wishes, society regulates the general production and thus makes it possible for me to do one thing today and another tomorrow, to hunt in the morning, fish in the afternoon, rear cattle in the evening, criticize after dinner, just as I have a mind, without ever becoming hunter, fisherman, shepherd, or critic'.[28]

This illustration maps pretty well the sort of working days Fourier outlined in his utopian scheme.[29] The pastoralism may well be ironical, since Marx had already, in the *1844 Manuscripts*, criticized Fourier for taking agricultural work as exemplary.[30] What is not ironical, apparently, is the general idea of such a solution to the division of labour. Yet one is struck by the fact that one does not overcome the present fragmentation of production by collating a heap of fragments.[31]

At all events, with the rejection of such Fourierism and the substitution of a relativized problem of continuing engagement with the imperatives of labour, the question of the relationship between free activity and material production becomes open. There are three possible solutions, each of which Marx toys with at some time. There is no space here to study in detail the ambivalence, and apparent contradictions, on the question in Marx's later writings. All we can do is to give some indication that he grapples with the problem.

The first alternative we have already seen, namely, the acknowledgement of the permanence of the realm of necessity, the distinction from this of the realm of freedom, and hence the view that labour remains man's curse. All one can hope for is the possible abolition of labour through total automation (a tendency anticipated by Marx in his *Grundrisse*).[32] The second alternative is to return unblushingly to the original perspective. This we find in one of Marx's last works, the critique of the Gotha programme, in which his vision of 'a higher phase of communist society' includes, besides the abolition of the division of labour, the remarkable claim that labour becomes 'life's prime want'![33] This seems to return us to Fourier. For Fourier, productive labour is a natural and spontaneous need; given a suitable social structure it becomes identical with self-enjoyment.

The third solution would refuse such an identity, but refuse also the unmediated opposition of self-activity and material production. It would be an attempt to try for a dialectical interpretation of freedom and necessity.[34] This idea can be found in Marx, when he goes for a middle way between Smith and Fourier, in his *Grundrisse*. Marx argues that because Smith has in mind only capitalist forms of employment he counterposes labour to freedom and happiness. In trying to envisage an alternative conception Marx first argues that an individual in his normal state of health *needs* to work; he then argues that this does not mean that such work is to be 'mere fun, mere amusement, as Fourier with *grisette*-like naïvety conceives it'; for 'really free working, e.g. composing,' is a serious business requiring 'intense exertion'. The key thing that brings it within the realm of freedom is when the aims that impose this discipline are not imposed from without but are posited by the individual himself.

In such a context, overcoming obstacles 'is in itself a liberating activity'[35] (a very Hegelian idea).

'Real economy', Marx declares, 'consists of the saving of labour time'. This of course depends on 'the development of the productive forces.' However, the free time won is in truth 'time for the full development of the individual, which in turn reacts back upon the productive power of labour as itself the greatest productive power'.[36] Given this, we cannot accept an abstract antithesis between 'direct labour time and free time'. This is an illusion grounded in 'the perspective of bourgeois economy'. Marx underlines Fourier's contribution in shifting the attention of socialists from questions of distribution to that of the mode of production; but he reasserts that 'labour cannot become play, as Fourier would like'.[37] Yet, because free time allows for 'higher activity' we get a different kind of subject entering production, an educated worker. In work Marx sees three aspects: the 'discipline' involved in the process of becoming human; the creative use of acquired knowledge and power; and even 'in so far as labour requires practical use of the hands and free bodily movement, as in agriculture, at the same time exercise'.[38]

The solution suggested in such passages to the supposed antithesis between free activity and materially determined production presupposes the whole ontology inaugurated (if not completed) in the *1844 Manuscripts*. Once the socially constituted unity in difference of man with nature is thought through, such an abstract antithesis must be rejected; even if, from the perspective of the existing estranged relationships, it seems all too plausible. Free activity (like alienated activity in fact) is constituted socially. Society in turn is constituted on the basis of material production. There is therefore a relationship between free activity and material production which it is the task of historical materialism to elucidate. As we have seen, this relationship is not simply *quantitative*, where free time depends on the shortening of the working day, although this is certainly important and rests on the potential of the productive forces available. It is also a matter of a growing mediatedness of the two sides such that the material practice through which man actualizes himself is a *unified* process which, though conditioned by existing wants and productive powers, also realizes both in itself, and in its grounding of other practices, human creativity and liberation. This process is open-ended in that new goals, new obstacles, and new powers, spring from it.

Freedom is not something given, it is won and re-won in the dialectic of history.

Summary

Marx's theory of alienation is not simply a materialist transformation of Hegel. None the less, the unity of man and nature is insufficiently problematized in 1844. Hence, the abolition of private property is identified with the abolition of 'labour' and the transition to free activity. Later, Marx recognizes that productive activity, even in socialism, is a labour caught up in the dialectic of freedom and necessity.

Appendix

Problems of Interpretation

In order to show the sheer difficulty of *reading* the text of 1844 (towards the overcoming of which these labours are directed), let us take as a case study a single passage and see how four different commentators respond to it. This passage is of peculiar importance because it is from the beginning of the section on 'estranged labour' in the first manuscript, that is to say, the place where Marx first introduces the idea of alienation. Marx writes:

> Labour produces not only commodities: it produces itself and the worker as a *commodity* . . . This fact simply means that the object that labour produces, its product, confronts it as *something alien*, as a *power* independent of the producer. The product of labour is labour embodied and made material in an object; it is the *objectification* of labour. The realization of labour is its objectification. Under these economic conditions this realization of labour appears as loss of reality for the workers, objectification as *loss of, and bondage to, the object*, appropriation as *estrangement*, as *alienation* . . . So much does the appropriation of the object appear as estrangement that the more objects the worker produces the less he can possess and the more he falls under the sway of his product, capital. All these consequences flow from a situation characterized by this: that the worker is related to the *product of his labour* as to an *alien* object.[39]

Ignorant writers, not worthy of particular notice, take 'objectification' here to carry a negative load, to be nothing but a synonym for alienation. They do this without knowing any Hegel. Yet even a sophisticated scholar like Pierre Naville tends to the same mistaken identification when he says that what we have here is a philosophical account borrowed from Hegel of the equation of objectification and alienation. He qualifies this merely by granting that Marx is anxious to give the idea 'a practical basis'.[40]

Lukács, by contrast, says of exactly the same passage that, while Hegel is not mentioned by name, 'even a cursory glance' reveals that these remarks amount to 'a fundamental critique of Hegel's philosophy'. This is because estrangement is sharply distinguished here from objectification in the act of labour.[41]

Erich Fromm equates the passage with one from *Capital*.[42] This arouses the ire of Ernest Mandel, who objects that 'Fromm does not notice that in the former what is being discussed is labour and the products of labour *in general*, whereas the latter begins with these very words: "Within the capitalist system . . .".'[43] Mandel avers that the passage in question does not seek the origin of alienated labour 'in a *specific* form of human society, but in *human nature* itself'.[44]

Mandel's reading is clearly wrong. The references to commodities and capital are clear enough. Furthermore, Marx cannot believe that alienated labour is rooted in human nature itself because the sequence of oppositions between objectification and loss of the object, etc. shows he is aware that specific economic conditions are responsible when appropriation appears as alienation. One reason why Mandel is led astray is that, as was explained in chapter 1, Marx uses 'labour' in his early writings in the same sense as does political economy, namely as productive activity formed by the present economic conditions, not as the more general notion Mandel takes it to be. Unlike political economy, Marx does *not* take such labour to be inherent in human nature. Hence he can look forward to the practical abolition of alienation.

11

The Continuing Importance of 1844

Introduction

It was in 1844 that Marx first embarked on 'the critique of political economy'; it was a task he never really completed. The only substantial result of his labours that he himself saw published was the first volume of *Capital* in 1867. A question arises immediately. If it took Marx 23 years' work before he could present the core of his findings in published form, of what value are the unpublished studies of 1844? The controversy about the 'young' and 'mature' Marx is well known. It is beyond the scope of this work to trace the development of Marx's thought throughout his entire opus, although some brief indications have been given earlier; the attempt here is solely to clarify the ideas of 1844. None the less, it is necessary to say something, however brief, in order to indicate the continuing importance of this turning point.

1844 and 1867

It must be conceded at the outset that there is no trace in the *1844 Manuscripts* of the specific concepts Marx employs in his subsequent scientific account of the capitalist economy. Most importantly, he has no adequate account of the capital relation and hence no theory of surplus value. The concept of alienation evidently embraces this; but Marx lacked the resources to spell out the more concrete determinations required.

Let us see how one or two sympathetic commentators deal with this issue. Allen Wood finds that Marx's mature theory 'does not assign to alienation the basic explanatory role projected for it in the early fragment'. Nevertheless, Wood also believes that 'Marx does not simply abandon the concept of alienation in his mature writings'. The position is that in the later works it is no longer explanatory but 'descriptive or diagnostic'.[1] It describes the effects of the existing mode of production rather than accounts for them; rather as a doctor might diagnose fever without yet having discovered the bacterium responsible.

On this view, then, we could say that in 1844 Marx goes as far as problematizing the private property relationship, but not explaining it. In spite of his claim to have explained the findings of the political economists to them, he merely accepts their results (the labour theory of value, the conflicts over distribution) and then draws attention to the paradox that everything is traced to labour, yet labour gets nothing and private property everything. But the private property relationship must be examined *in itself* to show not just that philosophical critique demands a resolution but that the real nature of the object itself is driving towards it.

Marx has grasped the elevation of capital to a pure form abstracted from content but he has not yet discovered the dynamic of the form itself and the way it really sustains itself on the basis of surplus labour. Capitalism as an ontologically distinct finite system of self-determination is not produced. He has not shown *how* the capital relation is reproduced. He cannot therefore *prove* that the private property relation is a dynamic contradictory one producing its own grave diggers. In 1867 we get a scientific account of the *inner nature*, as opposed to the *phenomenal results*, of the relation earlier problematized. Nevertheless, when his development of the theory of capitalist production is successful, we may argue, this does not mean a rejection of his early work, rather its adequate founding; the intuitions become solid arguments; the 'choreography' gets its infilling.

In my opinion there is more to the *1844 Manuscripts* than this. While the view outlined above would justify paying attention to the *1844 Manuscripts*, it does not give it an essential role, not just in posing problems, but in founding Marx's new science.

Alex Callinicos suggests that such a role may be elucidated by recourse to the distinction made by Popper and his followers between scientific and metaphysical propositions. According to this view, philosophical theories are metaphysical because they can never be conclusively tested, and attempts to establish their truth involve some *a priori* procedure. Metaphysical propositions may, nevertheless, serve a heuristic function in a scientific research programme. 'In so far as the hypotheses they generate are confirmed or refuted, such metaphysical statements may themselves be regarded as verifiable or falsifiable . . . .'.[2]

According to Callinicos, the *1844 Manuscripts* contain such a metaphysical theory (of man as a producer, and the analysis of estranged labour). This theory is not empirical but none the less inspires some of Marx's assumptions. 'For example, there can be no doubt that it partially motivated Marx's choice of social labour, rather than utility, as the homogeneous factor underlying the variety of commodities placed on the market.'[3] However, Callinicos hastens to add that 'the *truth* of the labour theory of value cannot be derived from the truth of Marx's theory of human nature, since the latter is treated as a metaphysical theory which can be neither confirmed nor refuted by experience; rather it depends upon the falsifiable empirical hypotheses derived from it'.[4]

Callinicos is right to say that Marx's philosophy of man should not be vindicated on *a priori* argument but on the success of the research programme it inspires. However, to label it 'metaphysical' simply expresses a certain narrow epistemological prejudice. What we are discussing are the ontological commitments implicit in any science. It is how things are that determines how they are known and not the other way around.

It is impossible to show here in detail how chapter after chapter of *Capital* can be understood as a further concretization of the ideas of 1844. What can be asserted in particular is that the thrust of *Capital* as a *critique* of political economy is made possible by the ontological framework established in 1844 and somewhat modified later in the manner discussed in chapter 10.[5] The movement of history is there understood as the outcome of the transformation of the man–nature relationship. In this way the concept of 'mode of production' is made possible.

On the basis of this ontological priority accorded to productive activity all modes of production and associated forms of social organization are opened to radical critique.[6] It is the interplay in Marx's theory between the permanent moment of mediated unity of man and nature, and the historically specific social forms this takes, that allows critical space for the diagnosis of the self-supersession of a given form. Certainly, in order to unmask the fetishized 'naturalness' of capitalist relations of production such an ontological framework is required. The critique of political economy requires a double movement. First the recognition that, as private property, labour-power and capital are estranged, each recalcitrant to appropriation by the other. This can be grasped only when the estranged forms are distinguished from the underlying man–nature unity. Then in turn the secondary mediations, exchange, wages, profit, can be represented as alien mediators reproducing rather than cancelling the estranged relationship. This critical understanding of the social form in which the man–nature dialectic is now worked out is possible only if alienated labour is grasped both in its non-identity with the primary mediation and also as the historically specific form taken by this underlying content considered as ontologically basic. The historical conditions of alienation can become the object of analysis only if they are situated in relation to that mediated unity which, in so far as it is *mediated*, allows for this alienation, and which in so far as it is a *unity*, allows a correct understanding of the existing system of social reproduction based on 'labour' (under the sign of private property) as an alien mediator.

The phenomena of estrangement must be understood in terms of the way in which the fundamental mediated unity of man and nature gives rise through specific historical processes to particular alienated forms of such mediation.

The form of value, for example, as Marx points out in his well-known letter to Kugelmann, must in some way enshrine, albeit in mystified form, the process of objectification and material reproduction.[7] It is not necessary to know this in order to adhere to a labour theory of value. This was possible for Smith and Ricardo. But it *is* necessary if the value-form of the product of labour is to become an object of criticism instead of being illegitimately naturalized, as it was in classical political economy which identified the two levels of mediation. At the same time, the labour theory of value cannot be articulated sufficiently on the basis of the ontological premises alone. To articulate correctly the forms of appearance of the content is no easy task. Marx had to expend enormous effort in working out the dialectic of the value-form itself, in solving the secret of surplus value and in disentangling the essence of the capital relation from its mystifying forms of appearance (interest, profit etc.). But it is only when the capital relation is conceived as a specific social form of material reproduction that the essential relation can be distinguished from the fetishized forms.

Although the failure of bourgeois economics may be explained politically, its intellectual limitations come down to its conflation of different levels of mediation, and its methodological individualism, that is to say, its failure to grasp the nature of social being: its weakness is in its ontology. Conversely, Marx's *Capital* is inconceivable without its ontological underpinning, and that was first opened up in the *1844 Manuscripts*.

We may say that anyone who fails to see the relevance of the *1844 Manuscripts* to *Capital* has simply not understood *Capital* itself. Some corroboration of this is that Althusser's theoretical anti-humanism is driven into a bizarre idealism of the structure, which treats particular individuals merely as bearers of its relations, in the same way as Hegel's 'concept' (*quelle horreur!*). In this way, far from providing a critique of reification, theoretical anti-humanism capitulates to it. But, to borrow Marx and Engels' words, structure 'fights no fight'; 'it is real living man who fights'.⁸ In proletarian revolution the workers precisely refuse to be bearers of the commodity labour-power any longer.

In comprehending such transformations the importance of an ontological framework against which to measure the shifting historical forms is clear. Otherwise critique would be reduced to contesting the validity of the existing order from the standpoint of a historically contingent utopian aspiration. By contrast, Marx's critique acquires a rootedness in material reality whereby it can ground the historical necessity of existing forms, while yet grasping their limits and the conditions of their supersession.

The Standpoint of Labour

Both in the *1844 Manuscripts* and *Capital* it is clear that the political location of Marx's critique is that of the proletariat.⁹ It is important to recognize that this is not a matter of a sympathetic identification with their problems. It flows from the identification of labour as the key social mediator. Furthermore, simply to say that Marx takes the standpoint of labour is inadequate. It has to be said also that Marx takes the *critically* adopted standpoint of labour, and that this is a matter not of mere partiality but of the place of labour in the social totality.

We have shown that, already in 1844, the standpoint of practical criticism is not man in general, but 'labour', that is to say, a definite pole of the system of estrangement. This is a political as well as a philosophical advance over Feuerbach's humanism because Marx explicitly links it to class-political communism, not just to the question of human essence. Significantly, the very first sentence of the *1844 Manuscripts* reads: 'Wages are determined through the hostile struggle between capitalist and worker.'¹⁰ The identification of the proletariat as the class of the future is no longer based on its universal suffering but on its strategic position in the economic order. However, in order to go beyond his sources in political economy, Marx has to unmask their identification of productive activity with wage-labour, and to grasp 'labour' as an estranged and alienating mediator falsely absolutized by Smith, and modelled in idealist philosophy by Hegel.

Hence the importance of characterizing Marx's position as that of the *critically* adopted standpoint of labour. At the same time this implies that Marx cannot be satisfied with a call for higher wages, or better conditions, in this way expressing the standpoint of labour against capital *within* the private property system. Because he grasps such 'labour' as a transient historical form of the productive activity that underpins the whole, he can envisage the proletariat abolishing itself *as* proletariat in the communist revolution.

Moreover, for Marx, such a revolution is to be no mere juridical rearrangement realizing 'justice', nor a narrowly economic matter of efficient allocation of resources to meet basic needs. It is a question of a fundamental transformation of social being, hence of individuals, their activity and their essential relations. It is a question of what socialism is all about – the emergence of a truly human society. The later scientific achievements, and the orientation to problems of political organization, never obliterated Marx's commitment to the profound insights of 1844.

Appendix

Problems of Translation

Entäusserung (and Entfremdung)

According to Lukács there is nothing novel about these terms: they are simply German translations of the English word 'alienation'. 'Alienation' itself, he points out, was used in political theory to refer to the renunciation of natural liberty implicit in the social contract. He says that *Entäusserung* was first used in philosophy by Fichte.[1]

We translate *Entfremdung* by 'estrangement' (but *fremd* as 'alien'), and *Entäusserung* nearly always by 'alienation'. As a matter of fact *Entäusserung* is a rather unusual German word. An illustration of this is that *Cassell's Dictionary* (12th ed., 1968) does not give it in the English section as an equivalent for those English words given under the entry for *Entäusserung* in the German section, preferring a more usual form, namely *Veräusserung*. Possible translations of *Entäusserung* include 'alienation', 'renunciation', 'parting with', 'relinquishment', 'externalization', 'divestiture', 'surrender'. Where alienation of property is concerned one can use *Entäusserung* but not *Entfremdung*, the latter is restricted to cases of interpersonal estrangement. There is indeed no reason not to use 'estrangement' to render *Entfremdung*, thus leaving 'alienation' free to render *Entäusserung*.

The closest translation of *Entäusserung* from a purely etymological point of view is 'externalization'. It is the usual choice of Miller in his translation of Hegel's *Phenomenology of Spirit*. The root '*äusserung*' means manifestation (from *äusser* – 'outer') and the prefix '*Ent*' indicates establishment of or entry into a new state or relinquishment of an old state; thus, in combination, the sense is that something is manifested in such a way as to change its state. Whereas *Veräusserung* – a more common equivalent of alienation, especially when it just means 'sale' – is a fairly neutral word, it is clear that Marx means *Entäusserung* to have a negative connotation.

The sense of relinquishment comes out strongly when Marx contrasts the root and its modification in connection with life: he says of private property that in it man's 'expression of life [*Lebensäusserung*] is his alienation/loss of life [*Lebensentäusserung*]'.[2] In other places Marx contrasts similarly '*Ver*' forms with '*Ent*' forms: 'In these economic conditions this realization [*Verwirklichung*] of labour appears as a loss of reality [*Entwirklichung*] for the worker.'[3] Again: 'Hegel conceives objectification [*Vergegenständlichung*] as loss of object [*Entgegenständlichung*].'[4]

Before the investigation in the *1844 Manuscripts* the aspect of alienation that had most impressed Marx was the universalization of market relations with the consequent reification of the human world. He says: 'Selling is the practice of alienation' ('*Die Veräusserung ist die Praxis der Entäusserung*'). This is because man can 'produce objects only by making his products and his activity subordinate to an alien substance and giving them the significance of an alien substance – money'.[5] Because Marx carefully distinguishes between *Vergegenständlichung* ('objectification') and *Entäusserung*, to translate the latter as 'externalization' creates a risk of confusion.

The question arises as to whether *Entfremdung* and *Entäusserung* are one concept or two. As we have already explained, *Entfremdung* is of narrower application, in that it could not be used with reference to transfer of property. Furthermore, it seems to have a less *active* connotation than *Entäusserung*. With Hegel's *Phenomenology* it is tempting to suggest that *Entfremdung* stands to *Entäusserung* as phenomenological *result* to the active *process* of spirit's positing of itself in otherness. This would conform with Marx's gloss: '*Entfremdung* . . . constitutes the real interest of this *Entäusserung*'.[6] Clearly this is not meant as a tautology, so Marx must be observing *some* distinction in Hegel. Richard Schacht[7] makes this point in criticism of T.B. Bottomore, who usually translates both terms as 'alienation' on the grounds that 'Marx (unlike Hegel) does not make a systematic distinction between them'.[8] But, since Marx is here referring precisely to *Hegel*, it is still possible that Bottomore is right. However, in order not to prejudge the question, they should certainly be distinguished in English translation.

As I explain in the text, Hegel finds something 'positive' in *Entäusserung*: this could hardly be so with *Entfremdung*, which is precisely the negative aspect of the movement. Probably Marx uses *Entäusserung* when he has in mind that man *loses* something of himself through alienation, and *Entfremdung* to mark its appearance as something *other* than himself.

As far as my own commentary is concerned, I use both 'estrangement' and 'alienation', not only for stylistic variation, but sometimes also to indicate a distinction between a state (estrangement) and a process (alienation).

APPENDIX

A table of translations of *Entfremdung* and *Entäusserung* in Marx's *1844 Manuscripts* and Hegel's *Phenomenology* is given below.

Marx's 1844 Manuscripts

M. Milligan: *Economic and Philosophical Manuscripts of 1844*, Moscow 1960, and also, revised by D. Struik, in *Marx-Engels Collected Works Volume 3*, London 1975.
Entfremdung = estrangement
Entäusserung = alienation (or externalization)

T.B. Bottomore: *Karl Marx Early Writings*, London, 1963.
Entfremdung and *Entäusserung* = alienation (or estrangement)

L.D. Easton and *Writings of the Young Marx*, New York, 1967.
K. H. Guddat: *Entfremdung* = alienation
Entäusserung = externalization

G. Benton: *Karl Marx Early Writings*, Harmondsworth, 1974.
Entfremdung = estrangement
Entäusserung = alienation (or externalization)

D. McLellan: *Karl Marx Early Texts*, Oxford, 1971.
Entfremdung = alienation
Entäusserung = externalization

Hegel's Phenomenology

A.V. Miller: *Hegel's Phenomenology of Spirit*, Oxford, 1977.
Entfremdung = alienation
Entäusserung = externalization. Miller warns that he 'departs from a rigid consistency in rendering . . . ' This is so: he has 'externalization' for *Entäusserung* in para. 804, but in para. 805 he has 'alienation', while in para. 806 he switches back.

J.B. Baillie: *Hegel's Phenomenology of Mind*, London, revised 2nd ed., 1949.
Entfremdung = estrangement
Entäusserung = various, he often resorts to a bracketed alternative, e.g. 'relinquishes (externalizes)'. (He also gives as an alternative to 'unhappy consciousness' the phrase 'alienated soul', which does not appear in the German (p. 251).)

Das Moment (moment)

This term of art Hegel generalizes from mechanics. With reference to the resultant force exerted by a lever, weight and the distance from the point of application, are called its moments. It is clear from this that it has nothing to do with a moment in time. In German Hegel can distinguish between *das Moment* (as an aspect of a dialectically structured whole or process) and *der Moment* (of time).

Aufheben

Hegel tells us in his *Science of Logic* that '*aufheben*' is one of the most important notions in philosophy. He says that it is not a question of reducing something to nothingness but of disposing of it as a result of mediation. He points out that in ordinary language *aufheben* means both 'to abolish' and 'to preserve' and that he intends to take advantage of this double meaning.[9]

According to W.T. Harris 'reduce to a moment' is the 'exact signification' of *aufheben* (although he uses 'cancel' himself).[10] In some ways this would be a good translation were it not for the implication of elevation in the term. I use 'supersede' when the stress is more on abolition, and when the stress is on preservation I use the slightly 'technical' term 'sublate', which was the choice of the *Logic*'s early translator J.H. Stirling (*The Secret of Hegel*). The dictionary definition of 'sublate' is 'to resolve in a higher unity'.

Der Mensch

Although this refers to human beings in general it is standardly translated as 'man'. But German also has '*der Mann*' where the male of the species is meant. Unfortunately, because English uses 'human' as an adjective it is not available as a noun. I have therefore followed standard practice in using 'man' as a generic both in the quotations and my own commentary. However, it should be noted that Marx's German is not as sexist as English translations make it appear. Where Marx discusses the relationship of man to woman each term is employed in its separate sense. Thus: 'The relation of *Mannes* to woman is the most natural relation of *Menschen* to *Menschen*.'[11]

Setzen (posit)

'To posit' is to put in place, set up, or establish. In an intellectual context it refers to the assertion or proof of some truth. However, Hegel and Marx use it in wider contexts, wherever something is brought into a specific place or relation. Thus the antithesis of property and propertylessness is 'posited by private property itself' when there is a real causal relationship between them – that one has property just because the other has not.[12]

Notes

Abbreviations

The following abbreviations are used in the notes. Further details of the works thus cited can be found in the bibliography. Throughout the notes a date in brackets is that of original publication; then follow details of the edition or translation consulted.

Marx and Engels

C.1 (Penguin)	Karl Marx, *Capital Volume 1*, Harmondsworth, 1976.
C.1 (Moscow)	Karl Marx *Capital Volume 1*, Moscow, 1961.
C.3 (Penguin)	Karl Marx, *Capital Volume 3*, Harmondsworth, 1981.
C.3 (Moscow)	Karl Marx, *Capital Volume 3*, Moscow, 1962.
C.W.	Karl Marx and Frederick Engels, *Collected Works*, London, 1975–.
E.W.	Karl Marx, *Early Writings*, Harmondsworth, 1975.
M.E.S.W.	Karl Marx and Frederick Engels, *Selected Works* (in one volume), New York, 1968.
New MEGA	Karl Marx and Friedrich Engels, *Gesamtausgabe*, Berlin, 1976–.
Werke Eb.	Karl Marx and Friedrich Engels, *Werke, Ergänzungsband, Schriften bis 1844, Erster Teil*, Berlin, 1968.

Hegel

G.W.9	G.W.F. Hegel *Phänomenologie des Geistes, Gesammelte Werke Band 9*, Hamburg, 1980.
P.R.	*Grundlinien der Philosophie des Rechts*, ed. J. Hoffmeister, Hamburg, 1955; *Hegel's Philosophy of Right*, trans. T.M. Knox, Oxford, 1965.

Feuerbach

F.B.	*The Fiery Brook – selected writings of Ludwig Feuerbach*, trans. Z. Hanfi, Garden City, NY, 1972.
K.S.II	Ludwig Feuerbach, *Kleinere Schriften II (1839–46), Gesammelte Werke Band 9*, Berlin, 1982.

S.W.2	Ludwig Feuerbach, *Sämtliche Werke Zweiter Band*, Stuttgart-Bad Cannstatt, 1959.

Lukács

Werke 8	Georg Lukács, *Der Junge Hegel*, *Werke Band 8*, Neuweid and Berlin, 1967.

Introduction

1 V.1. Lenin, 'The three sources and component parts of Marxism' (1913), in *Selected Works*, London, 1969, p. 20. This idea is not original to Lenin. Indeed, a tripartite division of this sort was elaborated as early as 1840 by M. Hess. In *Die europäische Triarchie* he said England would produce a revolutionary combination of German theory and French practice. Engels, in an article of 1846, puts in the mouths of the so-called 'true socialists' the following: 'Did we not assign to the Germans the sphere of theory, to the French that of politics, and to the English that of civil society?' *C.W.6*, 3.
2 Pierre Naville rightly points out that the matter is somewhat complex because the sources are already 'mixed' (*De L'Aliénation à la Jouissance*, Paris, 1957, p. 11); just one example: Marx could read political economy in Hegel through Hegel's own appropriation of it.
3 David McLellan, in *Marx Before Marxism*, London, 1970, says these elements appear in the Paris manuscripts 'together, if not yet united' (p. 206). I hope to show that there is more unity than is apparent.
4 *1844 Mss*: *C.W.3*,297; *Werke Eb.*,537.
5 'A synthesis *in statu nascendi*' says István Mészáro, *Marx's Theory of Alienation*, London, 1970, p. 15.

1: Alienated Labour

1 I use 'ontology' to indicate that set of fundamental categories through which the character of the social sphere is delimited and the general framework for theory construction established. I do *not* mean that *a priori* arguments establish the necessity of these categories, but I think that every research programme presupposes a commitment to some ontology. For Marx's ontology see Georg Lukács, *Ontology of Social Being: Marx* (1972), trans. D. Fernbach, London 1978; Carol C. Gould, *Marx's Social Ontology*, Cambridge, Mass., London, 1978; Scott Meikle, *Essentialism in the Thought of Karl Marx*, London, 1985.
2 I deliberately choose this phrase rather than 'labour' because the latter is open to some ambiguity of interpretation, as will be seen later in this chapter.
3 *Werke Eb.*, 512; *C.W.3*, 273; *E.W.*, 325.
4 *Werke Eb.*, 516; *C.W.3*, 276; *E.W.*, 328.
5 *Werke Eb.*, 517; *C.W.3*, 277; *E.W.*, 329.
6 *C.W.5*, 40.
7 *Werke Eb.*, 546; *C.W.3*, 306.
8 *Werke Eb.*, 541; *C.W.3*, 301.
9 *Werke Eb.*, 512–14; *C.W.3*, 272–4; *E.W.*, 322–6.

10 *Werke Eb.*, 515; *C.W.3*, 275.
11 *Werke Eb.*, 511–12; *C.W.3*, 272; *E.W.*, 324.
12 *Werke Eb.*, 514–15; *C.W.3*, 274–5.
13 *Werke Eb.*, 517; *C.W.3*, 277; *E.W.*, 329.
14 One should not be disturbed by Marx's borrowing the term 'species being' (*Gattungswesen*) from Feuerbach. The content is different (see Part Three below).
15 *Werke Eb.*, 515; *C.W.3*, 275; *E.W.*, 327.
16 *Werke Eb.*, 516; *C.W.3*, 276; *E.W.*, 328.
17 *Werke Eb.*, 516–17; *C.W.3*, 276–7; *E.W.*, 328–9.
18 *Werke Eb.*, 517; *C.W.3*, 277; *E.W.*, 329.
19 *Werke Eb.*, 520–1; *C.W.3*, 280; *E.W.*, 332.
20 *Werke Eb.*, 517–18; *C.W.3*, 277–8.
21 *Werke Eb.*, 546–7; *C.W.3*, 306; *E.W.*, 359. Hegel already explained that in bourgeois society 'the system of needs' multiplies indefinitely. He observes that 'the need for greater comfort . . . is suggested to you by those who hope to make a profit from its creation': *P.R.* (Knox), p. 269.
22 *Werke Eb.*, 547; *C.W.3*, 307.
23 *Werke Eb.*, 540; *C.W.3*, 300. But it is wrong to speak of Marx's 'producer's morality' (Eugene Kamenka, *The Ethical Foundations of Marxism*, London, 1962, p. 149) for he also values here 'human use'.
24 *Werke Eb*, 565–7; *C.W.3*, 325–6.
25 See S.S. Prawer, *Karl Marx and World Literature*, Oxford, 1976, pp. 76–85.
26 XLI – XLIII: *New MEGA I,2*, 318–22; *Werke Eb.*, 563–4; *C.W.3*, 323–4.
27 István Mészáros, *Marx's Theory of Alienation*, London, 1970, p. 79.
28 'Comment on James Mill' (1844): *Werke Eb.*, 446; *C.W.3*, 312. Also: 'It is not the *unity* of living and active humanity with the natural inorganic conditions of their metabolic exchange with nature, and hence their appropriation of nature, which requires explanation or is the result of a historic process, but rather the *separation* between these inorganic conditions of human existence and this active existence, a separation which is completely posited only in the relation of wage labour and capital.' (Marx, *Grundrisse*, trans. M. Nicolaus, Harmondsworth, 1973, p. 489).
29 *Werke Band 23, Das Kapital*, Berlin, 1962, p. 192; *C.1* (Penguin), 283; *C.1* (Moscow), 177.
30 *C.3* (Penguin), 964; *C.3* (Moscow), 804.
31 Georg Lukács: 'In seinem oekonomischen Betrachtungen zieht Marx an der Hand der Tatsachen des wirklichen Lebens scharf dis Grenze zwischen Vergegenständ-lichung in der Arbeit an sich und Entfremdung von Subjekt und Objekt in der *kapitalistischen Form* der Arbeit.' *Werke 8*, 674; also *The Young Hegel*, trans. Rodney Livingstone, London 1975, pp. 551–2.
32 'The foundations of historical materialism' (1932), quoted from Herbert Marcuse, *From Luther to Popper*, essays trans. Joris de Bres, London, 1983, p. 13; *Reason and Revolution* (1941), 2nd ed. London, 1954, p. 277. To cite a more recent account: Paul Walton and Andrew Gamble, in their book *From Alienation to Surplus Value*, London, 1972, put forward the view that Marx's 'ontological position' is grounded in 'the dialectics of labour' and they quote freely from all periods of Marx's work to establish this without noting any problems about the early terminology.
33 T.I. Oizerman, *The Making of the Marxist Philosophy* (1977), English trans., Moscow, 1981, p. 230.
34 Raya Dunayevskaya, *Marxism and Freedom*, New York, 1958, p. 61.

35 Erich Fromm *Marx's Concept of Man* (1961), New York, 1971, p. 40. Despite the fact that this book appears under Fromm's name, it consists mostly of Bottomore's translation of Marx's *1844 Mss*; Fromm's Preface attempts to popularize Marx by characterizing him as an 'existentialist' and a 'Zen Buddhist'.
36 Robert C. Tucker, *Philosophy and Myth in Karl Marx*, Cambridge, 1961 p. 134.
37 Mészáros, *Theory of Alienation*, p. 78.
38 Article on 'praxis' in *A Dictionary of Marxist Thought*, ed. T.B. Bottomore, Oxford, 1983, p. 386.
39 *Werke Eb.*, 471; *C.W.3*, 235.
40 *Werke Eb.*, 476; *C.W.3*, 240; *E.W.*, 288.
41 *Werke Eb.*, 477; *C.W.3*, 241; *E.W.*, 289.
42 *Werke Eb.*, 513; *C.W.3*, 273.
43 'Wir haben den Akt der Entfremdung der praktischen menslichen Tätigkeit, die Arbeit . . . ': *Werke Eb.*, 515; *C.W.3*, 275; *E.W.*, 327 gives a misleading translation of this sentence.
44 *Werke Eb.*, 515; *C.W.3*, 275.
45 *Werke Eb.*, 524; *C.W.3*, 285; *E.W.*, 336.
46 *Werke Eb.*, 542–3; *C.W.3*, 302–3.
47 *Werke Eb.*, 557; *C.W.3*, 317; *E.W.*, 369.
48 *C.W.5*, 46.
49 Ibid., 52.
50 Ibid., 77, 80, 87, 88, 205.
51 Ibid., 87.
52 *Werke Eb.*, 468; *C.W.3*, 232; Marx also gives credit to W. Weitling and to Engels.
53 Quoted from David McLellan, *The Young Hegelians and Karl Marx*, London, 1969, pp. 148–9.
54 Marcuse, *Reason and Revolution*, p. 293. For '*Aufhebung*', see Appendix.
55 Oizerman, *Making of the Marxist Philosophy*, p. 392.
56 The editors of the current English edition of the *Collected Works* simply ignore the problem and write in their Preface: 'Labour will be transformed from an activity people perform under compulsion into genuine self-activity of free people.' *C.W.5*, xxii.
57 *C.1* (Penguin), 126 n.4; *Das Kapital*, p. 50 n.4.
58 *C.1* (Penguin), 138 n.16; *Das Kapital*, pp. 61–2, n.16.

2: Private Property

1 *Werke Eb.*, 520; *C.W.3*, 279–80; *E.W.*, 331–2.
2 Dirk Struik, in the introduction to his edition of the *1844 Mss* (*The Economic and Philosophic Manuscripts of 1844*, New York, 1964), states: 'But the whole tenor leads to Marx's conclusion of the priority of property' (p. 45). In a private communication he says that this was a slip. The text meant is 'the priority of alienated labour'.
3 *Werke Eb.*, 521; *C.W.3*, 281; *E.W.*, 333.
4 *Werke Eb.*, 512; *C.W.3*, 272; *E.W.*, 324.
5 *Werke Eb.*, 520; *C.W.3*, 280; *E.W.*, 332. Proudhon in *What is Property?* (1841) says 'Property is Theft'.
6 *Werke Eb.*, 523; *C.W.3*, 283; *E.W.*, 335.
7 *Werke Eb.*, 484, 529; *C.W.3*, 247, 289; *E.W.*, 295, 341. See Adam Smith, *The Wealth of Nations* (1776), ed. E. Cannan, Chicago, 1976, vol. 1, p. 351.

8. *Werke Eb.*, 505; *C.W.3*, 266; *E.W.*, 318.
9. *Werke Eb.*, 506; *C.W.3*, 267; *E.W.*, 319.
10. *Werke Eb.*, 484; *C.W.3*, 247; *E.W.*, 295.
11. *Werke Eb.*, 506; *C.W.3*, 266; *E.W.*, 318.
12. 'We have forgotten . . . that cash-payment is not the sole relationship of human beings . . . ' Thomas Carlyle, *Past and Present*, London, 1843, p. 198. This passage is quoted by Engels in his review of *Past and Present* published by A. Ruge and Marx in their *Deutsch-Französische Jahrbücher*, Paris, 1844 (see *C.W.3*, 451). Evidently it was well known to Marx and Engels.
13. *C.W.6*, 487.
14. *Werke Eb.*, 554; *C.W.3*, 314; *E.W.*, 366.
15. *Werke Eb.*, 520; *C.W.3*, 280; *E.W.*, 332.
16. It is not surprising that commentators of an analytical rather than dialectical turn of mind prove unable to comprehend the interchanges of these determinations. The crucial passage is actually misquoted by Richard Schacht, *Alienation*, London, 1971, when he says that Marx 'contends that the dominance of the institution of private property "is the basis and cause of alienated labour", and thus also of the alienation of the product' (p. 108). In a private communication he admits that 'is' should have been *outside* the quotation from Marx. However, he defends his interpretation against the translation provided by Bottomore who gives: 'although private property appears to be the basis and cause of alienated labour, it is rather a consequence of the latter' (Karl Marx, *Early Writings*, trans. T.B. Bottomore, London, 1963, p. 131). The German is: *'wenn das Privateigentum als Grund, als Ursache der entäusserten Arbeit erscheint, es vielmehr eine Konsequenz derselben ist . . . '* Schacht suggests an accurate reading is: 'if private property appears as the ground, the basis of alienated labour, it is much more a consequence . . . ' In his book Schacht has to face the fact that just before the contested paragraph Marx writes: 'Private property is therefore the product, the necessary result, of *alienated labour*, of the external relation of the worker to nature and to himself.' In a footnote (n. 17 on p. 108) Schacht comments on this: 'But here he is thinking of the accumulation of possessions and capital, rather than of the *institution* of private property.' But Marx clearly sees the institution itself as coming to depend upon alienated labour. To view the capital relation as working within a pre-existing institution reifies the living social relation, instead of seeing it as *reproduced* by social practice, as the conditioned rather than the condition.
17. All we have of the second manuscript is pp. 40–3. The first two passages (pp. 1–3) of the third manuscript are further notes by Marx to pp. 36 and 39 of the second manuscript. All these passages are therefore closely related. *Werke Eb.*, 523–33; *C.W.3*, 283–94.
18. *Werke Eb.*, 524–5; *C.W.3*, 285; *E.W.*, 336. NB: 'object of activity' is mistakenly rendered in *E.W.* as 'object of labour'.
19. Bertell Ollman, *Alienation*, Cambridge, 1971, pp. 15, 17.
20. Ibid., pp. 164, 292 n.21.
21. See the introduction to Petry's translation of Hegel's *Philosophy of Nature*, 3 vols, London, 1970, vol. 1, p. 169.
22. G. Rose, *Hegel Contra Sociology*, London, 1981, p. 83. Hegel says that when the will is truly free it 'is released from every tie [*Verhältnis*] of dependence on anything else'. 'Its object is itself and so not an "other" or a barrier to be overcome.' (*P.R.*, para. 22–23). Later he says: 'The moral point of view is that of relation [*Verhältnis*], of ought-to-be [*Sollen*], or demand' (*P.R.*, para. 108).

23 Adelung notes that it is often 'nothing more than the factotum of classroom philosophers, who employ it in the purveyance of turgid and confused concepts' – quoted by Petry, *Philosophy of Nature*, p. 170. Incidentally, in *Das Kapital* Marx speaks of '*das Kapitalverhältnis*' (*Werke Band 23*, p. 604).
24 *Werke Eb.*, 526; *C.W.3*, 286; *E.W.*, 337.
25 *Werke Eb.*, 528–9; *C.W.3*, 288.
26 *Werke Eb.*, 525; *C.W.3*, 285.
27 *Werke Eb.*, 528; *C.W.3*, 288. Reading such lines one can hardly forbear thinking of Hegel's *Phenomenology*, where, in the chapter on 'Self-Estranged Spirit', the struggle of the noble and base consciousness, of enlightenment and superstition, is played out. Marx does not refer here to this material, although he does later on, and his sources are drawn not from the evidence of literature – Hegel uses Diderot's *Rameau's Nephew* – but of economists, jurists and historians.
28 *Werke Eb.*, 533; *C.W.3*, 293; *E.W.*, 344. Marx's discussion, in the Introduction of 1857 to his *Grundrisse*, of labour as 'indifferent' and as 'labour in general' is well known (*Grundrisse*, trans. M. Nicolaus, Harmondsworth, 1973, p. 104); here we see these ideas are present already in his first economic studies.
29 *Werke Eb.*, 533, *C.W.3*, 293; *E.W.*, 344.
30 *Werke Eb.*, 557; *C.W.3*, 317; *E.W.*, 369.
31 *Werke Eb.*, 533; *C.W.3*, 292–4; *E.W.*, 345.
32 *Werke Eb.*, 541, 562–3; *C.W.3*, 301, 322; *E.W.*, 352–3, 375.
33 *Werke Eb.*, 529; *C.W.3*, 289; *E.W.*, 341. This recalls a figure of Hegelian dialectic, whose abstract character is attacked by Marx in *Poverty of Philosophy* (1847), chapter 2, section 1: 'The yes becoming no, the no becoming yes, the yes becoming both yes and no, the no becoming both no and yes . . . '; see *C.W.6*, 164.
34 *Werke Eb.*, 530; *C.W.3, 290; E.W.*, 342.
35 *Werke Eb.*, 530; *C.W.3*, 290; *E.W.*, 341.
36 *Werke Eb.*, 530–1; *C.W.3*, 291.
37 *Werke Eb.*, 531; *C.W.3*, 292.
38 *Werke Eb.*, 520; *C.W.3*, 280; *E.W.*, 332.
39 *Werke Eb.*, 521; *C.W.3*, 280; *E.W.*, 333.
40 *C.W.4*, 35–6.
41 *C.W.4*, 36.

3: Communism

1 *Werke Eb.*, 535; *C.W.3*, 295; *E.W.*, 346.
2 *Werke Eb.*, 563; *C.W.3*, 322; *E.W.*, 375.
3 Ibid. Kostas Axelos, in *Alienation, Praxis and Techné in the Thought of Karl Marx* (1961), London, 1976, objects that Marx's project does not 'get beyond the horizon of appropriation' to 'play' (p. 278).
4 *Werke Eb.*, 536; *C.W.3*, 296; *E.W.*, 348.
5 Ibid.
6 Lloyd Easton and Kurt Guddat in the introduction to their translation of the *1844 Mss* (*Writings of the Young Marx on Philosophy and Society*, Garden City, NY, 1967) are quite wrong to give Proudhon and Fourier as Marx's examples (p. 18). Their names occur in his discussion under a distinctly different heading. It is a particularly gross libel on Fourier to associate him with 'crude communism', as Marx would have known. To what is the reference then? The editors of *C.W.3* (p. 602) draw our

attention to Engels' remarks on the French secret societies in his 1843 article 'Progress of social reform on the Continent' (see *C.W.3*, 396–7). Robert C. Tucker, in *Philosophy and Myth in Karl Marx*, Cambridge, 1961, suggests (pp. 154–5) that the source for Marx's characterization was Lorenz von Stein who coined the phrase 'raw communism' in his treatise *Der Sozialismus und Kommunismus des heutigen Frankreichs* (Leipzig, 1842).
7. *Werke Eb.*, 534; *C.W.3*, 294; *E.W.*, 346.
8. *Werke Eb*, 521, 534; *C.W.3*, 280, 294; *E.W.*, 333, 347.
9. *Werke Eb.*, 536; *C.W.3*, 296; *E.W.*, 347.
10. *Werke Eb.*, 534; *C.W.3*, 294; *E.W.*, 346.
11. *Werke Eb.*, 535; *C.W.3*, 296; *E.W.*, 347.
12. Fourier (1808) *Oeuvres Complètes*, Paris, 1966–8, *Tome I*, pp. 130–3.
13. Marx mentions Fourier on the same page as he discusses 'community of women'; but this (unreferenced) quotation from Fourier on women is used by Marx in *The Holy Family*, written later in the year 1844 in collaboration with Engels and published in 1845 (see *C.W.4*, 196).
14. *Werke Eb.*, 536; *C.W.3*, 296; *E.W.*, 348.
15. *Werke Eb.*, 583; *C.W.3*, 342; *E.W.*, 395.
16. *Werke Eb.*, 536; *C.W.3*, 297; *E.W.*, 348.
17. Ibid.
18. *Werke Eb.*, 546; *C.W.3*, 306; *E.W.*, 358.
19. For example: T.I. Oizerman, *The Making of Marxist Philosophy* (1977), Moscow, 1981, p. 246.
20. A solemn attempt to read 'crude communism' as a 'real phase', with truly bizarre results, is to be found in Tucker, *Philosophy and Myth*, pp. 154–6. Shlomo Avineri in *The Social and Political Thought of Karl Marx*, Cambridge, 1968, pp. 223ff, also takes 'crude communism' as a stage of future society and equates it with 'the first phase of communist society' of Marx's *Critique of the Gotha Programme* (1875) (in *M.E.S.W.*).
21. *Werke Eb.*, 544–6; *C.W.3*, 304–6; *E.W.*, 356–7.
22. *Werke Eb.*, 583; *C.W.3*, 341–2.
23. Erich Fromm, *Marx's Concept of Man*, New York, 1971, pp. 58–9.
24. *New MEGA, II, 1.2*, 392; *Grundrisse*, trans. M. Nicolaus, Harmondsworth, 1973, p. 488.
25. *Werke Eb.*, 521; *C.W.3*, 280.
26. *Werke Eb.*, 520; *C.W.3*, 279.
27. *Werke Eb.*, 522; *C.W.3*, 282.
28. 'Results of the immediate process of production', Ms. 466–7; *C.1* (Penguin), Appendix, p. 990.
29. István Mészáros, *Marx's Theory of Alienation*, London, 1970, p. 17.
30. When Proudhon demands 'equal possessions' he fails to transcend the estranged character of the object; he 'abolishes economic estrangement *within* economic estrangement', says Marx, in *The Holy Family*, (*C.W.4*, 43).
31. As Mészáros observes, p. 64. His *Marx's Theory of Alienation* is the best on the subject.

4: Marx and Hegel

1. *Werke Eb.*, 468; *C.W.3*, 232.

2 *Werke Eb.*, 467; *C.W.3*, 231.
3 *Werke Eb.*, 568; *C.W.3*, 326; *E.W.*, 379.
4 *Werke Eb.*, 468; *C.W.3*, 232. Following Marx's intentions therefore, most editions of the *1844 Manuscripts* bring together at the end the reflections on Hegel.
5 *New MEGA, I, 2*, 275, shows the transition mid-way down p. XI of the notebook. The Hegel material is on XI–XIII, XVII–XVIII, XXII–XXXIV. The Preface is on XXXIX–XL. (*C.W.3*, 602, misprints this as XXIX–XL).
6 *Werke Eb.*, 546; *C.W.3*, 305; *E.W.*, 357. *E.W.* gives 'his self-mediated birth' for '*seiner Geburt durch sich selbst*'; this rendering (and a similar one on the previous page) is over free.
7 *Phenomenology of Spirit*, trans. A.V. Miller, Oxford, 1977, para. 19.
8 *Werke Eb.*, 546; *C.W.3*, 306.
9 *Werke Eb.*, 574; *C.W.3*, 332–3.
10 *Werke Eb.*, 574; *C.W.3*, 333.
11 *Werke Eb.*, 570; *C.W.3*, 329; *E.W.*, 382.

5: Hegel's Phenomenology

1 *Werke Eb.*, 571; *C.W.3*, 329; *E.W.*, 383.
2 Hyppolite puts some stress on it in his *Genesis and Structure of Hegel's 'Phenomenology of Spirit'* (1946), Evanston, 1974. Lukács published his *Young Hegel* in 1948 but he did not know of Hyppolite when he drafted it in 1938, and he was not able to take account of him when publication became possible after the war. In his Preface (1954) to a new edition of his study, Lukács dismisses Hyppolite's reading as 'irrationalist' and says it had not given him cause to rework his arguments (p. xi). For Hyppolite's view of Lukács' book see his *Studies on Marx and Hegel* (1955), New York, 1969.
3 For example, H. Glockner did not even list '*Entäusserung*', or '*Entfremdung*', in his *Hegel-Lexikon* of 1935–39, a supplement to his Jubilee edition of Hegel's works (1927–30); the terms are still not present in the 2nd revised edition of the *Lexikon*, Stuttgart, 1957; nor does J. Hoffmeister include them in the index to his 1952 edition of the *Phenomenology*.
4 *Werke 8*, 658;, *The Young Hegel*, trans. Rodney Livingstone, London, 1975, p. 538.
5 Richard Norman, *Hegel's Phenomenology*, Brighton, 1976, p. 12.
6 *Phenomenology of Spirit*, trans. A.V. Miller, Oxford, 1977, para. 76.
7 Ibid., para. 78.
8 *G.W.9*, 14; *Phenomenology* (Miller), para. 11: 'the spirit in its formation'.
9 Georg Lukács in *The Meaning of Contemporary Realism* (1958), London, 1963, quotes (p. 112) Hegel on the social purpose of such educative experience: 'During his years of apprenticeship the hero is permitted to sow his wild oats; he learns to subordinate his wishes and views to the interests of the society; he then enters that society's hierarchic scheme and finds in it a comfortable niche.' Unfortunately Lukács gives no source for this remarkably cynical passage, so it is difficult to assess its relevance for the present discussion.
10 See the note in *Hegel: Texts and Commentary*, trans. and ed. W. Kaufmann, Garden City, NY, 1966, p. 21.
11 Josiah Royce, *Lectures on Modern Idealism*, New Haven, Conn., 1919, pp. 147–9.
12 Hyppolite, *Genesis and Structure*, p. 11.
13 *Young Hegel*, p. 566.
14 *Phenomenology* (Miller), para. 79.
15 Hyppolite, *Genesis and Structure*, p. 15.

16 *Phenomenology* (Miller), para. 80.
17 Ibid., para. 89.
18 Ibid., para. 79.
19 Ibid., para. 54.
20 Ibid., para. 85.
21 See the Introduction to his translation of Hegel's *Philosophy of Nature*, Vol. 1, London, 1970, p. 164. It is amusing to see that Vincent Descombes, *Modern French Philosophy* (1979), Cambridge, 1982, characterizes Kojève's anthropological reading of absolute knowledge as 'the end of *adversity*, the term which adequately translates Hegel's *Gegenständlichkeit*', p. 28.
22 *Phenomenology* (Miller), para. 36.
23 Frederick Engels, 'Ludwig Feuerbach and the end of classical German philosophy', *M.E.S.W.*, p. 600.
24 *Werke 8*, 577; *Young Hegel*, p. 470.
25 *G.W.9*, 422; *Phenomenology* (Miller), para. 788; *Phenomenology of Mind*, trans. J.B. Baillie, London, 1949, pp. 789–90.
26 *Werke Eb.*, 581–2; *C.W.3*, 340; *E.W.*, 393. For Hegel's *Logic* see *Wissenschaft der Logik, Erster Teil*, Hamburg, 1975, pp. 93–5; English trans. A.V. Miller, *Hegel's Science of Logic*, London, 1969, pp. 106–8.
27 *G.W.9*, 433; *Phenomenology* (Miller), para. 808.
28 *Werke 8*, 624, 632, 667; *Young Hegel*, pp. 508. 515, 546.
29 *Werke 8*, 632; *Young Hegel*, p. 515.
30 *Werke 8*, 624; *Young Hegel*, p. 508.
31 *G.W.9*, 431; *Phenomenology* (Miller), para. 804; *Phenomenology* (Baillie), 803–4.
32 *Phenomenology* (Miller), para. 85. The text itself can actually be divided according to the point of view in question – see the *Appendix* to Alexandre Kojève, *Introduction to the Reading of Hegel* (1947), ed. A. Bloom, trans. J.H. Nichols, New York, 1969.
33 *G.W.9*, 428; *Phenomenology* (Miller), para. 801; *Phenomenology* (Baillie), pp. 799–800. Compare this with Marx's account of scientific knowing in the Introduction (1857) to his *Grundrisse*, trans. M. Nicolaus, Harmondsworth, 1973.
34 *G.W.9*, 18; *Phenomenology* (Miller), para. 18.
35 *G.W.9*, 18; *Phenomenology* (Miller), para. 19; *Phenomenology* (Baillie), p. 81.
36 *Phenomenology* (Miller), para. 803.
37 *Phenomenology* (Miller), para. 808. Judith Shklar explains the inevitability of this conclusion by arguing that for Hegel retrospection was the only certain knowledge 'because it alone could reveal that men had made their knowledge and that it was the work of their own minds, and not an object to be seized' – 'Hegel's *Phenomenology*: an Elegy for Hellas'; in *Hegel's Political Philosophy*, Z.A. Pelczynski ed., Cambridge, 1971, p. 73.
38 *Phenomenology* (Miller), para. 36.
39 Ibid., para. 21.
40 Ibid., para. 797.
41 *F.B.*, 55–8.
42 Peter Singer, *Hegel*, Oxford, 1983, p. 71.

6: Marx's Criticism

1 *The Holy Family: C.W.4*, 192. As is well known, this theme recurs in Marx's Afterword to the 2nd edition of *Capital*.

NOTES TO pp. 59–65

2 Ibid; C.W.4, 139.
3 Werke Eb., 580; C.W.3, 339; E.W., 392.
4 Werke Eb., 573; C.W.3, 332; E.W., 385.
5 Werke Eb., 574; C.W.3, 332–3; E.W., 385–6.
6 Ibid.
7 Ibid.
8 The role of material labour as such in Hegel's *Phenomenology* is discussed in chapter 7.
9 Whether this is fair to Hegel is discussed in the following chapters.
10 Werke Eb., 575–6; C.W.3, 334; E.W., 387.
11 Werke Eb., 577; C.W.3, 335; E.W., 389.
12 *The Young Hegel*, trans. Rodney Livingstone, London, 1975, p. 516.
13 Werke Eb., 573; C.W.3, 332; E.W., 384–5. For a brief discussion of Hegel's later work, see chapter 8.
14 Werke Eb., 553; C.W.3, 313; E.W., 365.
15 Werke 8, 673–4; *Young Hegel*, p. 551. Livingstone's translation gives 'alienation and objectification in general'. This appears to be a mistake. For 'objectification' see the discussion below. Note that although Lukács' chapter heading refers to '*Entäusserung*', this point is made with reference to '*Entfremdung*'. For a Hegelian response to Lukács see Errol Harris's 1978 discussion 'Marxist interpretations of Hegel's *Phenomenology of Spirit*', in *Method and Speculation in Hegel's Phenomenology*, ed. M. Westphal, Atlantic Highlands, NJ, and Brighton, 1982.
16 Werke Eb., 580; C.W.3, 339; E.W., 392.
17 Werke Eb., 575; C.W.3, 333–4; E.W., 386–7.
18 Werke Eb., 580; C.W.3, 338; E.W., 391.
19 Werke Eb., 577–8; C.W.3, 336–7; E.W., 389–90.
20 See also the Appendix to this chapter.
21 Werke Eb., 572; C.W.3, 331; E.W., 384.
22 *Young Hegel*, pp. 551–2.
23 Werke 8, 671; *Young Hegel*, p. 549. Livingstone gives 'alienation is sharply distinguished from objective reality . . .', allowing the impression that alienation might be unreal.
24 For a defence of Hegel's equation of objectification and alienation see Hyppolite's review of Lukács' *The Young Hegel* in Jean Hyppolite, *Studies on Marx and Hegel*, trans. J. O'Neill, New York, 1955, pp. 87 ff. For a counter-attack on Hyppolite, see István Mészáros, *Marx's Theory of Alienation*, London, 1970, pp. 244–5.
25 Besides *The Young Hegel* compare Lukács' 1967 Preface to Volume 2 of his collected works, pp. 24–6, reprinted in the English translation of *History and Class-Consciousness* (1923), trans. Rodney Livingstone, London, 1971, pp. xxii–xxiv. Livingstone translates both '*Entfremdung*' and '*Entäusserung*' here as 'alienation' – in truth, Lukács seems to equate them.
26 Werke Eb., 573; C.W.3, 332; E.W., 385.
27 Joachim Ritter, in *Hegel und die französische Revolution*, Köln and Opladen, 1957, says that Hegel's treatment of the dichotomy of objectivity and subjectivity (the central problem of Hegelian philosophy) is now treated, under the influence of Marx, as a problem of estrangement. He adds (p. 61): 'what is important . . . is that one does not lose sight of the *positive* meaning of the dichotomy presupposed in estrangement' (*Hegel and the French Revolution*, trans. R.D. Winfield, Cambridge, Mass., 1982, p. 118). Dupré says that in 1844 Marx, for the first time, realized on re-reading Hegel that alienation is 'highly positive': it is 'the forward march of self-

creation' (*The Philosophical Foundations of Marxism*, New York, 1966, p. 122). Nathan Rotenstreich says 'Hegel set a positive value on alienation . . . ' (*Basic Principles of Marx's Philosophy*, Indianapolis, 1965, p. 156). Rotenstreich's chapter 'Concept of alienation and its metamorphoses' is interesting on the changing senses of 'alienation' in the history of thought. Unfortunately, there is a slip on p. 158 arising from a misreading of a critical gloss by Marx on Hegel as Marx's own view. Rotenstreich says: 'Having asserted that to abolish alienation is *ipso facto* to abolish the status of the object qua object, Marx said, in a marginal comment, that this follows from Feuerbach's line of reasoning. What Feuerbach sought to abolish was obviously not . . . objectivity (*Gegenständlichkeit*) but the fictitious status of pseudo-objects. Purporting to be based on Feuerbach's premises, Marx's conclusion – at least with regard to the existence of products of labour – is that the status of object qua object itself is to be abolished, since latent in its very existence is not the enrichment but the distortion of the creative subject.' The reference is not clear but it is probably the following passage: 'Abolition of *estrangement* is identified with abolition of *objectivity* (an aspect evolved by Feuerbach in particular)' (*C.W.*4, 665). This occurs under the head 'Hegel's Construction of the *Phenomenology*'. It is meant as a criticism of Hegel, first made by Feuerbach, and endorsed by Marx. The present discussion shows how absurd it would be to say that Marx wants to abolish the object 'qua object'. (It would be equally absurd in Feuerbach's case). Marx wants to abolish the object qua object alienated. Rotenstreich rightly goes on to a discussion of *Capital*'s characterization of the commodity form of the product of labour as a fetish; but this refers to its status, not as a natural object, but as a *value* (which 'has a purely social reality' and 'contains not an atom of matter'). It is interesting that in his 1844 notes on James Mill Marx says that '*value* is an *alienated* designation of [the product] *itself*, different from its immediate existence, external to its specific nature, a merely *relative* mode of existence of this' (*C.W.*3, 219).

28 *Werke Eb.*, 583–4; *C.W.*3, 341–2; *E.W.*, 395.
29 *Werke Eb.*, 581; *C.W.*3, 339; *E.W.*, 393.
30 For example: Jean-Paul Sartre, *The Problem of Method* (1960), London, 1963, p. 13; Mészáros, *Theory of Alienation*, p. 84.
31 'The foundation of historical materialism' (1932), in Herbert Marcuse, *From Luther to Popper*, essays trans. Joris de Bres, London, 1983, pp. 13, 45.
32 '*Vergegenständlichung*' is absent from J. Gauvin's *Wortindex zu Hegels Phänomenologie des Geistes*, Bonn, 1977. (P. Slater drew my attention to this point.) It is true that J.B. Baillie's translation (*Phenomenology of Mind*, London, 1949) uses the term, once (p. 86) in the Preface (but he is excessively free in his translation at that point) and again (p. 790) at the beginning of the last chapter (but this is a mistake for 'objectivity' – *Gegenständlichkeit*).
33 *Werke Eb.*, 572; *C.W.*3, 331; *E.W.*, 384.
34 *Werke Eb*, 581; *C.W.*3, 339; *E.W.*, 393.
35 *Werke* 8, 415–16; *Young Hegel*, p. 333.
36 *Werke Eb.*, 574; *C.W.*3, 333; *E.W.*, 386.
37 *Werke Eb.*, 513; *C.W.*3, 273; *E.W.*, 325.
38 *Werke Eb.*, 584; *C.W.*3, 342; *E.W.*, 396.
39 Ibid.
40 *Werke Eb.*, 583; *C.W.*3, 342; *E.W.*, 395.
41 *Werke Eb.*, 586; *C.W.*3, 344; *E.W.*, 398.
42 *Werke Eb.*, 553; *C.W.*3, 313; *E.W.*, 365.
43 *Werke Eb.*, 583; *C.W.*3., 341–2; *E.W.*, 395.

44 *Werke Eb.*, 570; *C.W.3*, 329; *E.W.*, 382.
45 *C.W.4*, 665.
46 e.g. J. Maguire, *Marx's Paris Writings: an Analysis*, Dublin, 1972, thinks Marx's account of Hegel less than fair.
47 Rose G., *Hegel Contra Sociology*, London, 1981, p. 150.
48 Ibid., p. 214.
49 *The Holy Family*: *C.W.4*, 139.
50 Richard Norman, *Hegel's Phenomenology*, Brighton, 1976, pp. 112–15. Hegel's admission is quoted in J.N. Findlay's Foreword to *Hegel's Logic*, trans. W. Wallace, 3rd ed., 1975, p. vii.
51 Rosen M., *Hegel's Dialectic and its Criticism*, Cambridge, 1982, p. 81.
52 *Werke Eb.*, 584; *C.W.3*, 342.
53 *Werke Eb.*, 578; *C.W.3*, 337; *E.W.*, 390.
54 Rose, *Hegel Contra Sociology*, p. 215.
55 *Werke Eb.*, 578; *C.W.3*, 337.
56 *G.W.9*, 765.
57 *Hegel's Logic*, para. 237. See Henri Lefebvre, *Dialectical Materialism* (1939), London, 1968, pp. 48–58.
58 *Werke Eb.*, 577; *C.W.3*, 336.
59 For a vigorous assertion of Hegel's difference from Fichte, and the claim that he is not 'idealist' but 'realist', see Alexandre Kojève, *Introduction to the Reading of Hegel* (1947), ed. A. Bloom, trans. J.H. Nicols, New York, 1969, pp. 150–4.
60 J.G. Fichte, *Science of Knowledge* (1794), trans. P. Heath and J. Lachs, Cambridge, 1982, pp. 231–2.
61 Ibid., p. 154.
62 Rose, *Hegel Contra Sociology*, pp. 152, 219.
63 For example: *Phenomenology of Spirit*, trans. A.V. Miller, Oxford, 1977, paras. 788, 803–8.
64 Ibid., para. 36.

7: The Influence of the Phenomenology

1 The following section is a reworking of my article on the subject, 'Hegel's master/slave dialectic and a myth of Marxology', *New Left Review*, 142 (1983), pp. 67–75.
2 Jean-Paul Sartre, *Being and Nothingness* (1943), trans. Hazel Barnes, London, 1958, p. 237. Marcuse, in a review (*Philosophy and Phenomenological Research*, March 1948) of *Being and Nothingness*, says that 'Sartre makes reference to Marx's early writings . . .': Herbert Marcuse, *From Luther to Popper*, essays trans. Joris de Bres, London, 1983, p. 188. In fact there is no such reference. Marcuse probably has in mind this remark about the 'master–slave' influence on Marx – a view held independently by Marcuse and which *he* had already linked to Marx's early writings (see below).
3 Jean Hyppolite, *Genesis and Structure of Hegel's 'Phenomenology of Spirit'* (1946), trans. S. Cherniak and J. Heckman, Evanston, 1974, p. 172. Also: 'the famous dialectic of *Master and Slave* that became the inspiration of Marxian philosophy', Hyppolite, *Studies on Marx and Hegel* (1955), trans. J. O'Neill, New York, 1969, p. 29.
4 Wilfred Desan, *The Marxism of Jean-Paul Sartre* (1965), New York, 1966, pp. 24, 50n.
5 *Critique*, nos. 195–6, 1963. The list is cited in Vincent Descombes, *Modern French Philosophy* (1980), Cambridge, 1982, p. 10n.

6 Interview with John Heckman; see his Introduction to the English translation of Hyppolite, *Genesis and Structure*, p. xxvi. Heckman is under the impression Sartre attended, p. xxiii.
7 Republished by Queneau, 'In Place of an Introduction', as the first chapter of his Kojève collection; the (partial) English translation of this collection of Kojève's lectures, *Introduction to the Reading of Hegel*, ed. A. Bloom, trans. J.H. Nicols, New York, 1969, includes it also as chapter 1.
8 Some examples: Dirk Struik, Introduction to K. Marx, *The Economic and Philosophic Manuscripts of 1844*, New York, 1964, p. 36; Walter Kaufmann, *Hegel: a Reinterpretation*, Garden City, NY, 1965, p. 137; W. Desan, *Marxism of Jean-Paul Sartre*, p. 34; G.A. Kelly, 'Notes on Hegel's "Lordship and Bondage"' (*Review of Metaphysics*, 1966), reprinted in *Hegel*, ed. A. MacIntyre, Garden City, NY, 1972, p. 190; Mark Poster, *Existentialist Marxism in Post-War France*, Princeton, NJ, 1975, pp. 13–15; Z. Hanfi, Introduction to *F.B.*, 42; Hans-Georg Gadamer, *Hegel's Dialectic*, New Haven, Conn., 1976, p. 73; Richard Norman, *Hegel's Phenomenology*, Brighton, 1976, pp. 53, 73; Joachim Israel, *The Language of Dialectic and the Dialectics of Language*, Brighton, 1979, p. 122; M. Petry, Introduction to *Hegel, The Berlin Phenomenology*, Dordrecht, 1981, p. lxxxix; Allen W. Wood, *Karl Marx*, London, 1981, pp. 242–3; R.C. Solomon, *In the Spirit of Hegel*, Oxford, 1983, p. 425.
9 Herbert Marcuse, *Reason and Revolution* (1941), 2nd ed., London, 1954, p. 115. In fact Marcuse had already said in his 1932 review of the *1844 Mss* that Marx's critical concepts point back to the ontological categories of 'labour' and 'domination and servitude' developed by Hegel in his *Phenomenology* (*From Luther to Popper*, pp. 13, 39). Pierre Naville gives prominence to Hegel's discussion but asserts that it is too simple to say this was Marx's source – *De L'Aliénation à la Jouissance*, Paris, 1957, p. 10. Those who do include Robert C. Tucker, *Philosophy and Myth in Karl Marx*, Cambridge, 1961, p. 147, and Joachim Ritter, *Hegel and the French Revolution*, (1956), trans. R.D. Winfield, Cambridge, Mass., 1982, p. 120.
10 The only occurrence of the phrase 'lordship and servitude' is when Marx copies out the entire list of contents of the *Phenomenology*.
11 *The Berlin Phenomenology* (Petry), pp. 86–9. *Der Knecht* counts as 'a member of the family'.
12 That is, '*eigner Sinn*' as against '*fremder Sinn*': *G.W.*9, 114–15; *Phenomenology of Spirit*, trans. A.V. Miller, Oxford, 1977, para. 195–6.
13 *Werke Eb.*, 574; *C.W.*3, 333; *E.W.*, 386. David McLellan, *Marx Before Marxism*, London, 1970, notes this (p. 197).
14 *Werke Eb.*, 574; *C.W.*3, 333; *E.W.*, 386.
15 *G.W.*9, 115–16; *Phenomenology* (Miller), para. 196; this is still clearer in *The Berlin Phenomenology* (Petry), pp. 86–9.
16 *Hegel's Philosophy of Mind*, trans. W. Wallace, Oxford, 1971, paras. 434–5; the Nürnberg *Propaedeutic* (1808–11) is mid-way in this respect; the transition is to Reason, as in the *Encyclopaedia*, but the importance of labour is still stressed; in J. Loewenberg's *Hegel Selections*, New York, 1929, p. 77.
17 *G.W.*9, 115–16; *Phenomenology* (Miller), para. 196.
18 The same comparison between Marx and Hegel is to be found in Charles Taylor, *Hegel*, Cambridge, 1975, p. 120; *Hegel and Modern Society*, Cambridge, 1979, pp. 50–1.
19 *Phenomenology* (Miller), para. 197.
20 *G.W.*9, 117; *Phenomenology* (Miller), para. 199.

21 Paragraph 435 of the 1830 edition.
22 *C.W.3*, 227.
23 *C.1* (Penguin), 990.
24 *Werke Eb.*, 573; *C.W.3*, 332.
25 J.N. Findlay, *Hegel: a Re-Examination*, London, 1958, p. 100.
26 For Jean Wahl in *La Malheur de la Conscience* (1929), Paris, 1951, this figure is paradigmatic of the whole *Phenomenology*. He argues that the dialectical method is based in the historical experience of humanity; 'and for Hegel is not this experience something more? Before being a philosopher he was a theologian' (p. vi).
27 For pertinent remarks comparing Hegel with Darwin, Malthus and Hobbes, see Marx's letter to Engels of 18 June 1862: *Selected Correspondence*, ed. S. Ryazanskaya, Moscow, 1965, p. 128.
28 *G.W.9*, 218; *Phenomenology* (Miller), para. 401.
29 Karl Löwith, *From Hegel to Nietzche* (1941), London, 1965, p. 265.
30 *G.W.9*, 220; *Phenomenology* (Miller), para. 405.
31 *G.W.9*, 223; *Phenomenology* (Miller), para. 409.
32 *G.W.9*, 224; *Phenomenology* (Miller), para. 411.
33 *G.W.9*, 224; *Phenomenology* (Miller), para. 412.
34 *G.W.9*, 224; *Phenomenology* (Miller), para. 413.
35 *G.W.9*, 225; *Phenomenology* (Miller), para. 413.
36 *G.W.9*, 227; *Phenomenology* (Miller), para. 418.
37 Findlay, *Hegel*, p. 113; Hyppolite, *Genesis and Structure*, p. 297; Kojève, *The Reading of Hegel*, p. 68.
38 *G.W.9*, 228; *Phenomenology* (Miller), para. 418.
39 *Werke Eb.*, 585; *C.W.3*, 343.
40 For a comparison of Marx's concrete universal with Hegel's see my essay 'Dialectics and labour' in *Issues in Marxist Philosophy*, vol. 1, ed. John Mepham and D.H. Ruben, Brighton, 1979.
41 *G.W.9*, 264–9; *Phenomenology* (Miller), para. 484–91.
42 J.-J. Rousseau, *The Social Contract*, trans. G.D.H. Cole, London, 1973, pp. 174, 194. For material on the influence of Diderot and Rousseau, see Stanley Rosen, *G.W.F. Hegel – an introduction to the science of wisdom*, New Haven, Conn., 1974.
43 *G.W.9*, 282; *Phenomenology* (Miller), para. 526.
44 *Phenomenology* (Miller), para. 521.
45 *C.W.3*, 331.
46 Norman, *Hegel's Phenomenology*, ch. 5 'History and alienation'.
47 *G.W.9*, 282; *Phenomenology* (Miller), para. 520.
48 Richard Kroner, Introduction, p. 50, to Hegel, *On Christianity: Early Theological Writings*, trans. T.M. Knox, New York, 1961.
49 Gadamer, *Hegel's Dialectic*, p. 71.
50 *C.W.4*, 36.
51 Shlomo Avineri makes this connection; *Hegel's Theory of the Modern State*, Cambridge, 1972, p. 97.
52 *P.R.* (Knox), p. 277.
53 'Zur Kritik der Hegelschen Rechtsphilosophie: Einleitung' p. 181, in *New MEGA, 1,2*. T.B. Bottomore's translation of Marx's *Early Writings*, London, 1963, started the fashion for rendering '*einer Klasse der bürgerlichen Gesellschaft, welche keine Klasse der bürgerlichen Gesellschaft ist*' as 'in . . . but not of . . . ' (p. 58) thus producing a rhetorical contrast not in the original straight contradition; *C.W.3* gives 'of' both times (p. 186).

54 For the debate on the influence of Stein on Marx see Kaethe Mengelberg's Introduction to her translation of Lorenz von Stein, *The History of the Social Movement in France 1789–1850* (1851), Totowa, NJ, 1964.
55 *Werke Eb.*, 536; *C.W.3*, 297; *E.W.*, 348. Compare also *C.W.3*, 313, 337.
56 For a somewhat exaggerated view of this parallel, see R.N. Berki, *Insight and Vision: the Problem of Communism in Marx's Thought*, London, 1983, p. 56.
57 *C.W.4*, 86.
58 Raya Dunayevskaya, *Marxism and Freedom*, New York, 1958. p. 38.

8: Hegel on Wage-labour

1 *C.W.3*, 604–5.
2 *Phenomenology of Spirit* trans. A.V. Miller, Oxford, 1977, para. 494.
3 *P.R.*, para. 194. On the background see Manfred Riedel, *Between Tradition and Revolution* (1969), Cambridge, 1984, ch. 1.
4 *Jenaer Systementwürfe I* (1803–4): *Gesammelte Werke Band 6*, Hamburg, 1975, pp. 323–4; *System of Ethical Life and First Philosophy of Spirit*, trans. H.S. Harris, Albany, NY, 1979, pp. 248–9. For the background to Hegel's thinking at this time see Bernard Cullen, *Hegel's Social and Political Thought*, Dublin, 1979, pp. 70–2.
5 Some of the argument below is condensed from my paper 'Personality and the dialectic of labour and property – Locke, Hegel, Marx' in *Radical Philosophy Reader*, ed. R. Edgley and R. Osborne, London, 1985.
6 *P.R.*, para. 194.
7 'Person and property' (1961), in *Hegel and the French Revolution*, trans. R.D. Winfield, Cambridge, Mass., 1982, p. 135.
8 *P.R.*, para. 59.
9 Ibid., para. 71.
10 Raymond Plant, *Hegel: an Introduction*, 2nd ed., Oxford, 1983, p. 155.
11 *P.R.*, para. 74.
12 Ibid., para. 43.
13 Ibid., para. 57.
14 *Hegel's Philosophy of Mind*, trans. W. Wallace, Oxford, 1971, para. 482.
15 *P.R.*, para. 57.
16 *C.1* (Penguin), 303, n.18.
17 *P.R.*, para. 66.
18 Ibid., para. 57 & Addition.
19 Ibid., para. 43.
20 'Hegels eigenhändigen Randbemerkungen' in *Grundlinien der Philosophie des Rechts*, ed. J. Hoffmeister, Hamburg, 1955, p. 330.
21 *P.R.*, para. 67. Ernest Mandel says that for Hegel material labour is alienating 'because labour is, *by its nature*, the externalizing (*Veräusserung*) of a human capacity, which means that man loses something that previously belonged to him': *The Formation of the Economic Thought of Karl Marx*, London, 1971, p. 155. Mandel seems to have in mind this paragraph of the *Philosophy of Right*, which deals with the *Veräusserung* (=alienation in the sense of sale) of human powers. If so, this is a misrepresentation of it. It is clear that Hegel does not say labour '*by its nature*' as 'externalizing' is alienating; rather, he says complex social *mediations* achieve alienation through setting labour in an (artificial) external relation to the person.

22 'If the whole and entire use of a thing were mine, while the abstract ownership was supposed to be someone else's, then the thing as mine would be penetrated through and through by my will and at the same time there would remain in the thing something impenetrable by me, namely the will, the empty will, of another' (*P.R.*, para. 62).
23 For Marx private property in general is an alien mediator estranging man from man. What is shown here is that even if one *accepts* Hegel's defence of private property it implies that *capitalist* property relations are contradictory. It is utterly absurd, however, to speak of 'Hegel's devastating critique of capitalist private property' and to equate him with Marx, as does David MacGregor, *The Communist Ideal in Hegel and Marx*, London, 1984, 189 *et passim*. Hegel's intentions are manifestly apologetic. Even when he recognizes that material to meet wants is barred to the needy because it consists of external objects held as private property by others, and hence 'its recalcitrance is absolute' (*P.R.*, para. 195), he seems to assume at this point that the problem is overcome through universal exchange. Later, when he concedes that modern society in fact creates 'a rabble of paupers' (*P.R.*, para. 244), he speculates on a solution through imperialism (*P.R.*, para. 246).
24 *P.R.*, para. 31.

9: Marx and Feuerbach

1 Georg Lukács, 'Moses Hess' (1926) in *Political Writings 1919–1929*, trans. M. McColgan, London, 1972, p. 203.
2 Michael Löwy, *Georg Lukács – From Romanticism to Bolshevism* (1975), London, 1979, p. 196.
3 Possibly the author was Feuerbach himself; for the debate see T.I. Oizerman, *The Making of the Marxist Philosophy* (1977), Eng. trans., Moscow, 1981, p. 124–5.
4 *The Life of Jesus* (1835) in *The Young Hegelians*, ed. L. Steplevitch, Cambridge, 1983, p. 48.
5 Marx's over-enthusiastic espousal of Feuerbach does not go *quite* as far as the stunning citation in H.P. Adams, *Karl Marx in his Earlier Writings* (1940), London, 1965, p. 104: 'Political economy owes its true foundations to the discoveries of Feuerbach'. What Marx actually says (in a deleted paragraph moreover) is that 'positive criticism as a whole' – and *therefore* 'criticism of political economy' – 'owes . . . ' etc. (*C.W.3*, 232).
6 *Werke Eb.*, 468; *C.W.3*, 232.
7 This standard classification is a bit simplistic. For the full story see J.E. Toews, *Hegelianism: Path to Dialectical Humanism 1805–1841*, Cambridge, 1980. For Young Hegelian materials in translation, see Steplevitch, *The Young Hegelians*.
8 Hegel to Niethammer 28 October 1808; in *Briefe von und an Hegel Band 1*, ed. J. Hoffmeister, Hamburg, 1952, p. 253.
9 *C.W.3*, 404.
10 The existence of this pamphlet is sufficient refutation of Alan White's claim that Engels was 'receptive' to Schelling's critique: see White, *Absolute Knowledge: Hegel and the Problem of Metaphysics*, Athens, Ohio, and London, 1983, p. 7. Equally mistaken is Alfred Schmidt's claim that Schelling's critique influenced the young Marx. Marx's contempt for Schelling's later work is evident in his letter to Feuerbach of 3 October 1843. Schmidt's reference to an allegedly Schellingian passage in the young Marx does not make it clear that it is *Hegel*'s view Marx is

      characterizing: see Schmidt, *The Concept of Nature in Marx* (1962), London, 1971, p. 20.
11 *Schelling and Revelation* (1842): *C.W.2*, 196.
12 *C.W.3*, 406. Compare with this the closing page of Engels' 1888 work *Ludwig Feuerbach and the End of Classical German Philosophy* (in *M.E.S.W.*).
13 Louis Althusser, *For Marx* (1965), trans. Ben Brewster, London, 1969, p. 65.
14 For the latest account of Hegel's accommodation see Ilting in *The State and Civil Society*, ed. Z.A. Pelczynski, Cambridge, 1984.
15 *C.W.1*, 84.
16 *Werke Eb.*, 581; *C.W.3*, 339.
17 *C.W.1*, 18.
18 Ibid., 11.
19 *Werke Eb.*, 608; *C.W.1*, 577; another translation is in M.A. Rose, *Reading the Young Marx and Engels*, London, 1978, p. 68.
20 'In a poem written in 1837 . . . preoccupation with the world of thought is contrasted with his own concern for the everyday life of man.' Bertell Ollman, *Alienation*, Cambridge, 1971, p. 274.
21 For a critical reading of this period, see Rose, *Reading*.
22 *C.W.1*, 18.
23 *Principles of the Philosophy of the Future*: *K.S.II*, 337; *F.B.*, 243.
24 *M.E.S.W.*, 602–3.
25 *C.W.2*, 237.
26 *M.E.S.W.*, 603.
27 *C.W.1*, 400; *New MEGA III, 1*, Briefe bis April 1846, p. 45.
28 Nathan Rotenstreich, *Basic Principles of Marx's Philosophy*, Indianapolis, 1965, p. 29.
29 See Marx's mini-autobiography in the Preface to a work of 1859: *M.E.S.W.*, 181 ff.
30 '. . . *die eigentümliche Logik des eigentümlichen Gegenstandes zu fassen*': *New MEGA I,2*, p. 101; *C.W.3*, 91; *E.W.*, 159.
31 Galvano della Volpe does not realize this and hence sees the 1843 critique of Hegel as more important than the *1844 Mss* in the development of Marx's new science. See 'For a materialist methodology' (1955–57), in Della Volpe, *Rousseau and Marx* (1964), London, 1978.
32 *K.S.II*, 332; *F.B.*, 238–9.
33 *C.W.3*, 168.
34 *New MEGA I, 2*, 178; *E.W.*, 252.
35 *New MEGA I, 2*, 181–2; *E.W.*, 256.
36 *New MEGA I, 2*, 177; *E.W.*, 251.
37 *New MEGA I, 2*, 182–3; *E.W.*, 257.
38 *New MEGA I, 2*, 177; *E.W.*, 251.
39 By M. Nicolaus, *Studies on the Left*, 7 (1967), no. 1, who believes this is carried through at least as late as the *Grundrisse*.
40 *Werke Eb.*, 467; *C.W.3*, 231.
41 *C.W.1*, 85.
42 *C.W.3*, 91.
43 *C.W.1*, 220.
44 Ibid., 216.
45 E.V. Il'enkov sums up the turn Marx's thought takes now as follows: 'Marx in 1842 did not turn to a formal analysis of contemporary communist ideas (they were indeed quite naïve), nor to a criticism of the practical attempts to implement them

(they were quite feeble), but rather he contemplated a theoretical analysis of the conflict within the social organism which spawned these ideas and the elucidation of that real demand which expressed itself in the form of ideas such as Utopian socialism and communism.' In *Marx and the Western World*, ed. N. Lobkowicz, Notre Dame, Indiana, 1967, p. 397.

46 *C.W.3*, 143.
47 Ibid., 297.
48 *C.W.5*, 49.
49 *Werke Eb.*, 468; *C.W.3*, 232.
50 *Werke Eb.*, 569; *C.W.3*, 328.
51 *Ibid.*
52 *Principles: S.W.2*, 276; *F.B.*, 205.
53 *S.W.2*, 276; *F.B.*, 206.
54 *S.W.2*, 301; *F.B.*, 229.
55 *Preliminary Theses on the Reform of Philosophy: S.W.2*, 227; *F.B.*, 157.
56 *Towards a Critique of Hegel's Philosophy: S.W.2*, 227; *F.B.*, 157.
57 *Principles: S.W.2*, 310–11; *F.B.*, 237.
58 *S.W.2*, 282; *F.B.*, 211.
59 *Hegel's Logic (Encyclopaedia I)*, trans. W. Wallace, 3rd ed., Oxford, 1975, para. 244.
60 *Philosophische Fragmente: S.W.2*, 363; *F.B.*, 270.
61 *Enzyklopädie der Philosophischen Wissenschaften im Grundrisse* (1830) Hamburg, 1975, para. 244. In Hegel's *Phenomenology* the same idea appears: 'spirit displays the process of its becoming spirit in the form of *free contingent happening*, intuiting its pure self as Time outside of it, and equally its being as Space. This last becoming of spirit, *Nature*, is its living immediate becoming . . . But the other side of its becoming, *History*, is a *conscious* self-*mediating* process – spirit emptied out [*entäusserte*] into time; but the externalization . . . is equally an externalization of itself; the negative is the negative of itself.' *Phenomenology of Spirit*, trans. A.V. Miller, Oxford, 1977, para. 807–8.
62 *Werke Eb.*, 585–6; *C.W.3*, 344; *E.W.*, 397–8.
63 *Werke Eb.*, 587; *C.W.3*, 345–6; *E.W.*, 398–9.
64 *Philosophy of Nature: Enzyklopädie* para. 247.
65 *Philosophy of Mind: Enzyklopädie* para. 381. For a defence of the incorporation of physical objects in 'infinite teleology' see Crawford Elder, *Appropriating Hegel* (1980), Aberdeen, 1981.
66 *Werke Eb.*, 588; *C.W.3*, 346.
67 Preface to the second edition of *The Essence of Christianity: F.B.*, 252.
68 *Werke Eb.*, 565; *C.W.3*, 325; *E.W.*, 377.
69 K. Marx, *Grundrisse*, trans. M. Nicolaus, Harmondsworth, 1973, p. 157.
70 *Werke Eb.*, 562; *C.W.3*, 321; *E.W.*, 374.
71 Lukács, *Political Writings*, pp. 210–12.
72 This aspect is well brought out by M. Wartofsky, *Feuerbach*, Cambridge, 1977.
73 Lukács, *Political Writings*, pp. 202–7; David McLellan, *The Young Hegelians and Karl Marx*, London, 1969, pp. 18, 112.
74 Lukács, *Political Writings*, p. 211; Lukács, *The Young Hegel*, trans. R. Livingstone, London, 1975, pp. 548, 559.
75 *C.W.4*, 665.
76 *Werke Eb.*, 562; *C.W.3*, 322.
77 *Principles: K.S.II*, 318; *F.B.*, 226.

78 *Werke Eb.*, 563; *C.W.3*, 322. Thus 'the science of man is a product of man's self-formation through practice', adds Marx; that is, man only knows what he is when he has become what he is in the totality of expressions. This view of science is parallel to that in Hegel's *Phenomenology*.
79 *Gesammelte Werke 5*, Berlin, 1984, p. 365; *Essence of Christianity*, trans. Marian Evans, New York, 1957, p. 217.
80 Erich Fromm, *Marx's Concept of Man* (1961), New York, 1971, p. 32.
81 *C.W.4*, 21.
82 *Essence: F.B.*, 262.
83 *Essence: Gesammelte Werke 5*, p. 377.
84 *Essence: Gesammelte Werke 5*, p. 71; *F.B.*, 127.
85 *Essence: Gesammelte Werke 5*, p. 71, n.3; *F.B.*, 133.
86 *Principles: K.S.II*, 301; *F.B.*, 209.
87 *On Feuerbach* thesis 11, *C.W.5*, 5.
88 Marcuse (1932) in Marcuse, *From Luther to Popper*, essays trans. Joris de Bres, London, 1983, pp. 21–2.
89 Louis Althusser, *Politics and History* (1970), London, 1972, p. 176.
90 Lukács, *Young Hegel*, p. 559.
91 Pierre Naville, *De L'Aliénation à la Jouissance*, Paris, 1957, p. 134.
92 *Werke Eb.*, 570; *C.W.3*, 329.
93 Marx to Feuerbach 11 August 1844: *New MEGA III,1*, Briefe bis 1846, 63; *C.W.3*, 354.
94 According to Engels, *C.W.38*, 22.
95 *K.S.II*, 441.
96 *C.W.5*, 57.
97 Wartofsky, *Feuerbach*, p. xx.
98 *C.W.3*, 254.
99 *C.W.4*, 139.
100 *C.W.4*, 39.
101 *C.W.5*, 530. Jindřich Zelený holds the *German Ideology* is also an implicit self-criticism of Feuerbachianism in the *1844 Mss*: *The Logic of Marx* (1968), Oxford, 1980.
102 See Engels to Marx, 20 January 1845: *C.W.38*, 16.
103 *C.W.5*, 3.
104 *C.W.5*, 29.
105 *K.S.II*, 18; *F.B.*, 54.
106 *Gesammelte Werke 5*, p. 28; *F.B.*, 97.
107 *C.W.5*, 31.
108 Marx to J.B. Schweitzer, 24 January 1865, *Selected Correspondence*, ed. S. Ryazanskaya, Moscow, 1965, p. 151.
109 *Selected Correspondence*, p. 100.
110 Marx to Engels, 11 January 1868: *Werke Band 32*, Berlin, 1965, p. 18; *Selected Correspondence*, trans. Dona Torr, London, 1934, p. 233.
111 Marx to Kugelmann, 27 June 1870. Marx's words (' . . . *das sie* – poor deer – *ihn langst begraben haben*') pose problems for translators because of the strange spelling and syntax: (*a*) *Werke Band 32* takes Marx literally and informs the German reader that Marx calls Hegel '*armes Tier*' (p. 686); (*b*) the English *Selected Correspondence* (1965) silently corrects to: 'that he – poor dear – had long been buried by them' (p. 240); Raya Dunayevskaya, in *Philosophy and Revolution*, New York, 1973, following the syntax, assumes Marx meant to be patronizing to the 'poor dears' Lange & Co. (p. 50).

112 Maximillien Rubel, *Marx Life and Works* (1965), London, 1980, p. 26.
113 24 April 1867: *Selected Correspondence* (1934), p. 217.
114 Alfred Schmidt, *History and Structure* (1971), Cambridge, Mass., notes the two distinct appropriations of Hegel (p. 61).

10:Towards an Assessment

1 Because he grounds human being in its objective relations Marx's ontology in the *1844 Mss* supersedes a mere anthropology; thus it is not touched by such claims on the part of Althusser, Sève and others.
2 Louis Althusser, *For Marx* (1965), trans. Ben Brewster, London, 1969, p. 197.
3 Ibid., p. 214.
4 Ibid., p. 198n.
5 *Werke Eb.*, 512–16; *C.W.3*, 273–6; *E.W.*, 325–8.
6 *Werke Eb.*, 516; *C.W.3*, 276.
7 *Werke Eb.*, 583; *C.W.3*, 341; *E.W.*, 395.
8 István Mészáros, *Marx's Theory of Alienation*, London, 1970, p. 45.
9 Ian Hunt and Roy Swan, 'A comparison of Marxist and Hegelian dialectical form', *Radical Philosophy* (1982), no. 30., pp. 36–7.
10 *Werke Eb.*, 536; *C.W.3*, 296.
11 *Werke Eb.*, 536; *C.W.3*, 297.
12 *Werke Eb.*, 538; *C.W.3*, 298; *E.W.*, 349.
13 *Werke Eb.*, 541; *C.W.3*, 301.
14 *Werke Eb.*, 543; *C.W.3*, 303.
15 *C.1* (Penguin), 283.
16 See Georg Lukács, *Ontology of Social Being: Marx* (1972), trans. D. Fernbach, London, 1978, p. 9.
17 *Enzyklopädie der Philosophischen Wissenschaften* (1830), Hamburg, 1975, para. 381.
18 *Werke Eb.*, 588; *C.W.3*, 346; *E.W.*, 399–400.
19 *Werke Eb.*, 541; *C.W.3*, 301. For a vigorous attack on neo-Hegelian Marxism for conceptualizing nature as unformed material for human practice see Peter Ruben, *Dialektik und Arbeit der Philosophie*, Köln, 1978.
20 *Werke Eb.*, 579; *C.W.3*, 337.
21 *Grundrisse*, trans. M. Nicolaus, Harmondsworth, 1973, pp. 409–10; see also Lukács, *Ontology*, pp. 8–10.
22 *C.3* (Penguin), 959.
23 For example, in the *German Ideology*, *C.W.5*, 49.
24 Mészáros, *Theory of Alienation*, p. 119.
25 *C.W.5*, 87–8. The last phrase is my attempt to give sense to '*Abstreifung aller Naturwüchtigkeit*' because *C.W.5* gives somewhat the wrong impression with 'casting off all natural limitations'.
26 Pierre Naville, in *De L'Aliénation à la Jouissance*, Paris, 1957, thinks Marx stuck to the aspiration to abolish labour in favour of free activity. J.R. Mailer, in *Actualité de Fourier*, ed. Henri Lefebvre, Paris, 1975, refutes Naville (pp. 264–87).
27 For a comparison see Janina Rosa Mailer, 'Fourier et Marx', in Lefebvre, *Actualité de Fourier*.
28 *C.W.5*, 47.
29 *Oeuvres Complètes Tome VI*, Paris, 1966–68, pp. 67–8.
30 *Werke Eb.*, 534; *C.W.3*, 294.

31 Kostas Axelos says that this is a 'transcendence of "differences" into a world of generalized indifference', unless it is reconceptualized as 'play': *Alienation, Praxis and Techné in the Thought of Karl Marx* (1961), trans. R. Bruzina, Austin, Texas, and London, 1976, p. 258.
32 *Grundrisse*, pp. 704–6.
33 *M.E.S.W.*, 324. See the analysis in Kate Soper, *On Human Needs*, Brighton, 1981, pp. 196 ff.
34 For remarks on this see Karel Kosik, *Dialectics of the Concrete* (1961), Dordrecht, 1976, pp. 123–7.
35 *New MEGA II, 1, Teil 2*, 499; *Grundrisse*, p. 611.
36 *New MEGA II, 1, Teil 2*, 589; *Grundrisse*, p. 711.
37 *New MEGA*, ibid.; *Grundrisse*, p. 712.
38 Ibid. The reference to discipline here perhaps recalls Hegel's definition of work as desire restrained and checked, and its role in the becoming of self-consciousness. It is amusing in the light of Marx's criticism of Fourier that contemporary French philosophy is still prone to celebrate 'the play of desire' as against 'productivism'.
39 *Werke Eb.*, 511–12; *C.W.3*, 272; *E.W.*, 324.
40 Naville, *De L'Aliénation*, pp. 148–9.
41 *Werke 8*, 631; *The Young Hegel*, trans. Rodney Livingstone, London, 1975, p. 549.
42 Erich Fromm, *Marx's Concept of Man* (1961), New York, 1971, pp. 51–2.
43 Ernest Mandel, *The Formation of the Economic Thought of Karl Marx* (1967), London, 1971, p. 165.
44 Ibid., p. 161.

11: The Continuing Importance of 1844

1 A.W. Wood, *Karl Marx*, London, 1981, p. 7.
2 Alex Callinicos, *Marxism and Philosophy*, Oxford, 1983, p. 41.
3 Ibid., p. 53. Scott Meikle goes so far as to say that, given the *1844 Mss*, 'the labour theory of value must follow': *Essentialism in the Thought of Karl Marx*, London, 1985, p. 55.
4 Callinicos, *Marxism and Philosophy*, p. 53.
5 See Georg Lukács, *Ontology of Social Being: Marx*, trans. D. Fernbach, London, 1978, pp. 10–15, on this.
6 See Gülnur Savran, 'Rousseau, Hegel and the Critique of Civil Society', DPhil. thesis, University of Sussex, 1983; the line of argument below is in agreement with her analysis.
7 11 July 1868: *Selected Correspondence*, ed. S. Ryazanskaya, Moscow, 1965, p. 208.
8 *The Holy Family: C.W.4*, 93. For useful discussions see Alfred Schmidt, *History and Structure*, Cambridge, Mass., and London, 1981, esp. pp. 61–2, and Norman Geras, *Marx and Human Nature: Refutation of a Legend*, London, 1983, esp. pp. 92–4.
9 'In so far as such a critique represents a class, it can only represent the class whose task is the overthrow of the capitalist mode of production and the final abolition of all classes – the proletariat': *C.1* (Penguin), 98.
10 *Werke Eb.*, 471; *C.W.3*, 235.

Appendix: Problems of Translation

1 *Werke 8*, 658; *The Young Hegel*, trans. Rodney Livingstone, London, 1975, p. 538.
2 *C.W.3*, 299.
3 *C.W.3*, 272.
4 *C.W.3*, 332–3.
5 'On the Jewish Question II', *E.W.*, 241.
6 *Werke Eb.*, 572; *C.W.3*, 331.
7 Schacht, *Alienation*, London, 1971, p. 72 n.7.
8 Karl Marx, *Early Writings*, trans. T.B. Bottomore, London, 1963, p. xix.
9 *Wissenschaft der Logik*, Hamburg, 1955, pp. 93–5; *Hegel's Science of Logic*, trans. A.V. Miller, London, 1969, pp. 106–8.
10 In *Hegel Selections*, ed. J. Loewenberg, New York, 1929, esp. p. 102n.
11 *Werke Eb.*, 536; *C.W.3*, 296.
12 *Werke Eb.*, 534; *C.W.3*, 294.

Bibliography

This bibliography assembles full details of works to which reference is made in the text and notes into five sections. The first covers editions and translations of Marx's *1844 Manuscripts*; the second gives other volumes of Marx and Engels' works cited here; the third gives the Hegel texts; the fourth lists other primary sources; the fifth contains the secondary literature referred to. A date in brackets is that of original publication; then follow details of the edition or translation.

1   Marx's 1844 Manuscripts

These manuscripts, written in Paris in 1844, are known by the title *Ökonomisch-philosophische Manuskripte*. They are referred to throughout this text as the *1844 Manuscripts*. A considerable part of the text has not been preserved; what remains comprises three manuscripts, each with its own pagination. There are marginal notes indicating Marx's intentions to reorder the material. Number 1 below contains the material reproduced as closely as possible from the original manuscripts. It also contains, quite separately, a lightly edited version. Number 2 contains a more thoroughly edited text attempting to follow Marx's intentions. This is the volume to which references are made throughout the text (*Werke Eb.*). Number 3 contains the standard English translation (based on numbers 5 and 6), to which quotations are also keyed (*C.W.3*). However, it should not be assumed that the renderings given follow this. For further comparison, references are sometimes given also to the translation listed as number 4 below (*E.W.*). Numbers 8 and 9 contain only partial translations of the *1844 Manuscripts*.

1   Karl Marx and Friedrich Engels, *Gesamtausgabe, Erste Abteilung Band 2*, Werke März 1843 bis August 1844, Dietz Verlag, Berlin, 1982.
2   Karl Marx and Friedrich Engels, *Werke, Ergänzungsband, Schriften bis 1844, Erster Teil*, Dietz Verlag, Berlin, 1968.
3   Karl Marx and Frederick Engels, *Collected Works Volume 3* (1843–44), trans. M. Milligan and D.J. Struik, Lawrence and Wishart, London, 1975.
4   Karl Marx, *Early Writings*, trans. Gregor Benton, The Pelican Marx Library, Penguin Books, Harmondsworth, 1975.
5   Karl Marx, *Economic and Philosophical Manuscripts of 1844*, trans. Martin Milligan, F.L.P.H., Moscow, 1960.

6 Karl Marx, *The Economic and Philosophic Manuscripts of 1844*, ed. Dirk J. Struik (revised version of Milligan trans.), International Publishers, New York, 1964.
7 Karl Marx, *Early Writings*, trans. T.B. Bottomore, Watts, London, 1963.
8 *Writings of the Young Marx on Philosophy and Society*, ed. and trans. Loyd D. Easton and Kurt H. Guddat, Doubleday, Garden City, NY, 1967.
9 Karl Marx, *Early Texts*, trans. David McLellan, Basil Blackwell, Oxford, 1970.

2 Marx and Engels

Karl Marx and Friedrich Engels, *Gesamtausgabe* (MEGA), Dietz Verlag, Berlin, 1976– .
Erste Abteilung Band 2, Werke März 1843 bis August 1844.
Zweite Abteilung Band 1, Manuskripte 1857–58.
Dritte Abteilung Band 1, Briefe bis April 1846.
Karl Marx and Friedrich Engels, *Werke: Band 23, Das Kapital, Erster Band*, 1962; *Band 32* 1965; *Ergänzungsband*, 1968, Dietz Verlag, Berlin.
Karl Marx and Frederick Engels *Collected Works*, Lawrence and Wishart, London, 1975–.
Volume 1, Marx, 1835–43.
Volume 2, Engels, 1838–42.
Volume 3, Marx–Engels, 1843–44.
Volume 4, Marx–Engels, 1844–45.
Volume 5, Marx–Engels, 1845–47.
Volume 6, Marx–Engels, 1845–48.
Volume 38, Marx–Engels, 1844–51.
Karl Marx, *Grundrisse*, trans. M. Nicolaus, Penguin Books, Harmondsworth, 1973.
Karl Marx, *Capital Volume 1*, trans. S. Moore and E. Aveling, F.L.P.H., Moscow, 1961.
Karl Marx, *Capital Volume 1*, trans. Ben Fowkes, The Pelican Marx Library, Penguin Books, Harmondsworth, 1976.
Karl Marx, *Capital Volume 3*, F.L.P.H., Moscow, 1962.
Karl Marx, *Capital Volume 3*, trans. D. Fernbach, The Pelican Marx Library, Penguin Books, Harmondsworth, 1981.
Karl Marx and Frederick Engels, *Selected Works* (in one volume), International Publishers, New York, 1968.
Karl Marx and Frederick Engels, *Selected Correspondence*, trans. Dona Torr, London, 1934.
Karl Marx and Frederick Engels, *Selected Correspondence*, ed. S. Ryazanskaya, Moscow, 1965.

3 G.W.F. Hegel

On Christianity: Early Theological Writings, trans. T.M. Knox with introduction by R. Kroner, Harper, New York, 1961.
Jenaer Systementwürfe I, Gesammelte Werke Band 6, Meiner, Hamburg, 1975.
System of Ethical Life and First Philosophy of Spirit, trans. H.S. Harris and T.M. Knox, S.U.N.Y. Press, Albany, NY, 1979.
Phänomenologie des Geistes, Gesammelte Werke Band 9, Meiner, Hamburg, 1980.
Phenomenology of Spirit, trans. A.V. Miller, Oxford University Press, Oxford, 1977.
Phenomenology of Mind, trans. J.B. Baillie, Allen & Unwin, London, 1949.
Wortindex zu Hegels Phänomenologie des Geistes, J. Gauvin, Bonn, 1977.

Hegel: Texts and Commentary, trans. and ed. W. Kaufmann, Anchor, Garden City, NY, 1966.
Briefe von und an Hegel Band 1, ed. J. Hoffmeister, Meiner, Hamburg, 1952.
Wissenschaft der Logik, Meiner, Hamburg, 1975.
Hegel's Science of Logic, trans. A.V. Miller, Allen & Unwin, London, 1969.
The Berlin Phenomenology, ed. and trans. M.J. Petry, Reidel, Dordrecht, 1981.
Enzyklopädie der philosophischen Wissenschaften im Grundrisse, ed. F. Nicolin and O. Pöggeler, Meiner, Hamburg, 1975.
Hegel's Logic (being Part I of the *Encyclopaedia of the Philosophical Sciences*) trans. W. Wallace, 3rd ed., Oxford University Press, Oxford, 1975.
Hegel's Philosophy of Nature, ed. and trans. M.J. Petry, 3 vols, Allen & Unwin, London, 1970.
Hegel's Philosophy of Mind (being Part III of the *Encyclopaedia of the Philosophical Sciences*) trans. W. Wallace, together with *Zusätze*, trans. A.V. Miller, Oxford University Press, Oxford, 1971.
Grundlinien der Philosophie des Rechts (*mit Hegels eigenhändigen Randbemerkungen*), ed. J. Hoffmeister, Meiner, Hamburg, 1955.
Hegel's Philosophy of Right, trans. T.M. Knox, Oxford University Press, Oxford, 1965.
Hegel Selections, ed. J. Loewenberg, Scribners, New York, 1929.
Hegel-Lexikon, H. Glockner, 2nd revised ed., 2 vols, Frommann, Stuttgart, 1957.

4 Other Sources

T. Carlyle, *Past and Present*, London, 1843.
L. Feuerbach, *Das Wesen des Christenthums* (1841), *Gesammelte Werke Band 5*, ed. Werner Schuffenhauer, Berlin, 1984.
L. Feuerbach, *The Essence of Christianity*, trans. Marian Evans, New York, 1957.
L. Feuerbach, *The Fiery Brook – selected writings of Ludwig Feuerbach*, trans. Z. Hanfi, Garden City, NY, 1972.
L. Feuerbach, *Kleinere Schriften II* (1839–46), *Gesammelte Werke Band 9*, ed. W. Schuffenhauer, Berlin, 1982.
L. Feuerbach, *Sämtliche Werke Zweiter Band*, new ed. W. Bolin and F. Jodl, Stuttgart-Bad Canstatt, 1959.
J.G. Fichte, *Science of Knowledge* (1794), trans. P. Heath and J. Lachs, Cambridge, 1982.
Charles Fourier, *Oeuvres Complètes*, Paris, 1966–68.
J.-J. Rousseau, *The Social Contract and Discourses*, trans. G.D.H. Cole, revised ed., London, 1973.
Adam Smith, *The Wealth of Nations* (1776), ed. E. Cannan (from 5th ed. 1789), Chicago, 1976.
L.S. Steplevich (ed.), *The Young Hegelians: an Anthology*, Cambridge, 1983.

5 Secondary Literature

Adams, H.P., *Karl Marx in his Earlier Writings* (1940), London, 1965.
Althusser, Louis, *For Marx* (1965), trans. Ben Brewster, London, 1969.
Politics and History (1970), London, 1972.
Arthur, C.J., 'Hegel's master/slave dialectic and a myth of Marxology' *New Left Review* (1983), 142.

Avineri, Shlomo, *The Social and Political Thought of Karl Marx*, Cambridge, 1968.
Hegel's Theory of the Modern State, Cambridge, 1972.
Axelos, Kostas, *Alienation, Praxis and Technē in the Thought of Karl Marx* (1961), trans. R. Bruzina, Austin, Texas, and London, 1976.
Berki, R.N., *Insight and Vision: the problem of Communism in Marx's Thought*, London, 1983.
Bottomore, Tom, (ed.), *A Dictionary of Marxist Thought*, Oxford, 1983.
Callinicos, Alex, *Marxism and Philosophy*, Oxford, 1983.
Cullen, Bernard, *Hegel's Social and Political Thought: an Introduction*, Dublin, 1979.
Della Volpe, Galvano, *Rousseau and Marx* (1964), London, 1978.
Desan, Wilfred, *The Marxism of Jean-Paul Sartre* (1965), New York, 1966.
Descombes, Vincent, *Modern French Philosophy* (1979), Cambridge, 1982.
Dunayevskaya, Raya, *Marxism and Freedom*, New York, 1958.
Philosophy and Revolution, New York, 1973.
Dupré, Louis, *The Philosophical Foundations of Marxism*, New York, 1966.
Edgley, Roy, and Osborne, Richard (eds.), *Radical Philosophy Reader*, London, 1985.
Elder, Crawford, *Appropriating Hegel*, Aberdeen, 1981.
Findlay, J.N., *Hegel: a Re-Examination*, London, 1958.
Fromm, Erich, *Marx's Concept of Man* (1961), New York, 1971.
Gadamer, Hans-Georg, *Hegel's Dialectic*, New Haven, Conn., and London, 1976.
Geras, Norman, *Marx and Human Nature: Refutation of a Legend*, London, 1983.
Gould, Carol C., *Marx's Social Ontology*, Cambridge, Mass., and London, 1978.
Hunt, Ian, and Swan, Roy, 'A comparison of Marxist and Hegelian dialectical form', *Radical Philosophy* (1982) No. 30.
Hyppolite, Jean, *Genesis and Structure of Hegel's 'Phenomenology of Spirit'* (1946), trans. S. Cherniak and J. Heckman, Evanston, 1974.
Studies on Marx and Hegel (1955), trans. J. O'Neill, New York, 1969.
Israel, Joachim, *The Language of Dialectic and the Dialectics of Language*, Brighton, 1979.
Kamenka, Eugene, *The Ethical Foundations of Marxism*, London, 1962.
Kaufmann, Walter, *Hegel: a Reinterpretation*, Garden City, NY, 1965.
Kojève, Alexandre, *Introduction to the Reading of Hegel* (1947), ed. A. Bloom, trans. J.H. Nichols, New York, 1969.
Kosík, Karel, *Dialectics of the Concrete* (1961), Dordrecht, 1976.
Lefebvre, Henri, *Dialectical Materialism*, (1939), London, 1968.
Actualité de Fourier, colloque d'Arc-et-Senans sous la direction de Henri Lefebvre, Paris, 1975.
Lenin, V.I., *Selected Works*, London, 1969.
Lobkowicz, Nicholas, (ed.), *Marx and the Western World*, Notre Dame, Indiana, 1967.
Löwith, Karl, *From Hegel to Nietzche* (1941), London, 1965.
Löwy, Michael, *Georg Lukács - From Romanticism to Bolshevism* (1975), London, 1979.
Lukács, Georg, *History and Class-Consciousness* (1923), trans. Rodney Livingstone, London, 1971.
Political Writings 1919–1929, trans. M. McColgan, London, 1972.
Der Junge Hegel (1948), *Werke Band 8*, Neuwied and Berlin, 3 Auflage, 1967.
The Young Hegel (1948), trans. Rodney Livingstone, London, 1975.
The Meaning of Contemporary Realism (1958), London, 1963.
Werke Band 2 (with new Preface), Neuwied and Berlin, 1968.
Ontology of Social Being: Marx (1972), trans. D. Fernbach, London, 1978.
Macgregor, David, *The Communist Ideal in Hegel and Marx*, London, 1984.
MacIntyre, Alasdair (ed.), *Hegel*, Garden City, NY, 1972.

McLellan, David, *The Young Hegelians and Karl Marx*, London, 1969.
  Marx Before Marxism, London, 1970.
Maguire, J., *Marx's Paris Writings: an Analysis*, Dublin, 1972.
Mandel, Ernest, *The Formation of the Economic Thought of Karl Marx* (1967), London, 1971.
Marcuse, Herbert, *Reason and Revolution* (1941), 2nd ed., London, 1954.
  From Luther to Popper, essays trans. Joris de Bres, London, 1983.
Meikle, Scott, *Essentialism in the Thought of Karl Marx*, London, 1985.
Mepham, John, and Ruben, D.H. (eds.), *Issues in Marxist Philosophy*, vol. 1, Brighton, 1979.
Mészáros, István, *Marx's Theory of Alienation*, London, 1970.
Naville, Pierre, *De L'Aliénation à la Jouissance*, Paris, 1957.
Nicolaus, Martin, 'Hegelian choreography and the capitalist dialectic', *Studies on the Left*, 7 (1967), No. 1.
Norman, Richard, *Hegel's Phenomenology*, Brighton, 1976.
Oizerman, T.I., *The Making of the Marxist Philosophy* (1977), English trans., Moscow, 1981.
Ollman, Bertell, *Alienation*, Cambridge, 1971.
Pelczynski, Z.A. (ed.), *Hegel's Political Philosophy*, Cambridge, 1971.
  The State and Civil Society: Studies in Hegel's Political Philosophy, Cambridge, 1984.
Plant, Raymond, *Hegel: an Introduction*, 2nd ed., Oxford, 1983.
Poster, Mark, *Existentialist Marxism in Post-War France*, Princeton, NJ, 1975.
Prawer, S.S., *Karl Marx and World Literature*, Oxford, 1976.
Riedel, Manfred, *Between Tradition and Revolution* (1969), Cambridge, 1984.
Ritter, Joachim, *Hegel und die französische Revolution* (1956), Köln and Opladen, 1957.
  Hegel and the French Revolution: Essays on the Philosophy of Right (1956–69), trans. R.D. Winfield, Cambridge, Mass., 1982.
Rose, Gillian, *Hegel Contra Sociology*, London, 1981.
Rose, Margaret A., *Reading the Young Marx and Engels*, London, 1978.
Rosen, Michael, *Hegel's Dialectic and its Criticism*, Cambridge, 1982.
Rosen, Stanley, *G.W.F. Hegel – an introduction to the science of wisdom*, New Haven, Conn., and London, 1974.
Rotenstreich, Nathan, *Basic Principles of Marx's Philosophy*, Indianapolis, 1965.
Royce, Josiah, *Lectures on Modern Idealism*, New Haven, Conn., 1919.
Rubel, Maximillien, *Marx Life and Works* (1965), London, 1980.
Ruben, Peter, *Dialektik und Arbeit der Philosophie*, Köln, 1978.
Sartre, Jean-Paul, *Being and Nothingness* (1943), trans, Hazel Barnes, London, 1958.
  The Problem of Method (1960), trans. Hazel Barnes, London, 1963.
Savran, Gülnur, 'Rousseau, Hegel, and the Critique of Civil Society', DPhil. thesis, University of Sussex, 1983.
Schacht, Richard, *Alienation*, London, 1971.
Schmidt, Alfred, *The Concept of Nature in Marx* (1962), London, 1971.
  History and Structure (1971), Cambridge, Mass., and London, 1981.
Sève, Lucien, *Man in Marxist Theory* (1974), trans. John McGreal, London, 1978.
Singer, Peter, *Hegel*, Oxford, 1983.
Solomon, R.C., *In the Spirit of Hegel*, Oxford and New York, 1983.
Soper, Kate, *On Human Needs*, Brighton, 1981.
von Stein, Lorenz, *The History of the Social Movement in France 1789–1850* (1851), introduced and trans. Kaethe Mengelberg, Totowa, NJ, 1964.
Taylor, Charles, *Hegel*, Cambridge, 1975.
  Hegel and Modern Society, Cambridge, 1979.

Toews, John Edward, *Hegelianism: Path to Dialectical Humanism 1805–1841*, Cambridge, 1980.
Tucker, Robert C., *Philosophy and Myth in Karl Marx*, Cambridge, 1961.
Wahl, Jean, *Le Malheur de la Conscience* (1929), Paris, 1951.
Walton, Paul, and Gamble, Andrew, *From Alienation to Surplus Value*, London, 1972.
Wartofsky, Marx, *Feuerbach*, Cambridge, 1977.
Westphal, M. (ed.), *Method and Speculation in Hegel's Phenomenology*, Atlantic Highlands, NJ, and Brighton, 1982.
White, Alan, *Absolute Knowledge: Hegel and the Problem of Metaphysics*, Athens, Ohio, and London, 1983.
Wood, Allen, W., *Karl Marx*, London, 1981.
Zelený, Jindřich, *The Logic of Marx* (1968), Oxford, 1980.

Index

Adams, H.P. 167
Adelung, J.C. 157
Althusser, L. 105, 121, 127–8, 144, 171
Avineri, S. 158, 165
Axelos, K. 157, 172

Baillie, J.B. 149, 162
Bauer, B. 33, 92, 123
Bauer, E. 119
Berki, R.N. 166
Bottomore, T.B. 148–9, 156, 165

Callinicos, A. 142–3
Carlyle, T. 24, 156
Cieszowski, A. 105
Cullen, B. 166

Darwin, C. 165
Della Volpe, G. 168
Desan, W. 78, 164
Descombes, V. 160
Diderot, D. 157, 165
Dunayevskaya, R. 14, 92, 170
Dupré, L. 161–2

Easton, L.D. 157
Elder, C. 169
Engels, F. 18, 31, 53, 107–8, 109, 123, 153, 155, 156, 158, 168

Feuerbach, L. 57, 59, 73, 105–26, 128, 132, 133–5, 145, 154, 162, 167
Fichte, J.G. 74–6, 105, 108, 147, 163
Findlay, J.N. 85, 165

Fourier, C. 11, 37, 136–8, 157, 158, 172
Fromm, E. 14, 39, 119, 140, 155

Gadamer, H.-G. 90, 164
Gamble, A. 154
Gans, E. 91
Gauvin, J. 162
Geras, N. 172
Glockner, H. 159
Goethe, J.W. 11, 51
Gould, C. 153
Guddat, K.H. 157

Hanfi, Z. 164
Harris, E. 161
Harris, W.T. 150
Heckman, J. 164
Hegel, G.W.F. 2, 5, 27, 45–135, 138, 139–40, 145, 157, 159, 163, 172
  Encyclopaedia 56, 75, 82, 83–4, 115–17, 132, 166
  First Philosophy of Spirit 95
  Lectures 79, 164
  Letters 107
  Phenomenology 1, 46–95, 107, 114–15, 121, 125–6, 128, 147–9, 157, 159, 162, 169, 170
  Philosophy of Right 54, 91, 94–102, 154, 156, 167
  Propaedeutic 164
  Science of Logic 54, 94, 125–6, 150
Hess, M. 11, 17, 41, 105, 106, 107, 123, 153

INDEX

Hobbes, T. 165
Hoffmeister, J. 159
Hunt, I. 130–1
Hyppolite, J. 51, 78, 159, 161, 165

Il'enkov, E.V. 168–9
Ilting, K-H. 168
Israel, J. 164

Kamenka, E. 154
Kant, I. 92, 108–9
Kaufmann, W. 164
Kelly, G.A. 164
Kierkegaard, S. 85
Knox, T.M. 91
Kojève, A. 77–8, 80, 81, 82, 160, 163, 165
Kosík, K. 172
Kroner, R. 90

Lange, F.A. 125
Lefebvre, H. 163
Lenin, V.I. 1
Locke, J. 52
Löwith, K. 85
Löwy, M. 105
Lukács, G.
  Contemporary Realism 159
  History and Class-Consciousness 161
  Moses Hess 105, 118, 169
  Ontology 153, 171, 172
  Young Hegel 2, 13–14, 49, 51, 54–5, 61, 62, 64, 68, 122, 140, 147, 159, 161
Luther, M. 31–2, 85

MacGregor, D. 167
McLellan, D. 153, 164, 169
Maguire, J. 163
Mailer, J.R. 171
Malthus, T. 165
Mandel, E. 140, 166
Marcuse, H. 14, 18, 66, 79, 82, 83, 121, 163, 164
Marx, K.
  Capital 2, 13, 18, 25, 31, 40, 84, 90, 98, 112, 125, 132, 133, 134, 136, 140, 141–6, 157, 160, 172
  Correspondence 107–8, 110, 122, 123, 124, 125, 144, 165, 167, 170

Critique of Gotha Programme 137, 158
Critique of Hegel 110–13, 126, 165
Dissertation 108, 112
1844 Mss. 1–50, 54, 59–95, 105–6, 108, 110, 112, 113, 114, 116–46, 148–50, 156, 159, 170
German Ideology 6, 13, 16–17, 25, 41, 113–14, 122–6, 136, 170, 171
Grundrisse 39, 137–8, 154, 157, 160, 169
Hegel Epigramme 108–9
Holy Family 33, 90–2, 109, 119, 123, 125–6, 144–5, 158, 160–1
On James Mill 84, 154, 162
On the Jewish Question 111, 148
Manifesto 24, 33, 126
Notebooks 72–3, 162
Poverty of Philosophy 125, 157
Rheinische Zeitung 110, 112–13
Theses on Feuerbach 110, 121, 123, 126
Meikle, S. 153, 172
Mengelberg, K. 166
Mészáros, I. 11, 15, 40, 129, 135, 153, 158, 161, 162
Miller, A.V. 147, 149

Naville, P. 122, 139–40, 153, 164, 171
Nicolaus, M. 168
Norman, R. 75, 90, 164

Oizerman, T.I. 14, 18, 158, 167
Ollman, B. 26–7, 168

Petrović, G. 15
Petry, M.J. 27, 52, 83, 164
Plant, R. 97
Popper, K. 142
Poster, M. 164
Prawer, S.S. 154
Proudhon, J-P. 22, 41, 113, 124, 155, 157, 158

Queneau, R. 78

Riazanov, D. 105
Ricardo, D. 1, 144
Riedel, M. 166
Ritter, J. 96, 161, 164
Rose, G. 27, 74–6
Rose, M.A. 168

Rosen, M. 75
Rosen, S. 165
Rotenstreich, N. 110, 162
Rousseau, J-J. 51, 88–9, 105, 111, 165
Royce, J. 51
Ruben, P. 171
Ruge, A. 110

Sartre, J-P. 38, 77–8, 162
Savran, G. 172
Schacht, R. 148, 156
Schelling, F.W.J. 107, 167
Schmidt, A. 167, 171, 172
Sève, L. 171
Shakespeare, W. 11
Shklar, J. 160
Singer, P. 57
Smith, A. 1, 21, 23, 31–2, 70, 95, 137, 144, 145
Solomon, R.C. 164
Soper, K. 172
Spinoza, B. 75

Stein, L. von 17, 41, 91, 158, 166
Stirling, J.H. 150
Stirner, M. 122, 123
Stoics, 72, 82–3
Strauss, D.F. 106, 123
Struik, D. 155, 164
Swan, R. 130–1

Taylor, C. 164
Toews, J.E. 167
Tucker, R.C. 14, 158, 164

Wahl, J. 165
Wallace, W. 83
Walton, P. 154
Wartofsky, M. 169
Weitling, W. 155
White, A. 167
Wood, A.W. 141–2, 164

Zelený, J. 170